PALGRAVE *Studies in Oral History*

Series Editors: Linda Shopes and Bruce M. Stave

The Order Has Been Carried Out: History, Memory, and Meaning of a Nazi Massacre in Rome, by Alessandro Portelli (2003)

Sticking to the Union: An Oral History of the Life and Times of Julia Ruuttila, by Sandy Polishuk (2003)

To Wear the Dust of War: From Bialystok to Shanghai to the Promised Land, an Oral History, by Samuel Iwry, edited by L. J. H. Kelley (2004)

Education as My Agenda: Gertrude Williams, Race, and the Baltimore Public Schools, by Jo Ann Robinson (2005)

Remembering: Oral History Performance, edited by Della Pollock (2005)

Postmemories of Terror: A New Generation Copes with the Legacy of the "Dirty War", by Susana Kaiser (2005)

Growing Up in The People's Republic: Conversations between Two Daughters of China's Revolution, by Ye Weili and Ma Xiaodong (2005)

Life and Death in the Delta: African American Narratives of Violence, Resilience, and Social Change, by Kim Lacy Rogers (2006)

Creating Choice: A Community Responds to the Need for Abortion and Birth Control, 1961–1973, by David P. Cline (2006)

Voices from This Long Brown Land: Oral Recollections of Owens Valley Lives and Manzanar Pasts, by Jane Wehrey (2006)

Radicals, Rhetoric, and the War: The University of Nevada in the Wake of Kent State, by Brad E. Lucas (2006)

The Unquiet Nisei: An Oral History of the Life of Sue Kunitomi Embrey, by Diana Meyers Bahr (2007)

Sisters in the Brotherhoods: Working Women Organizing for Equality in New York City, by Jane LaTour (2008)

Iraq's Last Jews: Stories of Daily Life, Upheaval, and Escape from Modern Babylon, edited by Tamar Morad, Dennis Shasha, and Robert Shasha (2008)

Soldiers and Citizens: An Oral History of Operation Iraqi Freedom from the Battlefield to the Pentagon, by Carl Mirra (2008)

Overcoming Katrina: African American Voices from the Crescent City and Beyond, by D'Ann R. Penner and Keith C. Ferdinand (2009)

Bringing Desegregation Home: Memories of the Struggle toward School Integration in Rural North Carolina, by Kate Willink (2009)

I Saw It Coming: Worker Narratives of Plant Closings and Job Loss, by Tracy E. K'Meyer and Joy L. Hart (2010)

Speaking History: Oral Histories of the American Past, 1865–Present, by Sue Armitage and Laurie Mercier (2010)

Surviving Bhopal: Dancing Bodies, Written Texts, and Oral Testimonials of Women in the Wake of an Industrial Disaster, by Suroopa Mukherjee (2010)

Living with Jim Crow: African American Women and Memories of the Segregated South, by Anne Valk and Leslie Brown (2010)

Gulag Voices: Oral Histories of Soviet Incarceration and Exile, by Jehanne M. Gheith and Katherine R. Jolluck (2011)

Detained without Cause: Muslims' Stories of Detention and Deportation in America after 9/11, by Irum Shiekh (2011)

Soviet Communal Living: An Oral History of the Kommunalka, by Paola Messana (2011)

No Room of Her Own: Women's Stories of Homelessness, Life, Death, and Resistance, by Desiree Hellegers (2011)

Oral History and Photography, edited by Alexander Freund and Alistair Thomson (2011)

Place, Writing, and Voice in Oral History, edited by Shelley Trower (2011)

Place, Writing, and Voice in Oral History

Edited by
Shelley Trower

palgrave
macmillan

PLACE, WRITING, AND VOICE IN ORAL HISTORY

First published in 2011 by
PALGRAVE MACMILLAN®
in the United States—a division of St. Martin's Press LLC,
175 Fifth Avenue, New York, NY 10010.

Where this book is distributed in the UK, Europe and the rest of the world, this is by Palgrave Macmillan, a division of Macmillan Publishers Limited, registered in England, company number 785998, of Houndmills, Basingstoke, Hampshire RG21 6XS.

Palgrave Macmillan is the global academic imprint of the above companies and has companies and representatives throughout the world.

ISBN: 978–0–230–62369–9

Library of Congress Cataloging-in-Publication Data

Place, writing, and voice in oral history / Shelley Trower.
p. cm.—(Palgrave studies in oral history)
ISBN 978–0–230–62369–9 (hardback)
1. Oral history. 2. Aural history. I. Trower, Shelley, 1975–

D16.14.P55 2011
907.2—dc23 2011018688

A catalogue record of the book is available from the British Library.

Design by Newgen Imaging Systems (P) Ltd., Chennai, India.

First edition: November 2011

10 9 8 7 6 5 4 3 2 1

Printed and bound in Great Britain by
CPI Antony Rowe, Chippenham and Eastbourne

Contents

Figures and Table

Figures

Chapter 1

Chapter 5

Chapter 6

Chapter 7

Chapter 8

Chapter 9

Table

Chapter 6

Contributors

Toby Butler is a lecturer in London History and Heritage at the University of East London and Birkbeck. His research interests include oral history, digital heritage, and the cultural history of London. Toby has created several websites that use oral history trails to explore place (see memoryscape.org.uk for details). He has directed and worked on oral history projects in India, the US, Wales, and England. He is co-editor of the *History Workshop Journal;* programme leader of an MA in Heritage Studies: Place, Memory and History, at the Raphael Samuel History Centre; and research associate at the Scottish Oral History Centre.

Sue Edney completed her doctorate at Bath Spa University, entitled "The Art of the Vernacular: Horticulture and Poetic Culture in the Poetry of John Clare and William Barnes." She has an article on Barnes and his dialect in the journal *English* (2009), and is currently employed at Bath Spa University as an assistant lecturer in English.

Rebecca Edwards is research assistant on the project "'It Was Forty Years Ago Today . . .': Locating the Early History of Performance Art in Wales 1965–1979," funded by the Arts and Humanities Research Council, UK. She completed her PhD at Swansea University on national identity and pop music in Wales. See www.performance-wales.org for more information.

Tim Fulford is a professor of English at Nottingham Trent University. He is the author of many books and articles on Romantic and eighteenth-century literature and culture, including *Romantic Indians* (2006) and *Literature, Science and Exploration* (2004). He is the coeditor of *The Collected Letters of Robert Southey.*

Steven High is Canada Research Chair in Oral History at Concordia University in Montreal, where he codirects the Centre for Oral History and Digital Storytelling. He is the author of *Industrial Sunset: The Making of North America's Rust Belt* (2003) and of *Corporate Wasteland: The Landscape and Memory of Deindustrialization* (2007).

Andrew Holmes is a researcher at the Environmental Justice Foundation in London. He completed his PhD at Cranfield University on the role of local knowledge in environmental research before focusing on the integration of oral history and ecology for the Ouse Project at Sussex University. Publications include *Storytelling, Floods, Wildflowers and Washlands: Oral History in the River Ouse Project* (forthcoming).

Leslie McCartney has an M.A. in cultural anthropology from Trent University, Peterborough, Ontario, Canada. She was the lead researcher of the Gwich'in Elders' Biographies Research Project and between 2002–2004 was the executive director of the Gwich'in Social and Cultural Institute. She was then project coordinator of the King's Cross Voices Oral History Project from 2004–2007. Since 2007 she has been employed at Trinity College, the University of Dublin, in Ireland.

Dafydd Moore is a professor of English at the University of Plymouth. He has published widely on *The Poems of Ossian,* including *Enlightenment and Romance in the Poems of Ossian* (2003) and *Ossian and Ossianism,* 4 volumes (2004). He is currently working on the *Edinburgh Companion to James Macpherson*, and on a book on Richard Polwhele and Romantic culture.

Heike Roms is senior lecturer in performance studies at Aberystwyth University. She has published on contemporary performance practice, particularly on work emanating from Wales. Her coedited volume, *Contesting Performance—Global Sites of Research,* was published in 2010. She is principal investigator on "'It Was Forty Years Ago Today…': Locating the Early History of Performance Art in Wales 1965–1979," a research project focusing on the historiography of early performance art, which is supported by a large research grant from the Arts and Humanities Research Council (UK). The project won the David Bradby TaPRA Award for Research in International Theatre and Performance 2011. (For more information see www.performance-wales.org)

Paul Thompson is professor emeritus in sociology at the University of Essex and a research fellow at the Young Foundation. He is founder–editor of *Oral History* and founder of the National Life Stories at the British Library. He is a pioneer of oral history in Europe and author of the international classic, *The Voice of the Past.* His other books include *The Edwardians, Growing Up in Stepfamilies,* and most recently, on migrants, *Jamaican Hands Across the Atlantic.*

Shelley Trower is a researcher at the University of Exeter and committee member of the Oral History Society. She has published several essays in journals and edited collections, and is the author of *Senses of Vibration: A History of the Pleasure and Pain of Sound* (forthcoming); coeditor of *Cornish Studies 17,* about sustainability and the clay country (2009), and editor of *Vibratory Movements*, a special issue of the journal *Senses and Society* (2008).

Series Editors' Foreword

This collection of ten essays, developed from papers presented at a 2008 conference at the University of Plymouth, England, breaks new ground for oral history. Essays in part 1 situate contemporary work within nineteenth-century efforts to preserve local oral cultures through the written word, suggesting an interesting interplay rather than a rigid demarcation between these two modes of communication. In part 2, they link oral history's traditional local focus to new work in environmental history, using it to document both changes in local environments over time and differences in the way local people view the same landscape—and changes to it. The essays in part 3 demonstrate how new modes of doing and presenting oral history—via performance, recorded memoryscapes, and websites—can restore the "oral" to oral history.

Themes of place, writing, and voice thus reverberate throughout the collection, intertwining in new and provocative ways. We read, for example, of nineteenth-century local dialects transformed into print, oddly prefiguring the current oral history practice—and problematic—of rendering vernacular speech in written transcripts; of an original project that draws upon both oral narratives and written texts to understand past land use practices, with the goal of flood alleviation and the restoration of biodiversity in rural Sussex, England; and of novel approaches to conducting and presenting interviews in situ.

Thanks to editor Shelley Trower's creative arrangement and thoughtful introductions, the whole of this book is more than the sum of its individual parts. Although most of these essays focus on work undertaken in England, if there is one overarching message here, it is that we can no longer consider oral history's often deeply local focus only as a kind of parochialism. All these essays broaden out to issues with remarkable global resonance – the move to literacy, postindustrial communities, ecological consciousness, the networked world.

The twenty-seventh book in Palgrave's *Studies in Oral History* series, *Place, Writing, and Voice* joins a growing number that are both deeply grounded in time and place and also open up new methodological and theoretical thinking in oral history, including Alessandro Portelli's *The Order Has Been Carried Out: History, Memory, and Meaning of a Nazi Massacre in Rome (2003); Remembering: Oral History Performance,* edited by Della Pollock (2005); Suroopa Mukherjee's

Surviving Bhopal: Dancing Bodies, Written Texts, and Oral Testimonials of Women in the Wake of an Industrial Disaster (2010); and *Oral History and Photography*, edited by Alexander Freund and Alistair Thomson (2011). In addition, books in the series aim to bring topically oriented oral history out of the archives and into the hands of students, educators, scholars, and the reading public. These volumes are based extensively on interviews and present them in ways that aid readers to appreciate more fully their historical significance and cultural meaning.

—Linda Shopes
Carlisle, Pennsylvania
—Bruce M. Stave
University of Connecticut

Acknowledgments

This collection derives from a conference held at the University of Plymouth, "Place, Writing and Voice" (September 5–6, 2008). I am grateful for funding from the university and from the Cornish Audio Visual Archive to support this conference and to my co-organizer, Dafydd Moore. This conference in turn derived from a symposium held in Cornwall, "Voices of the Clay Country," supported by the Heritage Lottery Fund (UK), which also partially funded my work on this collection. I am grateful to Garry Tregidga and Adrian Rodda for their invaluable support of the project in these early stages. I am also grateful to the Oral History Society and the Scottish Oral History Group, especially for the conference "Hearing Voice in Oral History" (2009), which helped me to develop ideas for this project and also introduced me to Steven High's work (in his keynote paper). In particular, I would like to thank Hilary Orange, Linda Shopes, Graham Smith, and Paul Thompson, for their generous intellectual input and support of my work in oral history. Above all, I would like to thank Nicholas Ridout, without whom this project, like many others, would not have been possible.

Introduction

Shelley Trower

Voices were once more closely bound up with particular places, or localities, than they are today. Before modern technologies of amplification, transmission and reproduction (such as telephones and record players), the oral was local in so far as it only reached those within earshot. It was necessary for balladeers and storytellers to travel in person to reach a wider audience. The voice itself, unlike the written text, could not be transmitted far beyond the locality in which it was spoken.

This book spans from oral traditions to oral history, observing differences between them while also allowing for connections. The relation between oral tradition and oral history is debatable and is changeable in different places, but for my purposes this book considers oral traditions to primarily include stories, songs, and dialects passed down through generations by word of mouth, whereas oral history consists more often of recollections from within a speaker's lifetime and usually makes use of technology to record and replay the sounds of the voice.[1] Oral traditions often seem to belong to a place—originating and surviving within a specific locality—but there is of course no clear division between oral traditions and oral history: folktales are recorded using digital audio technologies, for instance, while they are also written down and reproduced in print, and can thereby be transmitted far beyond any locality into the wider world. This book considers writing to be a kind of technology, much as sound recorders are, though with important differences. It considers changing perceptions of the oral and local, written and (relatively) global, from the eighteenth century to the twenty-first century. Early chapters consider how oral traditions were written down and transmitted to wider audiences beyond the locality where they were spoken. As a result of auditory technologies, the voice itself in oral history is now recorded and transmitted outside of any particular locality, but this book goes on to demonstrate how oral history can develop in-depth knowledge of localities, reestablishing the connection between the local and oral in new ways and with new relevance in a global context.

I thus hope to provide oral history with some of its own history, to provide a historical as well as a geographical framework for thinking about what it *is*—in terms of voice—and what it *does* in its engagement with place, bearing in mind the numerous projects out there that engage so closely with local communities and local history. Such engagement with the local is shared by the work of early oral historians such as George Ewart Evans, who wanted to record the ways of life of agricultural workers in an East Suffolk community at a time when these were being lost in the face of new farming technologies and social changes. Like many of the earlier folklorists, Evans focused on a specific place in his attempt to preserve something of a local oral culture that seemed to be dying out, although folklorists tended to ignore agricultural work (being more interested in tales, songs, and customs) and intervened as narrators and interpreters in the written text, while Evans directly recorded the voices of farm workers.[2] It is from his understanding of folklore, along with a strong tradition of local history, that Evans's work springs, and many more recent oral history studies have followed his lead, especially in England, in exploring and documenting rural locations, while there has also been a flourishing growth of interest in oral history projects in local communities in cities.[3]

Community-based oral history is not necessarily local, however. Alistair Thomson points out in his review of community oral history that in the 1970s and 1980s such projects broadened to include "communities defined by shared interest or identity which weren't necessarily linked to place."[4] Our present collection brings together a range of oral history projects, including community projects, but, in contrast to the general field of community history, these are all focused primarily on a particular place; what the different approaches share is a sense of place as, first and foremost, a specific geographical locality. Localities are not, however, to be understood as disconnected or separable from a wider world.

Its ability to work closely with specifics of place continues to be one of the most valuable strengths of oral history, as we shall see, though there can also be problems or limitations with place-based approaches. Oral history provides unique insights into places, but studies sometimes treat place in a rather superficial manner. As geographer Gavin Andrew and others observe, "A general focus 'on' a specific place simply frames the research and provides one of its parameters" in much work in oral history. Place is not often subject to theorization, though there are important exceptions.[5] Rather than simply doing oral histories in particular localities, then, I want to reflect on this practice, and to show how place and oral history can both have active, interactive roles. Oral history can help articulate how people experience places, can change perceptions and understandings of places, and can possibly even generate activities that physically change places; different places also actively shape oral history in various ways. This book is not a celebration but a critical investigation of place and voice and their relationship. I want to think about place in the context of a wider world. Attention to place-specific, personalized narratives can be used to productively disturb metanarratives with alternative strands of knowledge, as Mark Riley and David Harvey, among others, point out,[6] but individual local projects sometimes develop few if any connections with other projects, and at their worst may encourage an inward-looking lack of interest in the world beyond one's own neighborhood. Alistair Thomson observes that since the 1970s there has been a tension between "critical community history" and "parochial celebration," proponents of the former criticizing in particular the way in which personal stories are foregrounded, while there is a lack of engagement with "wider structural forces and social relationships [...] a focus on the local tended to neglect the national or global influences on local lives."[7] Thomson argues that it is an important continuing challenge for oral history to use personal testimony in ways that relate to wider social forces and dynamics.

An edited collection provides an ideal platform for framing a number of individual, local projects in relation to a wider historical and geographical context. It provides a way of framing connections between various projects and their localities, not least in this case through a consideration of factors that affect many parts of the world, including new communication technologies and environmental changes. Thus, although Britain and Canada are most central to this collection, the case studies are applicable to the practice of oral history internationally.

Oral history can be used to gather knowledge of localities, including knowledge that is part of local culture, by accessing people's firsthand experiences of and bodily involvement with specific physical environments, often as workers: as farmers and miners, for example. Riley and Harvey argue, however, that not only have oral historians rarely engaged with how geographers understand place; geographers in turn have neglected to use the methodologies of oral history (exceptions here include work by Gavin Brown among others).[8] They claim that despite the interest in subjective narratives following the "cultural turn" in geography, "historical and cultural geographers interested in issues of landscape meaning, rural transformation and cultures of the countryside" have carried out their studies largely "through the exploration of the writings (and artwork) of specific, and often privileged, individuals, leaving the methodological approach of oral history as a fairly neglected toolkit."[9] Along with the increased interest in subjective narratives, our contemporary context of environmental concerns gives new relevance to the work of George Ewart Evans. "Although Evans viewed the value of the oral material he collected as lying in their simple recording of past practices," comments Riley, "similar oral histories may play a significant role in contemporary nature conservation."[10]

Oral history is increasingly being used to explore peoples' relationship to their surroundings, including urban environments. Part two of this collection builds specifically on recent work that has considered the role of oral history in revealing perceptions and experiences of environmental history and issues ranging from nature conservation to global warming.[11] Among the chapters in part two, Andrew Holmes's (chapter 6) most directly draws on Riley's work, demonstrating how oral history, through interviews with farmers, can have a potentially active role in shaping agricultural practices in the context of recent environmental concerns. More generally, many of the chapters in our collection engage with oral narratives by rural and industrial workers, whose experiences of place—as a result of their working engagement with the countryside, or with mining landscapes, or in factories, for instance—differ considerably from writers, or tourists, or entrepreneurs, who are more likely to view such environments from a distance. As well as observing differences between the oral narratives and writings of "specific, often privileged, individuals," many chapters, through their consideration of written and oral narratives alongside each other develop connections and points of comparison.

This collection examines place on a number of levels. It engages with differing experiences and perceptions of particular localities and also explores how oral traditions and oral history interviews are themselves recorded and received, or *listened to,* in particular places. Steven High suggests that our focus on the interview means that we spend "remarkably little time thinking about what to do with the recordings."[12] I would like this collection to provide some balance between interviewees and their listeners, between the production and reception of voice. The process of interviewing can be an end in itself, but without listeners many projects may become pointless. Thus the focus shifts, finally, toward the audience and toward new technologies that offer new ways of making projects public and new ways of moving them into a wider, even global sphere.

Writing and Voice

The voice is responsive to place in that it reverberates against walls, or disappears into thin air. It is sensitive to architectural acoustics, to atmospheric conditions. It may even become, momentarily, a kind of place in itself, surrounding us; we can become immersed for a moment in the sound of a voice. In his historical study of orality and the development of writing and print, Walter Ong associates hearing with interiority:

> I gather sound simultaneously from every direction at once: I am at the center of my auditory world, which envelopes me, establishing me at a kind of core of

> sensation and existence. [...] You can immerse yourself in hearing, in sound. There is no way to immerse yourself similarly in sight.[13]

Ong suggests that hearing puts us in the middle of things. When we look at something, such as writing on a page, it is usually in front of us. It may be possible to become immersed in a book, but not in the same physical way as in sound. And it is this sense of being in the midst of an event—an event because "sound exists only when it is going out of existence"[14]—that was among other things lost in the shift to literate cultures, according to Ong. He defends oral cultures as primal, communal, in which people participate in a world of ongoing events, in contrast to the age of print media in which human beings are "situated in front of things,"[15] marking out a distance between individual humans and the world and each other. Historians and media theorists have explored such distance at some length, including Marshall McLuhan, who suggested that typography produced human "detachment and noninvolvement [...I]t was precisely the power to separate thought and feeling, to be able to act without reacting, that split literate man out of the tribal world of close family bonds in private and social life."[16]

Critics have accused writers like Ong of romanticizing the voice, at times privileging writing instead and thereby further intensifying the sense of a hierarchical division between voice and writing, which I wish this collection to avoid.[17] The chapters in part 1 of this collection contemplate how oral traditions are transformed into writing and print, but they are careful to acknowledge that attempts to preserve some kind of "pure" oral culture can idealize it as part of a conservative tradition that nostalgically mistakes change for decline. While these chapters indicate how the transformation of orality into print can involve loss—the loss, in particular, of distinctly local working-class voices as they are transmitted beyond their original locality for middle-class audiences—they resist the romanticization of orality and locality that print paradoxically tends to encourage. It was in the eighteenth century, when people began to fear that the proliferation of printed texts was destroying oral traditions,[18] that literature (most famously, probably, literary Romanticism, along with folklore collections, as we will see) began to idealize those very traditions, and to do so in the form of written, printed texts (the reproducibility of which made fame possible, beyond the mortal life of the unrecorded voice). We see a similar idealization in work by the early oral historian George Ewart Evans, who lamented how the local "dialect or *variety* of speech" was changing, losing its "purity" and its connection to place, to the soil: "it bears the accent of an older language and a much healthier one than current English, its unadorned purity being unpolluted by the numerous abstractions that have crept into our everyday discourse. [...] The language of the respondents is much nearer to the soil."[19] Evans here promotes a nostalgia for a mythical older world in which voice and place seemed bound up together, in which voice even seemed embedded in place, attempting to preserve something of that past not only through the audio recordings but also paradoxically through the written text. Evans's audio recordings were until recently far less readily available than his books, which consist largely of extensive extracts of the interviews.[20] I will shortly explore more recent uses of oral history with new technologies which make the voice itself more available, retaining qualities of sound such as described by Ong: its ability to surround, to immerse the listener. But this is not to privilege orality as somehow more pure or as belonging to a better, more communal world, than the written text.

There is no dramatic historical shift from orality to print,[21] but rather complex negotiation and interplay between various differing modes of communication. Writing and voice are related rather than opposed, as Alessandro Portelli, among others, has observed. In his foundational essay of 1979, "What Makes Oral History Different?," Portelli considers some of the formal differences between written and oral sources—including the sonic qualities of the latter, such as tone and volume, which contain "implicit meaning" in addition to that of words—but he observes that these different sources "are not mutually exclusive." As well as having specific qualities and functions, they share certain characteristics, and Portelli is particularly keen to emphasize that while a common prejudice tends to view written documents as more factually credible than oral sources, they can be equally subjective. He protests against any hierarchical assessment of oral sources as either inferior or superior: "the undervaluing and the overvaluing of oral sources end up by cancelling out specific qualities, turning these sources into mere supports for traditional written sources, or into an illusory cure for all ills."[22] In particular he argues that neither written nor oral narratives are more objective or authentic than each other. Portelli's later work, *The Text and the Voice,* develops a more thoroughgoing analysis of the interplay between the written and oral. Here he observes that it is literate societies that generate the nostalgic fantasies about "primitive orality," and that writers like Ong adopt a "binary approach" to orality and literacy, which are subjected to a linear model of history whereby the former is supposedly replaced by the latter. "Primitive orality," in Ong's model, is finally replaced by the "secondary orality" produced by electronic media, and especially by auditory technologies. Instead, Portelli proposes an additive approach whereby each new mode of communication does not abolish previous ones, "but adds to and modifies them, expanding possibilities and restructuring the whole field of communication."[23] Written and oral sources, quite simply, can do different things, which Portelli considers to be potentially complementary. Written texts can preserve words, can direct them toward a future audience, and give a sense of completeness, in the case of a finished artistic work, for instance, while the voice can be used to interact in real time with hearers (though technological developments have affected many such differences, including, for example, instant messaging or live chat, where writing becomes much more conversational). The chapters in this book bear out some of

Portelli's observations in this respect: they not only critique the romanticization of oral sources over written ones, but at times they encourage the use of both kinds of sources simultaneously, resulting in fuller, richer historical observations, archives, and exhibitions (see, for example, Steven High's chapter). With regard to community oral history, Alistair Thomson similarly points out advantages of using both oral and written sources. He proposes that we resist single-source community history, that we not only use photographs but work more with life writing, including:

> diaries, letters, autobiographical writings, many of which are out there and available to community history projects [...]. These other types of life story offer a different and equally useful angle on personal and collective experience. The relationships and motivations of life writing are different to those of oral history, and people may well write different stories to the ones they speak, not least because they have more control when they tell their own story as opposed to when you ask them to tell it to you.[24]

Thomson here seems to appeal against a tendency for oral historians to over-focus, understandably, on the oral narratives produced in interviews.

But although the voice is at times romanticized, or emphasized at the expense of written texts, the latter have also been overvalued at times. The rush to translate oral sources into written ones, which Portelli suggests is symptomatic, can certainly be problematic.[25] The various attempts, with their limitations and difficulties, to translate oral traditions into written texts in the eighteenth and nineteenth centuries, as documented in the first part of this collection, can provide historical background for more recent practices in oral history. Although the very term "oral history" would suggest that voice is central to this practice, its audio dimension has been notoriously underused. Historians tend to be more attentive to the words that are said than to the way they are spoken. The time-consuming practice of transcribing interviews, and the analysis and reproduction of interviews in written articles and books, provides evidence of this attention to words rather than to sounds. All these forms of writing of course have immense value, but it is also important to recognize their limitations. Transcriptions, for example, in many respects can be useful (they are readily searchable and can be easily scanned by the eye for purposes of research and analysis, for instance), but what is lost, of course, in the process of transforming speech into written words, includes different volumes, rhythms, intonations, and inflections. These dimensions of speech, Portelli observes, "carry implicit meaning and social connotations which are not reproducible in writing [...]. The same statement may have quite contradictory meanings, according to the speaker's intonation, which cannot be represented objectively in the transcript."[26] In the first issue of the *Oral History* journal, Raphael Samuel drew attention to the "Perils of the Transcript" in an article of that title (1972), pointing out that the editorial interventions made for transcripts can further distort the spoken word, by cutting pauses and repetitions, by inappropriately imposing grammatical forms such as paragraphs and punctuation, and even by rearranging and inserting words.[27]

Before technologies of sound reproduction, as I have said, the only way the spoken word could be preserved and transmitted, beyond the memories and locations of speakers and audiences, was in the form of the written text. Now, of course, the voice itself is recorded in the practice of oral history—it no longer has to be transformed by writing—so that while we continue to represent that voice in written texts (including this one) there are also multiple possibilities of reproducing and transmitting the actual voice. Our present collection does not analyze the sounds of the voice so much as the concept of voice itself, especially in terms of its differences from and relations to written texts and more recent technologies, and its relations to place. But I hope it will also help to contextualize future work that will focus in more detail on the sonorous textures of voice—not least some of the fascinating studies presented at an annual Oral History Society conference, "Hearing Voice in Oral History" (2009). Considering that voice is essential to oral history, we might do well to think more not only about what it says, but what it is, and how it says it.

Voice and Sound Technologies

Auditory and digital technologies make the voice accessible in new ways. The digitization of sound, in particular, challenges the dominance of transcription. Michael Frisch points out that the digital revolution has two major implications on our work with oral history interviews. First, digitization means that all forms of information (image, text, sound) become essentially the same: "All can be expressed as digital information that can be organized, searched, and integrated with equal facility." Second, digitization makes all points in the data instantly accessible: "One can move from point to point, anywhere in the data, without having to scroll or play forward or backward through the documentation in a linear way, as with tapes."[28] Frisch discusses a wide range of projects, from small-scale to large projects made available digitally on the Internet, including, for example, *The Virtual Oral/Aural History Archive* at California State University, Long Beach (http://salticid.nmc.csulb.edu/cgi-bin/WebObjects/OralAural.woa/), which presents oral history interviews in a highly searchable, user-friendly way. Such projects, Frisch shows, point the way toward increasing engagement with the "raw" documentation itself, which will also increasingly include video, as technological developments have made video interviews as easy to carry out and archive as audio interviews. (This book focuses on voice, but I would like to point out the importance of all that goes with it: gestures and body language and clothing and other visual and multisensory forms of communication, which are potentially as interesting and valuable to the meaning of interviews as the sound of the voice itself.[29]) There are now numerous examples of collections made available online from a range of different institutions and organizations including universities, museums, libraries, and community projects.[30] Often what is available are extracts from the collections, but they can be a useful starting point to then tracking down complete recordings using online catalogues. Digital technologies also make it easier for oral history to be heard—rather than or as well as being displayed as text—in public spaces such as museums and galleries.[31] In his discussion of community oral history, Alistair Thomson points out that the medium of oral history suits a variety of modes of publication, ranging from exhibitions to radio, film, and performance, along with print publications such as booklets. "Oral history," writes Thomson, "is aural (it's also visual in video interviews), it's people speaking and their faces and their voices; it's tremendously engaging and usable in a whole range of different forms of output." The use of new technologies need not and will not supersede the written text, as Thomson suggests with his emphasis on working more with life writing, but he nevertheless notes that it is "much harder to use life writing in new media."[32]

New technologies have allowed us to return in various ways to voice, and furthermore they have opened up new relations between voice and place. Binaural and three-dimensional sound systems are employed in museums and other exhibition spaces to create immersive sound environments (to return to the surround sound described by Ong), for example, and outdoor exhibitions and walking tours also employ location-based media.[33] A pioneering project in the UK is the public art installation, *Linked,* by artist Graeme Miller, which broadcasts oral history recordings of the testimonies of those who once lived and worked in the buildings demolished in the building of the M11 link road.[34] The voices are broadcast from transmitters mounted on lampposts on a route alongside the road, and they can be "tuned into" by walkers equipped with receivers and maps, which are available from local libraries and museums. As Toby Butler points out, self-guided walks and history trails are also run by museums and heritage organizations and tourist companies, but *Linked* pushes the boundaries of public oral history, turning the long urban street into a semipermanent exhibition space.[35] The transmitters are solid-state and are expected to last for decades, so the changing landscape will play a role in the future of the exhibition. Miller has also commented on this openness to an unknown future, which he sets in opposition to the closure of written texts. The broadcasts, he says, are

> not memories that you can write in stone anyway, they are almost deliberately sabotaged not to be a version of the truth because they are too incomplete to tell any coherent version, but they can arouse a lot of curiosity...[in the future] people will come and have another look at it, people change generation,

> outlook, landscapes change, it will be interesting how audio hieroglyphs stand up to test of time.[36]

The interviews are edited so that although most of the memories and stories are coherent, at times the broadcast seems to lose any clear meaning. So it is interesting that while the voices are given a degree of permanence (with the highly durable, solid-state transmitters) which we might traditionally associate with writing (above all, writing in stone), they retain an incompleteness, as well as an openness to the changes in people and the place. The most dramatic change in the forseeable future has surely already happened: the building of the motorway. And this is what the project attempts to capture and in a sense to undo, in its attempt to rebuild something of the past, of the demolished buildings. Oral history projects in general aim to preserve an aspect of the past through spoken memories, but Miller's has done more than this: it is not just about the preservation of meaningful testimonies and stories by people who lived and worked in the place, in the pre-motorway buildings, but that the very sound of their voices, in a sense, puts the houses back in place:

> I was going to put the houses back, I was going to put them back and do them in a way that would just project them back literally with radio waves, radio waves would fill up that space, so literally, that volume... because the road is a trench as well, it is going to be even more clear that it is an empty space rather than a flat plane, because it is carved down—it seems to occupy a certain volume, and that seems like the empty volume that you can pump full of radio waves and rebuild those houses.[37]

Butler, who collaborated on the oral history part of the project, later developed his own "memoryscapes," audience responses to which are discussed in chapter 9 in this volume. Numerous other audio trails have also been developed beyond the heritage and tourist sector by performance artists and sound artists, as well as, more recently, by oral historians[38] (in chapter 8 of this volume, Heike Roms and Rebecca Edwards also mention a plan to develop an audio guide to the history of performance in Wales, and in chapter 10, Steven High discusses his development of an online sound trail of a now-demolished paper mill in Ontario). Such trails clearly help listeners to engage with place in different ways, to change perceptions and to challenge assumptions, to make connections between the past and present of changing environments far more directly than would be possible for a listener sitting in a library or at home.

Sound trails are just part of what Steven High refers to as a wider move to embrace mobile methodologies and technologies (see chapter 10 of this book). As well as the walking audio tour, the walking interview is now being used increasingly by geographers and artists interested in place, so that the environment can act as a prompt, as it does also in Andrew Holmes's and Heike Roms's and Rebecca Edwards's chapters (6 and 8). In other words, interviewees/speakers as well as listeners are engaging with place in new ways, so that the voice is situated. In a project carried out with aboriginal people in New South Wales, Australia, for instance, information about place attachment was gathered from interviewees by visiting places they mentioned and by retracing routes across the landscape. In addition, the interviewers would roll out large aerial photographs during the interview process, and ask interviewees to plot places and pathways. The oral histories thus provided spatial detail, according to Maria Nugent, one of the historians working on the project, that "would be impossible to gain from other types of historical sources and from published histories and ethnographies."[39] The project was thus able to move well beyond the limits of written sources, and to map out place attachment despite the "*absence* of physical traces in places occupied by Aboriginal people [which] reflects their historical experience of dispossession and dispersal and the seasonal nature of their work patterns."[40] Although I would not want to suggest that the building of the M11, or the demolishing of the paper mill, involved an equally extreme level of destruction and injustice, Butler's and High's projects are similar in the respect that in their different ways they are intended to map out an absence resulting from dispossession and destruction, to replace a missing geography. In the case of Nugent's work, remembered places and routes were plotted out on maps—as they are in Roms and Edwards's chapter in this book—producing a textual and visual representation of collective autobiographical memory that can challenge how nonaboriginal people think about and represent the landscapes and places they own.

All such projects can thus help to articulate a sense of place, by and for disparate groups and purposes. They can enable certain groups to better convey their relationship to places and enable others to empathize with their experiences. They can help to establish an understanding of historical changes, and might even attempt to resist the obliteration of past places, whether through visual representations (as with the use of maps) or by harnessing voice so that it becomes a kind of place itself (as where radio waves "rebuild those houses").

A Global Sense of Place

Each chapter here considers how changes have taken place in a specific locality, and some also consider the changing ways in which oral history itself is recorded and listened to in particular localities. I want in this final section of the introduction to set out more precisely this book's approach to place, partly by defining it as distinct from the conceptions of earlier oral historians. I have already mentioned the work of George Ewart Evans, who was perhaps the first to demonstrate the capacity of oral history to reach for valuable, detailed understandings of specific localities. In this respect I would like to see this collection as continuing, as building on such work, but whereas Evans's approach to the local is to seek its unchanging, even ancient past, this is not an aim shared by contributors to this book. Evans repeatedly asserts that the revolutionary changes to life in the countryside have wiped out an earlier culture which continued unchanged since at least the early Middle Ages. This sense of continuity is tied up with a conception of localities as having boundaries, as being separate or protected from other locations. In *Ask the Fellows Who Cut the Hay,* Evans observes a sense of community and pride "among the old people" and seems to regret the influx of "strangers." He notes that "Newcomers, hardy enough to attempt to settle in the village, are at first regarded from a distance," and while they seem after a time to be accepted, recent innovations including council houses are "modifying the pattern of life and bringing more strangers into the village. Blaxhall is being swept late into the flood of twentieth-century change."[41] In contrast to this rather nostalgic ideal of capturing a (now lost) sense of place as stable or unchanging, and as securely bounded, I would like the cumulative effect of the chapters here, each of which observes specific, local changes, to be to ultimately destabilize place, and to emphasize how places are interconnected.

Two of the major kinds of change documented here result from postindustrialization and environmental damage, which of course affect many parts of the world in various ways. My own chapter, for example, explores an area of Britain, known locally as "the clay country," the economy and landscape of which were dominated by clay mining until the late twentieth century. Clay mining is an industry that has now all but vanished from the area. In its place, in one of the excavated, disused and sterile clay pits, an environmental project, the Eden Project, has been set up, consisting of two huge greenhouses (or biomes), which host plant life from other parts of the world, such as the Mediterranean. One of Eden's main stated purposes is to educate and to promote awareness of global environmental problems. In taking such changes into account—the move, in this case, from an industrial to a postindustrial environment—I have wanted to resist the ideal of uncovering or reviving a threatened place or local community with a once-stable essence. The lost industrial past for which many interviewees expressed understandable nostalgia was of course preceded, in turn, by a preindustrial past, the loss of which was previously lamented in many places in and beyond Britain, as the chapters in part 1 indicate. By situating my study within the framework of others, each can take on added implications. The clay industry (like the textile industry discussed in Sue Edney's chapter, for instance) was itself once the destroyer of previous ways of life, and of a certain kind of environment (moorland was transformed into vast infertile quarries), and was never ultimately sustainable, not least because mineral resources are finite. I want to emphasize that places are not fixed, static, preservable entities, but more like processes, and also that they are not bounded territories, but are permeable—they are both shaped by and they shape other parts of the world.

In this I am following Doreen Massey's influential proposal that we seek a global sense of place.[42] A sense of place, or locality, is in contrast sometimes set against the global. The search after place can be interpreted as an attempt to find rooted security, to establish fixed identities amidst—and in opposition to—the flux, fragmentation, and disruption of a postmodern world. As such, the idea of place is sometimes criticized as being a reactionary retreat, as the focus for a form of "romanticized escapism from the real business of the world." Occasionally, Massey argues, such a reactionary impulse can give rise to certain kinds of localism and nationalism, to sentimental and introverted preoccupations with sanitized "heritages," and to antagonism to "outsiders." She identifies a number of problems with the reactionary notion of place, including "the idea that places have single, essential identities," the inward-looking construction of their histories "based on delving into the past for internalized origins," and the drawing of boundaries.[43] We might find a version of this in certain local oral history projects as in Ewart Evans's attempts to preserve the olden, unchanging, "pure" heritage of Suffolk villages, which seems more essentially local, contained by boundaries, than the now modern villages with their changes brought about partly by "incomers." Evans's study could be considered an early version of the parochial, nostalgic celebrations carried out by some community oral history projects, which, Alistair Thomson notes, have been criticized for neglecting the "wider social forces [...] the national or global influences on local lives." Massey urges instead that places should not be idealized as static, but conceived of as processes. Along with this historical sense of places as ever-changing, they should not be conceived of geographically as having boundaries that define enclosures in counterposition to an outside—which is what seems to make them so vulnerable to invasion by newcomers—but rather should be defined precisely in terms of linkages to that outside.

To return to the case of the clay country, as well as understanding it in terms of its historical and ongoing changes, I want to frame it in relation to other places, to the "outside." Some of the people interviewed for this project expressed understandable hostility both to the Eden Project and to "incomers"[44]—both of which may seem to pose external threats to the locality—but while the substance of clay itself is found within the place and might be considered of internal origin, the industry was always dependent on external markets, and its collapse was due largely to competition from Brazil. Mining villages and towns and cities and landscapes can only be understood in terms of their linkages to places far beyond any regional or municipal boundaries. And it is not just that certain international or global forces shape such areas; there is movement in both directions, from outside in and from inside out. The clay country is not simply a passive victim of international markets or of global capitalism in the form of overseas competition, but has its own impact on other places. The impact of mining on the environment, for instance, is not restricted to local landscapes—rather, we have learned that ecosystems are interconnected, that the ravages of industry have a role to play in global environmental changes, which in turn variously affect different localities, such as those observed by Andrew Holmes and Leslie McCartney (chapters 6 and 7 of this book).

Rather than set the global and local in opposition to each other, then, or to claim that globalization causes the erosion of place, as earlier globalization theorists tended to do, Massey and others in the 1990s began to develop a new approach to the local in terms of connections or networks and movements. The global does not erode place, but produces new forms of localization. As Mike Savage, Gaynor Bagnall, and Brian Longhurst describe it in their helpful review, one way of construing global processes in these terms is to see that they "do not work at a general level, but operate through specific proximate ties and connections [...] there is no 'one' global, but an infinite multiplicity of global relationships, all constituted in various forms through particular local configurations."[45] Such a view retains a sense of the particularity of place. While Massey, Savage, and others have tended to focus on cities, such as the "world city" of London,[46] I have begun to briefly indicate here how other places, including rural postindustrial places, might also be viewed as interconnected. Considering that oral history projects are so often place-based, we might do well to take on board the connections and conceptions of place developed by geographers like Massey.

The chapters in this collection do not themselves focus on global networks or connections, but they offer a sense of how oral history can enrich the understanding of localities from the ground up, giving the substance of lived experience to some of the abstractions of globalization theory. Many of the chapters offer local perspectives of particular places that differ from those of visitors or tourists, resisting the romanticization of lost places of the past (whether preindustrial or industrial) and also drawing attention to some of the problems undergone by places in the face of global issues such as climate change, postindustrial economies, and indeed tourism itself. Together, the oral histories discussed here contribute to an understanding of how changes that can be mapped out on a vast, abstract scale are experienced differently in a range of specific localities, in everyday ways. Further, while an interest in particular localities can at the same time attend to a wider, international context, projects can themselves be projected far beyond any single locality, as my previous section of this introduction considered, especially through the use of the World Wide Web.

Communication technologies are of course often considered to be one of the facets of globalization, and can here at least be regarded as a tool by which oral history projects can attempt to transcend locality, to establish connections. In other words, I am keen to see local history projects making connections as part of an international oral history movement, both in the content of what they explore (seeking to understand localities in a relatively global context) and in the form through which they do it (seeking to make such understandings public on different levels, ranging from the local to the global). The chapters that constitute the final part of this collection, in particular, thus explore different forms of public oral history, ranging from the theater to sound trails to the Internet.

As Michael Burawoy argues, although the local was an appropriate defense against earlier forms of capitalism, the most effective responses to the kinds of global threats now facing many groups—particularly third-wave marketization and environmental crises—tend themselves to be able to operate on global as well as local levels.[47] This collection is in some respects itself rather locally focused (each of the essays concerns Britain or Canada), demonstrating the capacity of oral history to offer valuable insights into the particularities of place, but it can begin to push toward ways of reflecting on how the local can get beyond itself.

Notes

1. See, for example, Paul Thompson's *The Voice of the Past* (Oxford & New York: Oxford University Press, 1988), especially 22–71, for an account of oral tradition and oral history as connected and continuous as well as distinct, and Jan Vansina's *Oral Tradition as History* (Oxford: James Currey, 1985), especially 12–13, for an account of oral tradition which emphasizes its divisions from oral history. Vansina's understanding of oral history is now rather out-of-date but key points are still valid. Both Vansina and Thompson suggest that in some cultures in Africa, for example, oral traditions are far more prominent than in most parts of England or the US, where they are more clearly distinguishable from oral history. For a recent overview, see Lynn Abrams, *Oral History Theory* (New York & London: Routledge, 2010), 25–26.
2. Evans is best known for *Ask the Fellows Who Cut the Hay* (London: Faber and Faber, 1956). See also commentary by Stephen Caunce, *Oral History and the Local Historian* (London & New York: Longman, 1994). Many of his interviews can now be listened to using the British Library's online Sound Archive, at the George Ewart Evans Collection, http://sounds.bl.uk/Browse.aspx?category=Oral-history&collection=George%20Ewart%20Evans%20collection&browseby=Browse+by+interviewee&choice=S–Z (accessed January 23, 2011).
3. As Paul Thompson observes in *The Voice of the Past*, 66–67.
4. Alistair Thomson, "Oral History and Community History in Britain: Personal and Critical Reflections on Twenty-Five years of Continuity and Change," *Oral History* 36:1 (2008), 95–104 (98).
5. Gavin J. Andrews, Robin A. Kearns, Pia Kontos, and Viv Wilson, "'Their Finest Hour': Older People, Oral Histories, and the Historical Geography of Social Life," *Social and Cultural Geography* 7 (2006), 153–177. Mark Riley and David Harvey discuss this further in a later article, "Talking Geography: on Oral History and the Practice of Geography," *Social and Cultural Geography* 8:3 (2007), 345–351 (348). I will discuss further exceptions shortly below, but am thinking for now in particular of studies that use theories of nation to analyze the construction of national

narratives, such as Graham Smith and Peter Jackson's, which consider the work of Benedict Anderson and Homi Bhaba, for instance, in "Narrating the Nation: the 'Imagined Community' of Ukranians in Bradford," *Journal of Historical Geography* 25:3 (1999), 367–387. In challenging established narratives of nation, incidentally, Smith and Jackson's study could also indicate a further difference from attempts to collect and record oral traditions, which often feed into nationalist and regionalist histories and mythologies. See Paul Thompson for an account of the relationship between oral tradition/folklore and nationalism, *The Voice of the Past*, 61–65.

6. Mark Riley and David Harvey, "Talking Geography: on Oral History and the Practice of Geography," *Social and Cultural Geography* 8 (2007), 345–351 (p. 349).
7. Alastair Thomson, "Oral History and Community History in Britain," 99.
8. Riley and Harvey may overstate the extent to which geographers have failed to utilize oral history. Gavin Brown observes how cultural geographers increasingly use oral history "to explore individuals' subjective relationship with their environment." Brown used oral history in his own study to help balance the one-sided narrative provided by the few types of written record available for gay and lesbian history: police archives, court records, and medical case studies. He interviewed gay men to produce "cognitive," or "mental maps," of an area of London that reveal more about a place than "objective," cartographies, in "Listening to Queer Maps of the City: Gay Men's Narratives of Pleasure and Danger in London's East End," *Oral History* 29:1 (2001), 48–61. Another good example, focusing specifically on landscape meaning (prominent in this collection) and environmental issues is provided by the landscape architect Shelley Egoz, "Clean and Green but Messy: The Contested Landscape of New Zealand's Organic Farms," *Oral History* 28:1 (2000), 63–74.
9. Mark Riley and David Harvey, "Oral Histories, Farm Practice and Uncovering Meaning in the Countryside," *Social and Cultural Geography* 8:3 (2007), 391–415 (p. 392).
10. "Ask the Fellows Who Cut the Hay: Farm Practices, Oral History and Nature Conservation," *Oral History* 32:2 (2004), 45–53. Local historian Stephen Caunce similarly observes that "increasing awareness of the fragility of the environment has now made us more willing to listen and to see the value of a system that did not cause widespread pollution," in his *Oral History and the Local Historian*, 24.
11. See note 8 above. For further examples of oral history work both on the relationships between people and environments in general and on environmental concerns more particularly, see the articles in the two consecutive special issues of *Oral History* focusing on place: "Memory and Place," and "Landscapes of Memory," *Oral History* 28:1 and 28:2 (2000), and Stephen Hussey and Paul Thompson's edited collection, *Environmental Consciousness* (New Brunswick and London: Transaction, 2004).
12. See chapter 9. Steven High also makes this point in "Telling Stories: Oral History and New Media," *Oral History* 38: 1 (2010).
13. Walter Ong, *Orality and Literacy* (London & New York: Routledge, 2002), 71.
14. Ibid., 70. See also Ong, *The Presence of the Word: Some Prolegomena for Religious and Cultural History* (1969), where he writes: "The word is not an inert record but a living something, like sound, something going on" (12); "Sound is psychologically always something going on, something active, a kind of evanescent

effluvium which exists only so long as something or someone is actively producing it" (41–42).

15. Ong, *The Presence of the Word*, 28. See also Ong, *Orality and Literacy*, 72.
16. Marshall McLuhan, *Understanding Media: The Extensions of Man* (London: Routledge, 1964), 184–85.
17. Jacques Derrida is probably the best known critic of what he called "phonocentrism," the idealization of speech as superior to writing in Western thought, though he did not himself privilege writing instead—rather, he deconstructed the hierarchy. For commentary on the idealization of voice and the opposing position see, for example, Anne Karpf, *The Human Voice: The Story of a Remarkable Talent* (London: Bloomsbury, 2006), 202–08 and Penny Fielding, *Writing and Orality: Nationality, Culture, and Nineteenth-Century Scottish Fiction* (Oxford: Clarendon Press, 1996), 2–8.
18. See, for example, Ong, *The Presence of the Word*, 70–71; and Karpf, *The Human Voice*, 208.
19. George Ewart Evans, *Spoken History* (London & Boston: Faber and Faber, 1987), xv.
20. Many of Evans's interviews were made available online in 2010. See note 2.
21. Martin Jay's excellent account of the denigration of vision refers to arguments like Ong's as construing "visually imbued cultural and social practices" in "grandiose terms, such as a massive shift from an oral culture to a "chirographic" one based on writing and then a typographic one in which the visual bias of the intermediate stage is even more firmly entrenched." In Martin Jay, *Downcast Eyes: The Denigration of Vision in Twentieth-Century French Thought* (Berkeley, Los Angeles, London: University of California Press, 1994), 2. See also 66–69.
22. Alessandro Portelli, "What Makes Oral History Different?," in *The Oral History Reader*, 2nd ed., edited by Robert Perks and Alistair Thomson (London & New York: Routledge, 1998), 33–34.
23. Alessandro Portelli, *The Text and the Voice: Writing, Speaking, and Democracy in American Literature* (New York: Columbia University Press, 1994), 5
24. Alistair Thomson, "Oral History and Community History in Britain," 97–98.
25. In Portelli, "What Makes Oral History Different?," 33–38; and Portelli, *The Text and the Voice*, 7–11.
26. Portelli, "What Makes Oral History Different?" 34.
27. Raphael Samuel, "The Perils of the Transcript," *Oral History* 1:2 (1972), 19–22. For a recent discussion of the use of transcripts, and their difference from the oral text – pointing out that this is sometimes advantageous – see Abrams, *Oral History Theory*, 12–14.
28. Michael Frisch, "Oral History and the Digital Revolution," in *The Oral History Reader*, 2nd ed., edited by Robert Perks and Alistair Thomson (Oxon & New York: Routledge, 2006), 102–114 (103).
29. Ruth Finnegan provides one of the most comprehensive accounts of the various different ways in which human communication takes place, moving far beyond verbal forms of communication, in *Communicating: The Multiple Modes of Human Interconnection* (London & New York: Routledge, 2002).
30. For examples from the UK see extracts from Paul Thompson's Edwardian project as part of the University of Essex's Qualidata website, (http://www.esds.ac.uk/qualidata/online/data/edwardians/introduction.asp); extracts from the

Imperial War Museum's collection (http://collections.iwm.org.uk/server/show/ConWebDoc.6818); and full life-story interviews from various projects carried out at the British Library Sound Archive (http://www.bl.uk/reshelp/findhelprestype/sound/ohist/oralhistory.html) (all accessed September 21, 2010).

31. For discussion of oral history in public spaces and some examples see Perks and Thomson's *The Oral History Reader,* 336–37, and especially footnotes 29 and 30, p. 341–42.
32. Alastair Thomson, "Oral History and Community History in Britain," 97.
33. See Charles Hardy, "Authoring in Sound: Aural History, Radio and the Digital Revolution," in *The Oral History Reader*, 2nd ed., edited by Robert Perks and Alistair Thomson (Oxon and New York: Routledge, 2006), 393–405; see especially 396–97.
34. See http://www.linkedm11.net/index2.html (accessed September 21, 2010).
35. Graeme Miller and Toby Butler, "Linked: A Landmark in Sound, A Public Walk of Art," in *The Oral History Reader*, 2nd ed., edited by Robert Perks and Alistair Thomson (London and New York: Routledge, 1998), 425–433 (427–28).
36. Ibid., 428.
37. Ibid., 432.
38. For the Memoryscape Project, see http://www.memoryscape.org.uk/ (accessed September 21, 2010). Also, for excellent discussion of both *Linked* and *Memoryscape* and the context of sound art, see Toby Butler, "A Walk of Art: the Potential of the Sound Walk as Practice in Cultural Geography," *Social and Cultural Geography* 7:6 (2006), 889–908. Some of the best examples include, as well as the above, Mike Pearson's Carrland's project, http://www.carrlands.org.uk/ and Janet Cardiff, *The missing voice (case study B)*, London 1999, a good description and discussion of which can be found by David Pinder, "Ghostly Footsteps: Voices, Memories and Walks in the City," *Ecumene* 8 (2001), 15. For an excellent discussion of the history of sound art in terms of location see Brandon LaBelle, *Background Noise: Perspectives on Sound Art* (New York: Continuum, 2006), and related works as listed on the website http://www.errantbodies.org/main.html (accessed September 6, 2010).
39. Maria Nugent, "Mapping Memories: Oral History for Aboriginal Cultural Heritage in New South Wales, Australia," in *Oral History and Public Memories*, edited by Paula Hamilton and Linda Shopes (Philadelphia: Temple University Press, 2008), 59. Other studies have used comparable techniques with maps, such as Gavin Brown's method of asking gay men to map out places in a London borough that they perceived as especially "gay" or dangerous, as reported in "Listening to Queer Maps of the City."
40. Nugent, "Mapping Memories," 50.
41. Evans, *Ask the Fellows Who Cut the Hay*, 19.
42. Doreen Massey, "A Global Sense of Place," *Marxism Today* (June 1991), 24–29. Available at http://www.amielandmelburn.org.uk/collections/mt/index_frame.htm (accessed July 29, 2010).
43. Ibid., 24 & 26.
44. Attitudes to the Eden Project are discussed at the end of my chapter below (chapter 4). Some interviewees expressed negative views about people moving into the area. Such views also repeatedly feature on another oral history project I've

been working on as part of the Arts and Humanities Research Council-funded Mysticism, Myth, and "Celtic" Nationalism, in which we have interviewed 24 local Cornish people, many of whom identify "incomers" as a problem. One interviewee was opposed to the invasion of "the great arty English" at St. Ives, for example, changing its "essential nature," while he was also more generally concerned about incomers.

45. Mike Savage, Gaynor Bagnall, and Brian Longhurst, *Globalization and Belonging* (London: Sage, 2005), 6.
46. London far more powerfully shapes and is shaped by global processes than most other places, as Massey demonstrates in *World City* (Cambridge: Polity, 2010), but we might begin to think here about how rural places can also be viewed in terms of global networks. Savage et al. focus on Manchester in their study, *Globalization and Belonging*. See also Saskia Sassen, *The Global City: New York, London, Tokyo*, 2nd ed. (Princeton, New Jersey: Princeton University Press, 2001).
47. Michael Burawoy, "What Is to be Done? Theses on the Degradation of Social Existence in a Globalizing World," *Current Sociology* 56:3 (2008), 351–359. See also Michael Burawoy, Joseph Blum, Sheba George, et al., *Global Ethnography: Forces, Connections, and Imaginations in a Postmodern World* (Berkeley, Los Angeles, & London: University of California Press, 2000).

PART I

Introduction: Oral Tradition, Literature, and Locality

The three chapters in this first part consider how writers attempted to record voices in the form of written texts in the nineteenth century. Each chapter focuses on how a particular kind of writer took up certain aspects of local oral cultures—including folktales, songs, and dialect—and attempted to represent, to preserve and to transmit them through the written word. Each chapter considers what happens to local working-class voices when they are written down and transmitted to a wider audience, while they critique and resist the romanticization of locality and orality, as I noted in the introduction above. Literary studies here reveal long-standing connections between locality and orality and the working classes, which the rest of the volume will explore and develop in new contexts through oral history in the twentieth and twenty-first centuries. This will enable consideration of both continuity and change in the relation between the oral and local, the written and (relatively) global, and will develop links between literary studies and oral history.

In the opening chapter, Tim Fulford shows how Romantic literature, through its appropriation of oral tradition, plays a significant role in the heritagization of a particular locality in South West Britain, in its transformation into a "sacred place." The Romantic poets had always fetishized the oral. *Lyrical Ballads,* the book that famously established the new "Lake School" of poetry, deferred to two oral genres: the song and the ballad—valued as the voice of local peasantry. Fulford's chapter looks at the textual appropriation of unwritten stories of Dartmoor, its legends and tales, in the 1830s at the hands of Wordsworth's fellow Lake Poet, the laureate Robert Southey. Southey encouraged local authoress Eliza Bray to collect stories of the moor, and assisted in their publication. One result was to promote Dartmoor to the literary and touristic public as a Romantic region, akin to the Lakes and Snowdonia, in which a more primitive rural life could be accessed. Another was to fix local stories in a permanent, beautified, and moralized form fit for middle-class taste. As such, they came for many to represent the "real"ancient place they seek as a contrast to their ordinary urban lives—a place of superstition, magic, and ghosts. What was lost in this process, however, was the very locality of such tradition, its dialect, local references, and in-allusions, while the tales reached a far wider audience in their literary form. Bray's books entered literary tradition through Arthur Conan Doyle's renowned Sherlock Holmes story *Hound of the Baskervilles* and Christina Rossetti's classic "Goblin Market," and they have themselves been republished as recently as the 1990s, and are transformed into texts circulating on the World Wide Web, now peddling Dartmoor to tourists on the basis of their representation of an oral tradition that has largely vanished.

Oral historians have drawn quite extensively on the work of literary scholars—for example by employing concepts of narrative and genre in the analysis of interviews[1]—but literary critics rarely engage with oral history, and in my experience they tend to assume that it refers exclusively to oral traditions or culture. (Alessandro Portelli, whose work I discussed in this book's introduction, is an exception as a scholar of Anglo-American literature.) Many oral historians agree, however, that oral tradition is at the very least historically connected to the modern practice of oral history. Folklorists, among other kinds of collectors of various aspects of oral culture, including songs and dialects, were the first to develop comparable interests and techniques, such as in interviewing and recording working-class stories, providing a key point of connection with the early development of oral history. The nineteenth-century Cornish folklorist William Bottrell, for example, seems very much to anticipate the early priorities of oral history in so far as his work similarly emphasizes the importance of the oral culture of the "peasants" or "working classes":

> The folk-lore student, in collecting the myths, the proverbs, the traditions, the customs of the peasants of many lands, is doing an important work in accumulating facts bearing on the history of mankind; not the mere records of the wars and doings of kings and generals, but of the beliefs, aspirations, thoughts and feelings of the working classes of various nations.[2]

The field of literary studies, then, with its interests in a wide range of narratives, including folklore and dialect poetry, can allow us to explore the connections between oral traditions and history. Thus we might on the one hand be tempted to see a collector or recorder of folktales such as Bray as an early kind of oral historian, whose work helps to demonstrate the fertile potential of oral traditions if valued and recorded and translated into different forms—in this case literary, but new technologies create even more opportunities. On the other hand, Bray's approach could also serve to increase our understanding of the limitations of certain approaches, such as how the attempt to sanitize oral narratives in print can strip them of their local embeddedness, and can contribute to the consumption of a romanticized place by tourists. It is not that the romanticization of place or its construction for tourists is itself necessarily problematic (indeed, it might have certain benefits), but that oral historians need to think through the question of who oral history projects are for (community members or visitors, or both, for example), and their dangers as well as potential in recreating place. Postcolonial literature and criticism have also engaged creatively with the difficulties of translating oral traditions into written texts.[3] Oral historians and literary critics might thus exchange understanding of the possibilities, difficulties, and wide variety of forms of such translation.

Dafydd Moore and Sue Edney, in the second and third chapters of part 1, explore alternatives to the romanticization of voice and place. In doing so, they also pave the way for later oral history projects in their efforts to avoid or resist romanticization and touristic views (for example, they pave the way for Trower's and High's chapters). Moore takes up an interesting case of a county history, by Richard Polwhele, that resisted the tendency for literary representations of the oral to romanticize it. In contrast to the work of Polwhele's contemporaries such as William Borlase, who transformed and aestheticized oral traditions and the spoken language in his far more conventional history, Polwhele, in his compendious seven-volume *History of Cornwall*, managed to preserve something of the vitality of the spoken word—which constantly escapes every attempt to organize and to categorize. Polwhele's ambition was to be as inclusive as possible, and he was almost obsessively preoccupied with every last detail. Moore argues that Polwhele's efforts are thus both problematic, because the failure of a shaping and selecting editorial hand threatens the work's coherence, and a major part of the text's charm and value as a basis for Cornish history. Polwhele can be considered one of the most important local historians of the time, his techniques and work representing a significant advance of the form. By neglecting the standard narratives of eighteenth-century history in favor of the presentation of raw data, his open-handed *History* refuses the distancing and "museumizing" tendencies of his predecessors—and indeed, Moore suggests, of some twentieth-century oral historians—in favor of a teeming, untidy, but vital account of the spoken Cornish language. Moore demonstrates that Polwhele was in some ways very much of his time, a time when history broadened its horizons to include popular culture and the everyday. Yet, in his resistance to the narrative structures designed to contain those horizons, he was able—in a way that bears some (albeit limited) resemblance to oral histories in our time of "postdocumentary sensibility"—to avoid the romanticization of "noble savages" or "primitive societies," which tended to tame, to control, and to render them safe for consumption as heritage.

Rather than pursue a supposedly pure or authentic preindustrial orality with the ideal of fixing or freezing it in written form, in the final chapter of part 1, Sue Edney, like Moore, explores how printed texts can instead work with an ever-changing, living spoken language. Unlike the Romantic primitivists and folklorists and early oral historians like Evans, this isn't about the attempt to capture and preserve "a world about to be lost." Both Moore's and Edney's chapters demonstrate the absence of any clear division between the oral and written, which instead intermingle to produce new forms, aimed at a readership stretching beyond the locality being depicted. Edney focuses on the writings of dialect poets around mid-nineteenth-century Manchester, who took up and developed their own place-specific dialects, and on the range of ways in which they depicted the places themselves (both rural and urban), thus influencing the reception of place on a wider scale. Rather than attempting to capture some kind of preindustrial, previously unchanging essence of a place, the poets developed an adaptable "hybrid" form that straddles past and present, oral and written, and rural and urban. In this respect, Edney offers an alternative to the work of oral historians like Evans, who much more recently sought to capture rural dialects, which, he proposed, were losing their "purity" and connection to "the soil" (as discussed in the book's introduction above). Oral historians have continued to work with dialects—particularly with the understanding that these are often working-class voices—but are now far more ready to engage with urban as well as rural varieties and to recognize that they undergo constant change and intermingling with other voices, including those from immigrant communities, without mistaking change for decline or extinction.[4] The work of the dialect poets of the mid-nineteenth century, then, like that of Polwhele, is in some respects comparable to, or even paves the way for modern practices of oral history.

CHAPTER 1

Romanticizing the West Country: or, Hell-Hounds in Hard Cover and Pixies in Print

Tim Fulford

How does a space become a sacred place[5]—how does an area that was once disregarded and seen as waste become a heritage site, a tourist attraction for people seeking spiritual succor? Today, Dartmoor is such a place—a National Park, a shrine for literary tourists, and a pilgrimage site for the New Age, where nature discloses the supernatural, and the present is saturated with the spirits of the past. Oral lore, some ancient, some of modern invention, is recycled in print: pixies, druids, beasts of Dartmoor; hounds of the Baskervilles are transformed from local folktales to text circulating globally via the World Wide Web. What was once seen as being empty, as a dreariness, is now quested after: a zone brought into geographical focus and cultural meaning by people's desire to encounter the Other. Dartmoor is, that is to say, uncanny, its cultural purpose is to provide a physical trace of the noumenal—everything we think we cannot find in the urban, suburban, materialist world of motorways and retail parks—but be reachable by car. It offers a containable sublime where we can meet the ghosts of our own yearnings before driving back to the village for a B & B and cream tea.

The West Country[6] has its brochures and its blogs, its TV programs and its websites. In an economy desperate for tourist cash, it gets niche branding as a haunted land. An example is the website *Legendary Dartmoor*, a compendium of fascinating facts and folktales designed to attract visitors:

> The intention of this web site is to provide an overview of the many aspects of Dartmoor in the hope that they will inspire people to visit the moor and discover the numerous "*Gems in a Granite Setting*" for themselves. Some of the tales and stories within this site date way back in time whilst others literally happened yesterday but all go together to make an ever evolving heritage of Dartmoor. Albeit natural or supernatural, human or spiritual, everything will in some small way leave its mark, many of which now lie firmly in the written tomes and oral history of Dartmoor. So, I hope you enjoy your visit to Legendary Dartmoor and find something of interest but check back regularly as there are new pages being added all the time. Please visit the sponsored adverts, wherever possible they are local Dartmoor businesses and also by doing so you will help towards the ever-increasing costs of maintaining this site—thank you.[7]

My concern in this essay is the origin of a region's heritigization, its retro-marketing as a place of spiritual encounter, a traditional place in which Britons can proudly discover a natural supernaturalism that is native to their land—in effect, the West Country's romanticization. Often, I shall show, this is a matter of the conversion of oral testimony and oral tradition into marketed text. Sometimes, it's a matter of the invention of history—the creation retrospectively of a prior tradition that gives a vacant space the dignity of tradition, making it speak to the cultural imaginary of the present—making it, in short, a place.

The story begins in 1831, not in the southwest but the northwest, with Poet Laureate Robert Southey. Already nationally famous as a Lake Poet, Southey was an authorial embodiment of the romanticization of mountain country as a national heritage. Like Wordsworth and Coleridge, he had made the Lakes a place where a sublime and a beautiful that were native to "British ground" (to borrow Wordsworth's term[8]) could be encountered. Wordsworth romanticized the Lakes (which already featured in scores of tour guides and picturesque sketches) mainly in poetry; Southey did so chiefly in prose. His *Letters from England*[9] (1807) gave a detailed walking tour of the Lakeland fells; in 1829 his *Colloquies*[10] described his favorite routes, views, and spots, adding beautiful engravings by the artist William Westall to his loving descriptions. Importantly, the *Colloquies* not only celebrated landscape, they also commemorated the chivalric deeds done in that landscape in the remote past. Like Walter Scott's, Southey's romanticism was historical: he endowed a place with the aura of the heroic that he found in the tales and stories about its medieval lords and ladies.

It was as a romanticizer of history that the Devon author Eliza Bray wrote to Southey in 1831. A historical novelist, she sent Southey, an expert on Iberia, a story set in Portugal and another set around Dartmoor. He preferred the novel written about home turf and advised her to collect the traditions and stories of her locality and to write them up:

> If you would stoop from Fancys realms to truth, I should like to see from you—what English literature yet wants, a good specimen of local history;—not the antiquities only, nor the nautical history, nor both together (as in Whites delightful book about Selbourne) nor the statistics,—but *every thing* about a parish that can be made interesting,—all of its history, traditions & manners that can be saved from oblivion (for every generation sweeps away much) the changes that have been, & that are in progress: everything in short, that belongs to the pursuits either of historian, biographer, naturalist, philosopher or poet,—& not omitting some of those "short & simple annals" of domestic life, which ought not to be forgotten. Such works in general have been undertaken by dull men,—but there are few tasks upon which a lively, & feeling, & spiritual mind might be more agreeably, or usefully employed.[11]

Bray acted on his advice, collecting stories and sending them in a series of long letters to Southey, who suggested she reuse this correspondence in a publication. He then helped get them published and he favorably reviewed them in the eminent journal, *The Quarterly Review.*[12] Bray was, then, a protégée of Southey's, and her book was a response to his wish to turn a little-known country into a romantic place—that is, into a culturally significant area, given geographical meaning by virtue of the unique stories and histories that it had prompted through the ages.

It's clear that when Bray published, Dartmoor was not yet a name that people could be expected to recognize. Not yet a place. *A Description of the Part of Devon Bordering on the Tamar and the Tavy* appeared in 1836 (henceforth referred to in this chapter as Bray, *A Description).*[13] In 1838, a larger version followed, with the cumbersome title *Traditions, Legends, Superstitions, and Sketches of Devonshire on the Borders of the Tamar and the Tavy... in a Series of Letters to Robert Southey.*[14] It turned out to be an important book, the founding volume[15] of the reconfiguration of the southwest that made Dartmoor and Cornwall romantic regions that were sought out by travelers, that appeared in fiction, that featured on tourist maps, and were preserved as National Parks. Bray's book brought her locality to public notice as a romantic landscape. It succeeded by publicizing in print a less antiquarian version of moorland and West Country tradition than was included in the earlier county histories written by William Borlase and by Richard Polwhele.[16] This was the oral tradition about local instances of the supernatural: ghosts, pixies and phantom hounds, of whom Bray collected stories told by village women. She filled half her book with these stories and later republished the pixie legends in stand-alone format for children as *A Peep at the Pixies, or Legends of the West.*[17]

Bray's methodology as a collector of oral tradition is significant. As a gentlewoman, she felt too remote from the cottagers to collect the stories herself. She took them from her husband, who had heard them as a child, or from the local gentry, who had been told them by their nurses, or she took them from a servant specially deployed to interview "the village gossips" (Bray, *Traditions*, 180). Whether this reluctance to communicate directly with the local storytellers stemmed from distaste or from a modest sense that they would be unlikely to unbutton to their social superior, she does not state. Bray then sent the stories to Southey in letters: it was these manuscript letters that she then published as a book and that captured the imagination of Victorian readers. One, in particular, has resonated ever since—being perhaps the first published version of the legend of the huge spectral hound that later, in Conan Doyle's Dartmoor novel, became famous throughout much of the world. The legend concerned the evil Lady Howard, as Bray recounted:

> All I knew of her then was, that she bore the reputation of having been hard-hearted in her lifetime. That for some crime she had committed (nobody knew what) she was said to be doomed to run in the shape of a hound from the *gateway of Fitz-ford* to Oakhampton park, between the hours of midnight and cock-crowing, and to return with a single blade of grass in her mouth whence she started; and this she was to do till every blade was picked, when the world would be at an end.
>
> Dr. Jago, the clergyman of Milton Abbot, however, told me that occasionally she was said to ride in *a coach of bones* up the West-street towards the Moor; and an old man of this place told a friend of mine the same story, only adding that "he had seen her in it *scores of times!*" A lady also who was once a resident here, and whom I met in company, assured me that, happening many years before to pass the old gateway at Fitz-ford, as the church clock struck *twelve,* in returning from a party, she had herself *seen the hound start!* Now I verily believe the lady told truth; for my husband's father, many years ago, rented Fitz-ford; it was the residence of his hind or bailiff, and there the late Mr. Bray used to keep a pack of hounds: it is, therefore, nothing improbable that one of them might have slipped the kennel, and ran out as the church clock struck twelve, and so personated, in the eyes of imagination, the terrific spectre *of the old* tale. My husband can remember that when a boy it was a common saying with the gentry at a party "Come, it is growing late, let us begone, or we shall meet Lady Howard as she starts from Fitz-ford." (Bray, *Description*, 319–20)

In collecting this oral story, to which even the local gentry subscribed (albeit, some of them, in jest), Bray gave national circulation and the respectability of the print medium to a tale that originated in cottagers' superstitious beliefs that death was not accidental but fated and that evil deeds received supernatural punishment. The early deaths of Lady Howard's several husbands, and the cruelty of some of them, made her, after her own death, the subject of superstitious stories that coalesced into the legend of her ghostly transformation from lady to beast. The eeriness of the dark nighttime moorscape also shaped the legend, which, after Bray publicized it, then found voice in the "Ballad of Lady Howard," a song about an uncanny, deathly Other that was collected in the later Victorian period by the Reverend Sabine Baring-Gould from the singing of "old . . . Anne Bickle of Bratton Clovelly, circ. 1838–40." Baring-Gould's transcribed version, which he noted was "remembered by me" much later, seems influenced by the Romantic pseudomedieval ballads written by Thomas Percy (see *The Reliques of Ancient English Poetry,* 1764), Robert Southey (see "The Old Woman of Berkeley" and "The Devil's Thoughts") and by Samuel Taylor Coleridge (see "The Rime of the Ancyent Marinere"). Baring-Gould's version:

My ladye hath a sable coach,
And horses two and four;
My ladye hath a black blood-hound
That runneth on before.
My ladye's coach hath nodding plumes,
The driver hath no head;
My ladye is an ashen white,
As one that long is dead.

"Now pray step in," my ladye saith,
"Now pray step in and ride."
I thank thee, I had rather walk
Than gather by thy side.
The wheels go round without a sound
Or tramp or turn of wheels;
As cloud at night, in pale moonlight,
Along the carriage steals.

I'd rather walk a hundred miles
And run by night and day
Than have the carriage halt for me
And hear the ladye say:
"Now pray step in, and make no din,
Step in with me and ride;
There's room I trow, by me for you,
And all the world beside."[18]

Here the manner is literary: the rhetorical gestures (eg. the pseudo-antique spellings and diction) pertaining to the written occlude the oral, even though the ballad was once sung (as it still is), and it defers to old ballads that were oral before they were textual. It is, however, itself derived from Baring-Gould's knowledge of print—of Bray's book and of the ballads of her poet mentors. Southey's friend Walter Scott, for instance, balladized a legend of a specter-hound in his *Lay of the Last Minstrel*:

> For he was speechless, ghastly, wan,
> Like him, of whom the story ran,
> Who spoke the spectre-hound in Man.[19]

Bray did not only include the story of Lady Howard in her factual prose. As she reminded Southey, she had already used the local legend in her 1830 fiction *Fitz of Fitz-ford*, transforming the spectral hound into a real bloodhound (just as it turns out to be in *The Hound of the Baskervilles*). Bray commented:

> The above anecdotes were all I knew about her, when I determined to make her take a part in my story; but *the hound,* the gateway, and *the coach of bones, were all* fine hints for imagination to work upon. I walked down to Fitz-ford with Mr. Bray and reconnoitred the spot, and there, such is the bewitching power of locality, all seemed to rush at once into my mind. The plot was formed with ease, and I went home determined to connect the adventure of Fitz and Slanning, under the gateway, with Lady Howard; to give her a real hound, a blood hound, instead of turning her into one; and then the coach *of bones* and her riding in it after death, might be made a legend, in consequence of a great crime which, by an evil passion, she had been led to determine on committing whilst riding in her own coach, in all her pride, to the house of the person she had it in view to betray to ruin here on earth. This rude sketch of a plot was soon worked into shape and committed to paper. Mr. Bray named the hound *Redfang,* as a significant appellative for a dog whose instinct was to become the agency in assisting to bring about the catastrophe (Bray, *Description*, 320–21)

In *Fitz of Fitz-ford,* Redfang, the enormous hound, follows the scent of blood across the moor, baying, and then becomes a symbol of Lady Howard's evil violence.[20]

Redfang, and Bray's rendition of the specter-dog on which Redfang is based, inaugurate in print the uncanny hound that still persists in contemporary myth as the Beast of Dartmoor and Bodmin Moor. The monstrous animal is also an embodiment of the moor's eeriness, making it a Romantic place in the manner of Southey, who had featured specter-hounds hauling his hero through a frozen wilderness at the climax of his Gothic poem *Thalaba the Destroyer* (1801):

And lo! beneath yon lonely pine, the sledge...
And there they stand the harnessed Dogs,
Their wide eyes watching for the youth,
Their ears erected turned towards his way.
They were as lean as lean might be,
Their furrowed ribs rose prominent,
And they were black from head to foot,
Save a white line on every breast
Curved like the crescent moon.
And he is seated in the sledge,
His arms are folded on his breast,
The bird is on his knees;
There is fear in the eyes of the Dogs,
There is fear in their pitiful moan,
And now they turn their heads,
And seeing him there, Away

(Robert Southey, *Thalaba,* Book 11, lines 179–94)[21]

Ever fascinated by tales of ghouls and ghosts (he introduced the zombie and the vampire to English fiction[22]), Southey welcomed Bray's gothicization of the moor and its folktales. He wrote in a June 1832 reply to her latest communication of local legends:

> Your Pixies are pleasant creatures. I knew them of old by Coleridge's poem about them, which was written before he & I met in 1794: but your stories were new to me, & have amused my fire side greatly. We have no playful superstitions here, or if there are any they have not come to my knowledge: but I suspect that the popular superstitions of mountainous countries are generally of a sterner character than such as belong to milder regions. The Welsh, late as they possessed their country, have left few vestiges here,—the Danes many. Boggles & Barguests are the only supernatural beings we hear of in these parts:—to what class they belong I cannot tell you, but the Barguest which I believe generally appear in the shape of some quadruped, may possibly in its origin have simply been a Mountain Spirit.
>
> Large towns, & large manufacturies in the country, destroy all superstitions of this kind. (12 June 1832)[23]

The *barguest* is a northern version of the spectral, monstrous animal on the loose—often seen as a wild hound.

Southey was not alone in enjoying Bray's rendition of the tale: Arthur Conan Doyle encountered the story of a spectral hound roaming Dartmoor from his Devon-educated friend Bertram Fletcher Robinson in March 1901. The two men toured the moor together, visiting Grimspound, Child's Tomb, and Fox Tor

Mires. Conan Doyle then composed the novel he called "a real creeper," developing, from the various legends of the hell-hound, a plot that owes something to Bray's use of the Lady Howard legend in *Fitz of Fitz-ford.* Conan Doyle's dog, like Bray's, is not in the end supernatural, although it seems to be so, so bloodcurdling are its bayings. Like Bray's, too, it is used to tracking a hunted man across the moor. And while we cannot be certain that Conan Doyle knew Bray's (by then obscure) work, it is certainly the case that her factual account had entered the knowledge of all educated people brought up, as Robinson was, near the moor. Bray's print version of the story may have reentered oral culture, circulating in stories read aloud, or told, by parents and nurses to their children.

The strange relationship between oral and written that Bray's specter-hound embodies is also unexpectedly present in another, very different, part of her book. *Traditions* incorporates, as well as her own versions of local legend, her husband's discussions of his efforts to trace the vestiges of ancient Druids and bards. An obsessive antiquarian, Edward Bray was determined to fill Dartmoor's emptiness with a human prehistory that conveyed significance and sublimity upon its oakwoods and standing stones. He sought evidence on the tors and the menhirs (rough, upright monoliths) for an original British and oral culture that worshipped on the moor—a Celtic culture that preceded the Romans and was driven into rural fastnesses by them. The part of the moor called Bair Down, which Bray's father had enclosed and improved, Bray concluded, was a holy site, sacred to the Druids and bards who had made it their last sanctuary from Roman power. The place was still resonant with the ceremonial words sung there by priests and poets to guide the Celtic Britons: in an act of imaginative reconstitution, Bray endowed it with an oral power that he, as its historian, could discern and perpetuate, thereby positioning himself as the renewer of its local tradition, a man deeply enough rooted in the place to deliver to his own age the ancient spirits that he sensed still inhabiting it. This intense appropriation of a place and its past was, Bray knew, a Romantic fantasy: he compared Bair Down's bards with the bards of Southey's poem *Madoc* (1805) and with those of poets Ossian and Gray. But he was committed to the fantasy, so strong was his desire to imbue the land his father had bequeathed him with the historical and spiritual significance that poetry, particularly oral poetry, conveys. Thus he imagined a *gorsedd,* or bardic meeting, taking place at Bair Down in medieval times:

> In their bards, also, the Britons heard the voice of "other times," the history of their forefathers, the legends and traditions of their country. Such recitals could elevate or soften the souls of their auditors, as they sat around with the glistening eye, the suppressed respiration, and the varying and accompanying feeling to each modulation of their song, that could nerve the arm to action, or melt the heart to pity, as the subject arose to energy, or, chord by chord, died away in low sounds as the melody of melancholy spoke with irresistible power

> in the cadence of their harp. And when he, too, should be no more, the hardy British chief looked to the genius of the bards as the bulwark of his fame. The mossy stone and the cairn might mark the spot where rested the mortal fabric of his body, but his more enduring monument was in immortal verse. (Bray, *Traditions*, 107)

Not content with writing about the bards in his journals, Bray began an extraordinary project on the ground. He employed a local mason with a pickax to cut inscriptions into the granite rocks of Bair Down. These inscriptions, composed by Bray himself, were dedications to the poets who inspired him in his bardic visions, verse couplets celebrating the place's history, and runic letterings intended to seem as if they had been left by ancient Druids. I reproduce here one of the few still discernible in 2008, after two centuries of weathering and lichen-growth (Figure 1). Bray's wording expresses his feelings about poetry's power to endow a wilderness with sanctifying human associations: "Sweet Poesy! fair fancy's child! / Thy smiles imparadise the wild."

The paradox inherent in Bray's project was that it was in written inscriptions that he recorded his reverence for the orality of an ancient culture—a token of its organicism and of the centrality accorded to poetry within it. Bray's Britons were admirable because they were not alienated from their leaders: politics, religion,

Figure 1 A granite rock with inscription composed by Bray, "Sweet Poesy! fair fancy's child! / Thy smiles imparadise the wild."

and poetry were united in the spoken words of the bards. Neither were they alienated from their land, for the poetry was an immediate oral response to the place in which they met. But, lacking any oral community of his own, Bray could offer tribute to this unity only in the form of text, text, moreover, that lacked a community of readers. The chiseled inscriptions remained almost unread, because they were unknown to any save Bray and his family, until Mrs. Bray published them in *Traditions.* But at least they possessed what Bray craved: permanence, a lasting mark of his emotional investment in the place he owned, which conferred upon it a greater historical significance than the personal. The inscriptions placed him at the end of a true British tradition.

Bray's textualized rocks, even when published in his wife's book, brought few visitors to the moor. Today they are almost totally obscured by moss, even when one spends hours standing in the Cowsick River, getting soaked as one scrapes away at promising-looking boulders. They remain a fascinating but limited version of bardic romanticism, much influenced by Southey, but bound to antiquarian book-history in their understanding of the past and ignoring local oral testimony.

Bray was solicitous of his distance, as a gentleman, from the oral voices and lore of the present-day peasants. His journal records his snobbish attitude to contemporary oral lore: he finds using the local dialect distasteful and vulgar and so does not properly ask local peasants for the stone he's searching for:

> Perhaps I might have obtained the information I wanted long before, had I asked for what I was told to ask; namely, for a stone that was placed over a shoot. But, absurdly, I confess, I have always had an objection to the word; because, in one sense at least, it must be admitted to be a vulgarism even by provincialists themselves. The lower classes in Devon shire, almost invariably, say shoot the door, instead of shut the door. And when it is used by them to express a water-pipe, or the mouth of any channel from which is precipitated a stream of water, I have hitherto connected it with that vulgarity which arises from the above *abuse of* the word. But if we write it, as perhaps we ought, *shute,* from the French chute, which signifies fall, we have an origin for it that may by some, perhaps; be considered the very reverse of vulgar, and have, at the same time; a definite and appropriate expression for what, otherwise, without a periphrasis, could hardly be made intelligible. (Bray, *Traditions*, 131)

This contempt ensured that Bray's respect for the oral remained an idealization of the past: he was tied to texts—to books and to marks in the landscape of a long-vanished culture.

Mrs. Bray's attitude to the oral sources of her written texts was less clear-cut than her husband's, though still influenced by the Lake Poets. In one pixie story, she cites the lyrical ballad in which Wordsworth most visibly prefers the untutored oral knowledge of a local girl to the conventional authority of the educated adult, "We Are Seven." '"Six more eggs!" said the child, "then pray ma'am, be so good as to give them to me; for I have in all six brothers and sisters at home, and all very hungry;" and, like Wordsworth's little girl, Mrs. Bray added, "We are seven" (*Peep at the Pixies*, 34). Wordsworth's child-speaker in "We Are Seven," however, confounds her middle-class adult questioner. Thus Wordsworth, although presenting his *Lyrical Ballads* in print, defers to the oral, making the unlettered peasant child wiser than the educated man. *Lyrical Ballads*, he wrote, were based on a "spontaneous overflow of powerful feelings": his poetry echoed speech, song, and the folk ballad.[24] For Wordsworth, orality configured liberty, tradition, and nobility, all qualities he believed to be destroyed by the advancing culture of consumer capitalism of which textuality—even including published poetry—was increasingly a part.

Mrs. Bray, despite her allusion to Wordsworth, was far more conservative and class-bound, especially when she republished the pixie stories that her servant had collected in a new format as children's stories. In the introduction to *A Peep at the Pixies,* she made sure her juvenile readers were reminded of their social superiority to the families who were the oral sources of the tales:

> The people who live in these humble dwellings are not very nice, for the pigstye is generally near the door, and the children are not much cleaner than the pigs. It is the more discreditable to their mothers to let them be so, as there is water enough around to wash and keep clean all the children in Devonshire (Bray, *Peep at the Pixies*, 4)

Within the stories themselves, Mrs. Bray included distancing remarks, designed to condescend to the women who were her oral sources. Their tales, it is thus implied, are unreliable specimens of primitive superstition, amusing for children so long as it is understood they are old wives' tales rather than proper sources of knowledge. The process is clearly visible in Bray's rendition of "The Belfry-Rock, or the Pixies' Revenge," a transcription that both mythologizes Dartmoor and declares its origin in the unreliable narrations of an "old gossip, the narrator of this wonderful history" (*Peep at the Pixies,* 80). In this tale, Bray's repeated references to the scene of telling both glamorize a bucolic scene and warn the reader not to accept the story's authority on trust. Thus Bray fixed the pixie stories as local old wives' tales, setting them in the aspic of genteel print—a permanent, gentrified, and beautified form fit for middle-class taste, ensuring that the people who voiced the stories she printed were condescended to.

If Mrs. Bray was imitating the German folk-story collectors—"doing a Grimm," as it were—she was sanitizing the stories in the process, making oral tradition conform to poetic justice and conventional morality. What was lost in this process was the very locality of such tradition, its dialect, local references and in-allusions.

Mrs. Bray related tales of Tintagel, on the Cornish coast, in the same polite prose as she narrated stories from Tavistock. She turned the pixie tales into moral lessons for children, teaching them conventional picture-book history. Nevertheless, there remained sufficient residue of socially and morally improper matter for the stories to intrigue other writers. Indeed it may have been *because* Bray enclosed such matter within a conventional frame that her stories seemed safe, as well as tempting, for proper Victorians to imitate. One who did was Christina Rossetti, who wrote of her poem "Goblin Market" (1862): "In the first instance I named it 'A Peep at the Goblins' in imitation of my Cousin Mrs. Bray's 'A Peep at the Pixies'...but my brother Dante Gabriel Rossetti substituted the greatly improved title as it now stands."[25]

Rossetti, according to her biographer Jan Marsh,[26] almost certainly derived her poem from Bray's "The Lady of the Silver Bell." Set in St. Nathan's Kieve (the present-day National Trust site St. Nectan's Glen/Rocky Valley) near Tintagel, this story recounts the pixie enchantment of the young girl Serena, in a mossy ravine where the stream plunges over a waterfall to the sea. Bray's version of the folktale emphasizes that the enchantment is an oral affair in which people hear magical voices:

> But at that very moment she heard strains of the most enchanting music. Nothing earthly seemed to mingle with those sounds. "O Serena! Serena, quickly turn, hark to the vesper bell." She fancied that a voice above the rocks spoke these words. But, alas! she neglected the friendly warning. She looked this way, that way, up the ravine, among the trees, and could see no one; whilst every step she advanced, the music of the unseen musician appeared to move on before her. "I will but tarry a few minutes to see who it is plays thus sweetly, and where the sounds come from," said Serena, "I shall yet reach the chapel yonder, before the bell has done ringing" (Bray, *Peep at the Pixies*, 72)

The pixie music and the male body arouse illicit female desire: Serena is fascinated by a sleeping "young man, of a very good person, and handsome features, with light brown curly hair":

> Serena gazed till her admiration of the manly beauty and splendid attire of the youthful sleeper became as great as that which she had felt, a little while before, for the music; and far exceeded her admiration of the beauties of the scene. She thought that, if ever she married, it should be to just such a beautiful youth...
>
> Serena...looked about her, and seeing an opening in some rocks near at hand, that were overshadowed by thick and pendant boughs, she determined to conceal herself and to survey more at her leisure the noble features and the splendid adornments of the sleeper; hoping that, when he awoke, he would again touch the strings of his lute. (Bray, *Peep at the Pixies*, 74)

In Bray's version, Serena is condemned for "being led into folly by her vain and idle curiosity" (p. 78); misled by a wizard, she falls down the waterfall to her death as she tries to lift the pixies' spell by uttering an incantation there: another instance of the magical power of orality in the tale.

Rossetti adapted the story, retaining its emphasis on gazing and on the male body and female desire, but intensifying the sensuous orality. Rossetti's goblins tempt the young women with "Figs to fill your mouth, / Citrons from the South, / Sweet to tongue and sound to eye" (lines 28–30).[27] Meanwhile, the sound of the verse replicates the orality for the reader: lines such as "Plump unpeck'd cherries, / Melons and raspberries, / Bloom-down-cheek'd peaches, / Swart-headed mulberries, / Wild free-born cranberries, / Crab-apples, dewberries, / Pine-apples, blackberries" (lines 7–13), with their complex deployment of assonance, alliteration, internal rhyme, half-rhyme and rhythmic irregularity, are tongue-twisters to say, both mimicking the chewing of fruit and reminding the reader that utterance is a sensuous act. The goblin's cry is a cornucopia of orality in form as well as content: it leads Laura to succumb to desire for the pleasures of the male, expressed as delightful, erotic but illicit orality: "She dropped a tear more rare than pearl, / Then sucked their fruit globes fair or red" (lines 127–28). In Rossetti's poem, the enchantment of orality moves from the alluring sound of voice to the sensual taste, smell, and sight of the mouth—the lips of the speaker savored indirectly through the fruit that he offers and directly through the kiss that he entreats. Rossetti is more licentious than Bray: not only does she emphasize the erotic more heavily, but she does not finally condemn her heroine for succumbing to it. Laura is saved by her sister Lizzie, who resists the goblins' oral pleasures: she "would not open lip from lip / Lest they should cram a mouthful in" (lines 431–32). Enchantment by their fruit is overcome, and replaced by a renewed sisterly bond (both oral and erotic): "Hug me, kiss me, suck my juices / . . . / Eat me, drink me, love me / Laura make much of me" (lines 468–72).[28]

Rossetti's is by far a greater work than Bray's, an intense fiction that explores some of the deepest and most taboo desires and anxieties produced by Victorian sexual mores and gender roles. But it could not have been written without Bray's prior romanticization of the folktale—and, perhaps, it was Bray's very containment within a conventional moral frame of material that, had it been endorsed, might have breached taboos too openly that gave Rossetti, herself a "proper lady," license. Oral tradition, via Southey's promptings of a local author, had been transformed not once but twice into one of the most highly crafted, and most literary, poetic expressions of innocence, temptation, sexuality, and guilt to be written after the example of *Christabel*, the folk-romance of Southey's friend Coleridge.

It's extraordinary that Mrs. Bray's letters to Southey inspired two of the most potent fictions of the Victorian age, helping thereby to introduce symbolic figures that haunt modern culture beyond the text: millions of people who have never read Sherlock Holmes know of the hound of the Devon moors; just as many are fascinated by West Country fairies, goblins, and pixies. Dartmoor and the Cornish coast, meanwhile are firmly fixed in the cultural imaginary as spiritually authentic places haunted by legends: today in Rocky Valley, New Age pilgrims leave offerings next to some rock carvings which they want to believe are ancient, so resonant is their location, even though they may be the doodles of a nineteenth-century mill worker; while people regularly sight enormous black beasts—some say panthers; some pumas; some, Newfoundland dogs—running free on the moors. Mrs. Bray, conventional though she was, let loose in the West Country beings that configure people's hidden fears and desires. Devon and Cornwall, as a result, are places of superstition, magic, and ghosts, places to be away with the fairies, places imbued with a traditional spirituality people seek as a contrast to their ordinary materialist lives—which, ironically enough, gives a retail opportunity to local shopkeepers and the Chinese factory-workers who, in today's globalized local economy, make the souvenirs they sell. The author of *Legendary Dartmoor* understands the shtick even as he contributes to it, if I am right in seeing an ironic relish beneath his words:

> Perhaps the elusive piskie does not only dwell in the minds of the old moor people, drive past Pixies Holt on a summer's day and see all the visitors clutching their purchases of "lucky Dartmoor pixie" ware and maybe it is possible that the little people's influence stretches further than thought. As I write this at my desk I am surrounded by old brass "Dartmoor pixie ware," there are candlesticks, letter knife, bottle opener, door knocker, shoe horn, ash tray, pin tray, horse brasses and ink wells all of various ages that date from the 1920's onwards. Clearly not only are the piskies part of the Dartmoor tradition, they are part of the Dartmoor economy. Visit the e-bay site and search for "Dartmoor Pixie," today there are two toasting forks, two bottle openers, a key rack and two pixie jugs all with Dartmoor piskies on them. Again, proof that the Dartmoor piskie is alive and well in 2007.[29]

Mrs. Bray is herself again on sale: in 1999, Oakmagic Publications published a selection from her books under the title *Dartmoor Superstitions.* It's fitting that her work can be found on the shelves of the gift shops of the place that, like the legendary hounds and the mythical pixies, would never have come into the cultural imaginary without her transformation of local oral lore into the transferable medium of standard-English print. Bray's text is remanufactured and reworked for a new age, just as she reworked an oral tradition and, in the process, manufactured a romantic region.

Notes

1. See, in particular, *Narrative and Genre,* edited by Mary Chamberlain and Paul Thompson (London: Routledge, 1998). See also the discussion by Lynn Abrams,

in chapter six of *Oral History Theory* (New York & London: Routledge, 2010), 106–129. (Much of Abrams's discussion concerns a structuralist approach, however, which is rarely still used by contemporary literary scholars since the 1980s and is, as Abrams indicates, more pertinent to linguistics.)

2. William Bottrell, *Stories and Folk-lore of West Cornwall* (Penzance, 1880), p.iii.
3. For a good overview of such work see chapter four, "Orality," of Justin D. Edwards, *Postcolonial Literature: A Reader's Guide to Essential Criticism* (London: Palgrave, 2008).
4. See, for example, the inclusion of urban dialect and immigrant communities in Graham Smith's interview, "Voices on Radio: Billy Kay the Maker of Odyssey," *Oral History* 13:1 (1985), 54–60. For some theoretical context on the role of orality in Scotland's attempts to establish a sense of nationhood in the nineteenth century, and reflection on how the oral is always about to be lost, see Penny Fielding, *Writing and Orality: Nationality, Culture, and Nineteenth-Century Scottish Fiction* (Oxford: Clarendon Press, 1996). This study also contains a discussion of James Hogg's and Walter Scott's "different attempts to represent oral storytelling in print," attempts which differ considerably from but are comparable to those discussed in part one of this collection (101 ff).
5. Re. sacred space, I adopt the distinction from Paul B. Carter, *The Road to Botany Bay: an Essay in Spatial History* (London: Faber, 1987). Space becomes place by virtue of acts that confer on it cultural meaning—acts that mark the earth directly, including pathfinding and homesteading and acts that represent it, including mapmaking and writing.
6. The West Country is the term often used in Britain for the area of South West England, usually incorporating the counties of Cornwall, Devon, Dorset, Somerset, and the city of Bristol.
7. "Legendary Dartmoor," http://www.legendarydartmoor.co.uk/index.htm (accessed 29/08/08).
8. "British ground" is from line 5 of Wordsworth's "View from the Top of Black Comb" (1811).
9. Robert Southey, *Letters from England; by Don Manuel Alvarez Espriella. Translated from the Spanish* (London: Longman, 1807).
10. Robert Southey, *Sir Thomas More: or, Colloquies on the Progress and Prospects of Society*, 2 vols. (London: Murray, 1829).
11. From the MS in the Robert Southey Collection, Special Collections, Rush Rhees Library, University of Rochester.
12. Robert Southey, review in *Quarterly Review*, 59 (1737), 275–312.
13. Eliza Bray, *A Description of the Part of Devonshire Bordering on the Tamar and the Tavy; its Natural History, &c., in a Series of Letters to R. Southey, Esq.*, 3 vols. (London: Murray, 1836).
14. Eliza Bray, *Traditions, Legends, Superstitions, and Sketches of Devonshire on the Borders of the Tamar and the Tavy, Illustrative of its Manners, Customs, History, Antiquities, Scenery, and Natural History, in a Series of Letters to Robert Southey, Esq.*, 3 vols. (London: Murray, 1838).
15. Bray's collection of folk stories was used as a source by later writers on the moor, including Thomas Keightley, *The Fairy Mythology, Illustrative of the Romance and Superstition of Various Countries* (London: Bohn, 1850) and *Popular Romances of*

the West of England: or, the Drolls, Traditions, and Superstitions of Old Cornwall, 3rd ed., edited by Robert Hunt (London, Chatto and Windus, 1903).

16. William Borlase, *Antiquities, Historical and Monumental, of the County of Cornwall*, 2nd ed. (London: W. Bowyer and J. Nichols, 1769), 116; Richard Polwhele, *The History of Devonshire*, 3 vols. (Exeter: printed by Trewman and Son, for Cadell, Johnson, and Dilly, London, 1793–1806). Polwhele's *History of Cornwall* is the subject of the next chapter in this book, by Dafydd Moore.
17. Eliza Bray, *A Peep at the Pixies, or Legends of the West* (London: Grant and Griffith, 1854).
18. See the Sabine Baring-Gould song collection, Plymouth Central Library, Killerton MS, vol. 1, at p. 78, number 30.
19. Walter Scott, *The Lay of the Last Minstrel*, canto V, part xxvi, lines 15–17. From *The Poetical Works of Sir Walter Scott… Complete in One Volume* (Edinburgh: Cadell, 1841).
20. Eliza Bray, *Fitz of Fitz-ford*, vol. 4 of *The Novels and Romances of Anna Eliza Bray*, 10 vols. (London: Longman and Brown, 1845), 462.
21. *Thalaba the Destroyer*, vol. 3 of *Robert Southey: Poetical Works 1793–1810*, gen. ed. Lynda Pratt, 5 vols. (London: Pickering and Chatto, 2004).
22. Southey introduced the zombie in his *History of Brazil*, 3 vols. (London, 1810–19), 25–26. He introduced the vampire in *Thalaba the Destroyer*, vol. 3 of *Robert Southey: Poetical Works 1793–1810*, 120, 264–69.
23. From the MS in the Robert Southey Collection, Special Collections, Rush Rhees Library, University of Rochester.
24. Wordsworth's definition appeared in the Preface to *Lyrical Ballads* (1800).
25. Rossetti is cited by Dennis Low in *The Literary Protegées of the Lake Poets* (Aldershot & Burlington: Ashgate, 2006), p. 178 note 7.
26. Jan Marsh, *Christina Rossetti: a Writer's Life* (London & New York: Viking, 1994), 230.
27. "The Lady of the Silver Bell" is from *The Complete Poems of Christina Rossetti*, vol. 1, edited by R. W. Crump (Baton Rouge and London: Louisiana State University Press, 1979–1990).
28. See Lexi Stuckey, "Christina Rossetti and Anna Eliza Bray—Fashioning a New Form of Fairy Tale in 'Goblin Market,'" On *The Victorian Web: Literature, History and Culture in the Age of Victoria*, http://www.usp.nus.edu.sg/landow/victorian/authors/crossetti/stuckey.html (accessed August 31, 2008).
29. http://www.legendarydartmoor.co.uk/index.htm (accessed August 29, 2008).

CHAPTER 2

"The *Romance* of Real Life": Richard Polwhele's Representation of the Literary Culture and Language of Cornwall

Dafydd Moore

Richard Polwhele's reputation, at least in literary studies, rests on his spectacularly vindictive assault on radical women writers, *The Unsex'd Females* (1798). He was equally forthcoming with his political views in the pages of the conservative press, and was a frequent contributor to, amongst others, the *Anti-Jacobin Review*. That said, while *The Unsex'd Females* might give a not unrepresentative indication of his poetic talents, it is less typical of his poetic subject matter. Over a prolific 60 years, Polwhele's career encompassed a wide number of genres and preoccupations, but was most notably devoted to exploring the importance of what, in a lengthy poem of the same name, he termed the "influence of local attachment," and to creating a legendary history of Cornwall in the manner of Walter Scott. Reactionary politics and indifferent poetry, pursued either in concert or separately, were only two of Polwhele's interests. More significant (to him and certainly subsequently) were his works of antiquarian and county history: *Historical Views of Devonshire* (1793), *The History of Devonshire* (1793–1806), and *The History of Cornwall* (1803–1808). Collectively they are, according to Mark Brayshay, "magnificent studies" that "scarcely have an equal" in their time.[1]

Brayshay's verdict is in part a response to the comprehensiveness of Polwhele's work at its best. His coverage (especially in the second Devon publication, *The History of Devonshire)* may be in places patchy, but what he does cover, he covers in exhaustive detail. Polwhele's work gives ample testimony to what Mark Salber Phillips has termed the "enlargement of the boundaries of the historical" in the eighteenth century, and to the challenges to form and order posed, Phillips suggests, by the conviction that the subject matter and purposes of historiography were wider than previously allowed by classical models.[2] The very exhaustiveness is the most striking, and the most strikingly difficult, thing about the seven-volume *History of Cornwall.* It is not necessarily easy to read or follow, and, judged by any measure of organization or firm argumentative purpose, it is likely to be found wanting. Ill-constructed, at times seemingly randomly organized or bordering on stream of consciousness, these volumes suggest a failure on Polwhele's part to come to grips with his material.

This chapter addresses this paradox and suggests that the scattergun nature of what A. L. Rowse called Polwhele's "abounding gallimaufry," or confused jumble, is both its greatest strength and greatest weakness: the value of the work comes as a result of features that are constantly threatening its structural integrity.[3] On the face of it, the *History of Cornwall* follows a structure not unlike the one adopted by Robert Henry's *History of Great Britain* (1771–93), held by Phillips to be a classic example of the ways that the narratives of history changed as a response to "the problem of representing worlds of social experience and inward feeling that were hard to translate into the traditional narrative conventions" of classical public history.[4] Polwhele too follows a pattern whereby each period is covered by a range of chapters discussing different features of the times and different histories of the time (civil, religious, political, cultural, social). But where Henry manages to keep to his interlocking narratives set aside and picked up according to the logic of the overall historical progression in such a way that the reader is able "to take advantage of the systematic arrangement of his chapters to construct his own path through the history," Polwhele's powers of organization seem to fail him, and his *History of Cornwall* collapses into something far more eclectic and random but also, I would suggest, of vital interest and importance.[5] What follows owes a significant amount to Phillips's suggestive account of eighteenth-century historiography, but is particularly interested in what happens when a historian fails to brace his interest in everything against established historiographical narratives.

As I have hinted, Polwhele's work covers a great deal of ground, but this essay will restrict itself, as much as possible, to a consideration of the way in which language and literature figure in his *History of Cornwall.* It should be acknowledged at the outset that Polwhele was not in any straightforward or indeed identifiable sense an oral historian or folklorist. However, the issues to do with the rendering of place, writing, and voice raised by Polwhele's activities in relation to the standard methods of eighteenth-century scholarship make him of relevance to this book. Polwhele's deployment of oral sources within his history is interesting in terms of the development and nature of oral history and its relation with "conventional" historiography, given that in this period the two are more usually seen as coming apart.[6]

The most efficient way of identifying the qualities of Polwhele's treatment of Cornish literature and language is by comparison with that of the great figure of mid-eighteenth-century Cornish antiquarianism and topographical history, William Borlase, in his *Natural History of Cornwall* (1758). When Borlase turns his attention to the language and literature of Cornwall he does so in entirely conventional terms, under a series of predictable headings. Most tellingly, he has no interest in the spoken or living language.

Borlase stakes a claim for Cornish as the most aesthetically satisfying of Celtic languages, a status that is a result of the moral character of the people. So Cornish is "reckoned more pleasing in sound because less guttural than the Welsh, and indeed than the other dialects."[7] But if Welsh is guttural, then Breton is "muttering" and Irish "whining," both "ill qualities contracted," Borlase suggests, on account of the "servitudes and much subjection" suffered by the speakers of these languages (314). This slip from an aesthetic to a moral or even political discourse is the most obvious example of the way in which Borlase's attitude to language is intimately connected with the discourse of civic humanism. Cornish thus is "manly and lively spoken," and "elegant and manly, pure, short and expressive" (314).

For Borlase, the language is an index of the Cornish people, who are "healthy, strong and active" (292), hardened by the Cornish weather and the physical exertion associated with the key economic activities of fishing and mining. It is not just the day job though that rears this kind of people. Borlase spends a deal of time discussing the "manly exercises of wrestling and hurling" that he claims are "more generally practiced in this county than in any part of England" and he is not slow to remind his readers of the importance placed upon wrestling by the ancient Greeks as a way of encouraging the attitudes and aptitudes necessary in the active warrior citizen (299). Across the board, then we might suggest that Borlase associates Cornish culture with the ideals of civic humanism.

Borlase also discusses the key Cornish text, the cycle of passion plays known as the *Ordinalia*. He cites a passage in Cornish with parallel translation and offers some analysis of its meter, which it turns out is "trochaic heptasyllable" or "trochaic diameter cataletic," a meter Borlase suggests was also used by Aristophanes, Horace, Shakespeare, and Dryden. Be that as it may, what is certain is that "the language suits the metre; [and] as the subject is sublime, the composition is not unsuitable" (296). As such, Borlase places and explains the text in terms of a respectable literary tradition.

Overall, Borlase's treatment of Cornwall and the Cornish can be related to a host of other eighteenth-century engagements with the language, culture, and literature of what were perceived as less polished or primitive peoples. Alien literary forms could, through the invoking of formal parallels, be established within the terms of canonical literature, as for example and perhaps most famously Joseph Addison had done with his essays on "The Ballad of Chevy Chase" in *The Spectator* in 1711 (or as the more disreputable figure of James Macpherson did in back-engineering his Celtic epic poet Ossian in such a way as to create the "Northern Homer"). A strange language and people could be rendered intelligible and valuable within the discourse of active citzenship and virtue as vigorous, strong, simple, and sublime and might even be the subject of a degree of cultural wish fulfillment. Cornish is both manly and elegant, qualities that significant quarters of eighteenth-century society were inclined to feel, with regret, bordered on the oxymoronic. More than one primitivist fantasy was predicated on the reconciling of politeness and power, sensibility and active citizenship.[8]

However, it is significant that the virtues of manly activity and implied political independence (only implied, because Borlase only refers comparatively to the subjugation of other Celtic peoples, rather than the explicit independence of the Cornish) are entirely displaced into the realm of the aesthetic. Karen O'Brien's analysis of William Robertson's use of "the classical language of virtue, military self-reliance and heroic independence," and his "occasional mood of carefully contained nostalgia" in his *History of Scotland* (1759) is suggestive here. Such things, O'Brien suggests, need to be understood in literary rather than political terms, as a "largely aestheticised celebration of an obsolete Scottish culture not otherwise endorsed by the modern, progressive sensibility of the Enlightenment historian."[9] Similarly, Borlase quarantines his references to the manly independence of (the) Cornish within an aesthetic appreciation of a language he then consigns to history itself. After all, the single most noticeable thing about Borlase's attitude to Cornish is his lack of interest or investment in the language as a living entity. He praises the efforts of Edward Lluyd in his *Cornish Grammar* (1707), and indeed he continued these efforts himself. Yet he is quite clear that the point of such an exercise is to be in a position to correct defective extant texts, rather than to revive the language in any way. The overall point of constructing a Cornish vocabulary is so that "we may attend it to the grave." Borlase noted:

> This language is now altogether ceased, so as not to be spoken any where in conversation; but as our ancient towns, castles, rivers, mountains, manors, seats and families, have their names from the Cornish tongue, and as most of the technical names of mining, husbandry, fishing and indeed some terminations of lands are in Cornish, it will in all ages be entertaining, and upon many occasions useful and instructive for this county to have as correct and copious a vocabulary of its ancient language, as can be procured from the materials now extant. (William Borlase, *Natural History of Cornwall,* 316)

It would be 20 years yet before Dolly Pentreath, the supposed last speaker of Cornish (about whom more shortly) died. But this literal preempting of the death of the language is not the most dubious thing about the passage. Far more important, and damaging, is the way he closes the door on the revival of the language in that final phrase, and perhaps more important still is the overall cultural dynamic being described here. That is to say, it exemplifies a dynamic whereby a language becomes commodified as a question of entertainment, its "use" and "instruction" within the realm of intellectual curiosity, rather than vital experience. Borlase both pays tribute to the continuing power of the language, its interweaving within the fabric of the people, place and land—it is impossible to know Cornwall, its places and its practices without a sense of the meaning of Cornish words—and simultaneously consigns it to the past and to learned rather than lived discourse. Cornish becomes the subject of learning (or idle curiosity), and perhaps the object of sentimental emotion as the observer is invited, in the words of one commentator on the cultural politics of Highland primitivism, to "a delicious sense of readerly involvement in the gloaming of a world about to be lost."[10] Thus it is that Borlase stands accused, by Emma Mitchell, for example, as one of a number of writers who wrote off Cornish as a dead language, a stable point of reference in a changing world, and in doing so conspired in an act of cultural colonization that they purported to be describing.[11]

If we turn to Polwhele, it is possible to discern significant differences in terms of emphasis and interest. Polwhele's interest in Cornish is both more cursory and more vital than Borlase's. He refers to other authorities (including Borlase) on the nature and extent of Cornish, content to suggest that "little else remains, but to notice its extent, and to observe its gradually contracting limits, till we see it reduced to a mere point, though not sure of its utter extinction."[12] Polwhele goes on to quote at length from Danes Barrington's famous account of his seeking out and meeting with Dolly Pentreath, and he discusses further the final decay of the language.[13] To the extent that he labors the point about the language verging on extinction, he falls squarely into the category of antiquarians such as Borlase (though it is notable that some 50 years after Borlase had declared the language dead, Polwhele is "not sure of its utter extinction" and is careful to note, though without further comment, that Dolly Pentreath was living within four miles of Borlase at the time he was administering the last rites). But in laboring the point, Polwhele also confuses it by offering other examples of people who knew some Cornish to speak or write (including the person who composed the Cornish inscription for Dolly's headstone). He also cannot resist reproducing a squib of Peter Pindar's on the subject of Mevagissey ("Mennygizzy") and Mousehole, the first famed for pilchards and the latter for "old Doll. Pentreath, / The Last who jabber'd Cornish—so says Daines," which finds time, in amongst making fun of the absurdity of expending so much scholarly energy on the point, to make clear that Barrington was also wrong in his belief that Dolly was the last speaker of Cornish.[14]

Later Polwhele asserts that he does not believe "that there now exist two people who can converse, for any continuance, in the Cornish" (*History of Cornwall,* vol. 5, 20), but only three pages later in a note on his Cornish glossary he talks of "those ancient persons" who still, in his phrase "pretend to jabber at it," and from whom he collected words (vol. 5, 23). Polwhele's final position is confused and confusing, not helped by the fact that the context of this last comment is in fact a complaint that these "ancient persons" are uneducated illiterates and therefore rather inconveniently ignorant of the orthography and etymology of that which they "pretend to jabber."

To see matters generously would be to credit Polwhele with some determination to distinguish the shared knowledge needed to converse in a language from the ability to know the Cornish words for things. Contradiction and confusion ensue because Polwhele has an insufficiently sophisticated theoretical language with which to discuss these linguistic questions, but Polwhele's messy, inconclusive register of leads and hints does undermine the neat narrative of extinction on the death of Dolly in 1777. As such it denies the "last of the race" primitivism and the tendencies towards cultural heritage-making invested in such narratives, and in its own way comes close to the picture as described in most modern histories of the county, which agree that people with some knowledge of the language were around well into the second half of the nineteenth century.[15]

Having left the "genius" of Cornish to other authorities, Polwhele does not dwell over long upon it. In fact he had in an earlier volume printed a "Cornish idyll" with translation, which he thinks "is not much unlike, I think, the twenty-seventh idyllium of Theocritus."[16] As I suggested earlier, to associate an unfamiliar text with one of the standard works, forms, or writers of literary tradition, is a standard manoeuver, but the qualities emphasized by this comparison are not those of the manly sublime vigor Borlase saw in the *Ordinalia,* but "flippancy, familiarity, and the rudest rusticity" (*History of Cornwall,* vol. 3, 32). He also reproduces a number of the short poems and riddles of early eighteenth-century writers of Cornish, and elsewhere in volume 2 prints the Lord's Prayer in seven different Celtic languages (for no obvious or stated reason, it has to be said). However the focus of Polwhele's linguistic interest is his Cornish–English Vocabulary, published as volume 6 of the *History of Cornwall.* It represents a selection from a full vocabulary he drew up from his own collecting and from the papers of, amongst others, Borlase and William Pryce, and his friend John Whitaker, famous as the fiery-tempered historian of Manchester and less famous for but no less fiery in his role as rector of Ruan Lanythorne in Cornwall.

Like everything Polwhele wrote, the vocabulary is heavily footnoted. Indeed, the footnotes themselves are heavily footnoted. For example, the word for "sea" is accompanied by notes that extend for three pages (*History of Cornwall,* vol. 6,

58–61). Generally speaking, these notes point in three directions. First, they seek to connect Cornish and the culture it represents with other ancient languages and cultures of the world, Classical, Biblical and Eastern. So the similarity of the Cornish word for "plough"—*arat*—to the Latin *aratrum* is noted and leads to a lengthy note on the farming practices of the county, its peculiarity, and its "high antiquity" (vol. 6, 8). Second, particularly given the emphasis upon words drawn from the "occurrences of ordinary life" (vol. 6, v), the notes demonstrate the continuity of the culture signified by these words into living memory (the point of the note on farming is that this is how it was still being done); and third, the notes are stalking horses for Polwhele's own concerns and preoccupations.

In this way, the word for "people"—*bobyl* or *poble*—prompts a lengthy rant on the rebelliousness, disrespectfulness, and ingratitude of the common sort and two sonnets on the pleasures of nature occasioned by his escape from what he terms "the roaring of the rabble / The strut of apes, the corporation-squabble—/ From all the radical astounding din" (vol. 6, 18–19). On the other hand, the explanation of the Cornish word for "supreme" asserts the unquestioned loyalty of the ancient Cornish to "Kings, Dukes, and Chieftains" and leads to a disquisition on the right and proper ends of Conservative Associations in defending the aristocracy. The note on *dun* or "hill" gives Polwhele an opportunity to print a poem written in the time of the French invasion threat, emphasizing the strength and independence of the ancient Cornish. Conversely, the note on "mountain" (*Bray*, *Brê* or *Brea*) prompts an anecdote about Polwhele's satire on a correspondent of the *Cornish Gazette* with firm opinions on the series of momentous battles fought on Carnbrea outside Redruth by "Britons, Romans, Saxons, Danes, Cornish-boys, and Englishmen." His poem, he tells us, had originally appeared in the *West Briton* after the "cross old driveller" of an editor of the *Gazette* had objected to Polwhele's "sportive muse." The note ends with Polwhele's satiric poem on antiquarian delusion and self-indulgence, itself complete with mock learned footnotes; that all of this occurs in a footnote on a word in a dictionary is just about the best proof one could wish for Swift's famous contention that satire is a mirror in which men see all things but themselves.

It is tempting to write this all off as an ill-disciplined, editorially lamentable mess, eccentric even by the standards of an age where lexicographical description was considerably more free-wheeling than we might expect today. We might conclude that in his efforts to ape the witty style of the eighteenth-century lexicographers and philologists he admired, he got it hopelessly wrong.[17] Yet however we account for it, the result is interesting. The overall effect is, in its eccentric way, to make the glossary much more of a living, vibrant document than a list of words in a dead tongue, living on merely in the names for things. Cornish remains—or is reinvested as—a site of contention and controversy, not a museum exhibit.

There is more to volume 6 of the *History of Cornwall* than the Cornish–English vocabulary, however. As well as a list of local names of Saxon derivation, "a curious monument" says Polwhele, "of the battle between the Cornish and the Saxon languages on the banks of the Tamar" (vol. 6, v), he includes what he calls a "provincial glossary" for Cornwall and Devon, dialect words which he suggests are "almost confined to the vulgar; though often of no mean origin" (vol. 6, v). As with the Cornish, he draws up the glossary from a number of sources. He takes the language from both oral and written sources, including proverbs; riddles; family mottos and epitaphs; manuscript collections of a number of figures including Jeremiah Milles, Cornish president of the Society of Antiquarians; and dialect poems, including the rather intriguingly titled "A Dialogue in the Devonshire dialect between Robin and Betty, in 3 parts by a niece of Sir Joshua Reynolds," in which Polwhele notes that the "rustic characters and manners are delineated with much simplicity and humour" (vol. 6, v). It is one of these sources that he refers to as "the romance of real life" (vol. 6, v), testament I think to his enduring interest in the everyday. Ultimately it is Polwhele's interest in the English as spoken by the people in Cornwall (and Devon) that makes his interest in the oral and written culture of the county most interesting.

Where Borlase had been more or less silent on the English of the region, Polwhele seeks multiple opportunities to bring it to the readers' attention. He distinguishes Devonian and Cornish English, citing a number of authorities as far back as Carew who held the Cornish variety more pure and elegant than that of Devon or other regions (speculating that this was because it was imported by those with access to a more refined world and one step up the social ladder from Cornish–Cornish). He reproduces two "Cornish Eclogues" that he says have "long circulated in MS in the West of Cornwall" and have spawned many imitators. This is the opening of the first, "A Cornish Dialogue between 2 Old Men," and it gives a flavor of the earthy humor and immediacy of this reported conversation, offered to the reader without the tidying up and polishing that is a feature of other contemporary attempts to render vulgar traditions for a polite readership:

Job Munglar
Loard! Uncle Jan Trudle dost a hire the news
How belike we shall stompey in temberen shoes?
For the Franchman and Spangars be coaming they saey
For to carry us ale from ould Inglant away!

Jan Trudle
Hould tha toang, tha' great Toatledum pattick og Newlyn's,
What becaze the ould wemmen be dwaling and druling,
And fright'ning one tother with goblins and goastes,
And a squaling "The Franchmen be got 'pon the coastes!"
Soar thee beestn'n sich a whit-liver'd saft-bak'd Timdoodle,

(in Richard Polwhele, *History of Cornwall*, vol. 6, p. 24n)

He then gives examples of Devonian English by way of contrast, "An Exmoor Scolding,"and "An Exmoor Courtship" (both of which, he notes, are also inflected with Somerset English) and two extracts from poems of Peter Pindar, from canto III of the *Lousiad* and "The Plymouth Bribery." The following is from the *Lousiad*, and purports to be from "the manuscript performance of one John Ploughshare" commemorating George III's visit to Exeter in 1789:

> In comm'd the King at laste to town,
> With doust and zweat az nutmer brown,
> The hosses all in smoke;
> Huzzaing, trumpeting, and ringing,
> Red colours vleeing, roaring, dringing,
> Zo mad zeem'd all the voke
>
> (in Richard Polwhele, *History of Cornwall*, vol. 6, 53)

Polwhele is interested not only in distinguishing the similarities and differences between Cornish and Devonian English (though he is on the whole content that his readers observe and work this out for themselves), but also in registering the Cornish English spoken in different parts of the county. He suggests that the primary occupations of the people are key to differences of language and pronunciation, and picks out the differences between the mining and farming communities for particular attention. Thus the English spoken in Breage is "broad-mouthed;" Polwhele comments that "the same words which I have heard in St Agnes and Piran-zabulo, have a very different effect in Breage, owing to a full and hoarse enunciation, and a sort of guttural harshness" (vol. 5, 24). These internal distinctions are perhaps the most significant, since they suggest not only that attention to detail mattered to Polwhele (indeed detail is something that he is never short of), but that his view of Cornwall is not one that irons out distinctions and differences in the interests of a monolithic notion of Cornishness. Equally, while the "harshness" of industrial Cornish English strongly implies an aesthetic value judgment, Polwhele notably stops short of distinguishing an "authentic" or more "pure," pre-industrial/pastoral version of the language. Polwhele does not seem to fall into the trap Philip Payton identifies as a historic tendency amongst observers of Cornwall when they "mistake cultural change for cultural extinction."[18]

English–Cornish verse crops up in other places within the *History of Cornwall*. Polwhele's account of the religious practices of the ancient Cornish lead him into a lengthy discussion of the festivals still extant in Cornwall that he fancies hark back to pagan times. For example, his detailed account of the Helston Furry of the eighth of May not only contains speculation on the derivation of the word "furry," but also records some stanzas of one of the traditional songs at the event:

Ro—bin – Hood – and – lit—tle – John
They – both – are gone – to – Fair – O –
And we – will to – the merry – green wood
To see – what they – do – there – O –
And – for – to – chase – O –
To chase – the Buck – and – Doe
With – Ha – lan – tow
Jolly rumble – O

(in Richard Polwhele, *History of Cornwall*, vol. 1, p. 42n)

The most striking thing about this is its attempt—presumably—to represent the tune of the song, that is to say its oral performance, in the presentation of the words.[19] The extract is presented with little preamble or editorial mediation on the part of Polwhele, and with little engagement with the texture of the poem. He quotes a correspondent's conjectures on the origin of the word "halantow," but there are none of the usual fancied comparisons with classical or other canonical literature for the song itself. And while this means that no claim is staked for this Cornish material in terms of the recognized canon, it also means that the work is not appropriated by or assimilated within accepted standards of taste and sensibility. The Helston Furry song is not some second-rate Theocritus, Spenser, or Shakespeare, but only—and triumphantly only, that is to say, uniquely—the Helston Furry song.

Polwhele also reproduces six pastoral poems written for the furry of 1796, "which was celebrated in that year with more than usual spirit." Below is the beginning and end of the poem "The Fadé," describing that part of the festivities when the revelers "fadé" into the countryside to adorn themselves with flowers and oak branches:

White-vestur'd, ye maidens of *Ellas*, draw near,
And honour the rites of the day:
'Tis the fairest that shines in the round of the year;
Then hail the bright Goddess of May.
O Come, let us rifle the hedges, and crown
Our heads with gay garlands of sweets:
[…]
The nymph who despises the furry-day dance,
Is a fine, or a *finical* lady–
Then let us with hearts full of pleasure, advance,
And mix, one and all, in the *Fadé*!

(in Richard Polwhele, *History of Cornwall*, vol. 1, 46)

Taken together, these poems offer a striking juxtaposition between the polite and the vulgar, between the textual rendering of oral tradition and the text-bound neoclassical formalities of late eighteenth-century poetry. As such, the furry emerges from the *History of Cornwall* as a site of living, evolving tradition, not a remnant or museum piece. Neither is there any romanticizing of a pure oral tradition with its concomitant opposition between primitive oral and polished literate culture so beloved by late-eighteenth-century commentators and so influential from that point on. Rather, the furry appears as evidence of what Adam Fox, arguing against this "crude binary," calls the "dynamic continuum" between oral and literate culture, between the folk or popular and the elite, characterized by "webs of interpenetration and mutual infusion."[20]

This lack of editorial or critical interpretation becomes more marked in volume 5 as Polwhele moves onto the "apothems, adages, and epitaphs" that he says, echoing a truism that can be traced as least as far back as William Camden's *Britannia* (1586), marks the "genius of a people" (vol. 5, 34).[21] Accordingly, he offers over twenty pages of riddles, sayings, and expressions, and family mottos and epitaphs in Cornish and Cornish–English, with explanation where necessary (and, it has to be said, occasional censure: as a vicar Polwhele takes a professional interest in the epitaphs adorning Cornish churchyards and the reader is given to understand that a few he cites would not have been allowed in the churchyard at Manaccan on his watch). So we learn, for example, that in Cornwall the phrase "to send him to St. Columb" equates to the more widely known, "to send him to Coventry," or to socially ostracize an individual.[22]

What strikes the reader encountering this material is the sheer amount of data being indiscriminately presented. Examples are piled up one after another with very little effort to connect them together into an overall argument. Polwhele's addiction to footnotes and notes to footnotes means that the scraps of verse and expression are not even braced by the grammar and paragraph structures of his discursive style. The overall effect is more akin to a scrapbook or collage than a systematic survey. The result is both curiously compelling and in places almost totally unreadable. But beyond both of these possible responses lies the sense of immersion within a culture that is teeming and vibrant, and cannot be compartmentalized or categorized.

This essay is concerned with literary culture, but it is worth recording that this tendency is continued in all aspects of the *History of Cornwall.* Indeed, the volume entitled *The Language, Literature and Literary Characters of Cornwall* ranges far and wide in and of itself. It moves on from the literary productions of the county to lengthy analysis of the education system of the county, including 11 pages on Truro Grammar School, its headmasters, notable old boys, and Polwhele's personal recollections as a pupil, replete with the Shandy-esque preservation of Polwhele's father's views of various characters. There is also an account of printing in Cornwall and in particular its newspapers, of the private libraries and literary societies in the county and of its great men of letters and arts, poets, painters and musicians.[23] In these accounts, nothing seems to be deemed too trivial or irrelevant to mention if it adds local color. For example, we are informed that one Bennet, organist at Truro and sometime composer in the mid-eighteenth century, though blind, "played whist with facility" (vol. 5, 206). In this way, the *History* has much in common with what Mark Salber Phillips notes as a particularly Scottish preoccupation with cataloguing everyday life at the end of eighteenth century.[24]

By way of conclusion, I want to consider the features of Polwhele's *History of Cornwall* in relation to some recent thinking about the representation of writing and voice. Polwhele's work could be considered neither folklore collection nor oral history in any more than a rather factious way (though he did correspond with those engaged in such work in the West Country and elsewhere, including Eliza Bray, the folklorist discussed in chapter one of this book).[25] It does, however, resonate in many of the ways characteristic of study in these fields. Polwhele offers an interesting case study or evidence of a number of recent insights.

A number of recent readings of historiography in the period offer suggestive comments about Polwhele's *History of Cornwall.* As we have seen, in its content it offers support for Phillips's analysis of the ways in which history becomes wider in its scope and subject, and in its structural failure, *The History of Cornwall* also offers support for Phillips's accompanying sense of the challenges such an understanding of the subject pose for the structure and coherence of historical narrative. In these terms, Polwhele's *History of Cornwall* is very much of its moment, in step with a current of historiographical thought that emphasized the quotidian, that sought to encompass custom and manners as well as—indeed, instead of—politics. Certainly it is striking how Polwhele also engaged with a number of the other historical genres that Phillips identifies as symptomatic of this perspective, in particular, memoir and anecdote.[26]

That said, there are other views of eighteenth-century historiography. For Daniel Woolf, Polwhele's interests would represent one of the "recessive genes of historiography," bred out during the eighteenth century but resurfacing in the "current vogue for a social and cultural history focussed on the material, anecdotal, and mundane."[27] The answer might lie in this question of form—or perhaps, of formlessness. That is to say, Polwhele evinces the eighteenth-century interest in the material but not an eighteenth-century interest in interpreting, organizing, and otherwise controlling it. In this way, it is even possible to read the absence of coherent editorial mediation in the *History of Cornwall* in terms of what Michael Frisch terms a "post-documentary sensibility" that denies "the assumption of pathed linearity" and of the "inevitability and indeed [...] the indispensability of editorial intervention, selection, shaping, arrangement and even manipulation."[28] That said, to advance Polwhele as some sort of proto-postmodernist oral or popular historian would be too farfetched. His *History of Cornwall* might demonstrate what Alessandro Portelli terms the "spontaneous uncontrollable mass of fluid, amorphous material" characteristic of an engagement with orality, but it is hard to feel that his failure to come to grips with it is anything other than a failure, and certainly not a conscious decision to go with the flow.[29] If anything, its continued flirting with incoherence merely illustrates the justice of Frisch's starting point concerning the "indispensability of editorial intervention" in a pre-digital age. More than just being farfetched, however, such a reading would also distract attention from the more significant lessons Polwhele's *History of Cornwall* might illustrate.

If we find it hard to swallow the idea of Polwhele as a prophet of postmodernist oral history, we are on safer ground relating these preoccupations to the Romantic interest in what he terms "the romance of real life." It is tempting to interpret this in terms of Wordsworth's interest in "incidents and situations from common life" told "in a selection of language really used by men" and in terms of a certain Romantic interest in the everyday as a force of aesthetic and political liberation.[30] Except it needs registering that Polwhele was not particularly interested in either of these sorts of liberation—he was writing neoclassical verse epistles well into his sixties in the 1820s, and in his seventies getting into a public row with the editor of the Truro *West Briton* over whether he had *exactly* said from the pulpit that a recent cholera outbreak was God's punishment for agitation in favor of Reform.[31]

This is not in itself an insurmountable objection: we have moved beyond a time where we demand that all aspects of a historical figure's career and thinking fall into a neat box; we can allow that people are complicated and at times contradictory (in fact, there is significant evidence for his interest in the plight of the poorest in society and his efforts to defend their interests, however misguided his political model might seem today). However there are other reasons why we should not rush to type Polwhele within the tradition of radical oral history. Mark Salber Phillips reminds us that Samuel Johnson's preference for biography over history is part of a conventional Protestant Christian sense of the importance of everyday life, while Paul Thompson's personal belief that "the richest possibilities for oral history lie within the development of a more socially conscious and democratic society" does not prevent him from acknowledging that a "telling case" can be made for a conservative position that sees the value of oral history in preserving "the full richness and value of tradition."[32] Adam Fox offers an example of this in his discussion of the attraction of the study of proverbs for early modern historians (and as we have seen, for Polwhele) and the retreat from such study in the eighteenth century. Proverbs were, Fox notes, "grist to the mill of anyone seeking to identify enduring continuity in English attitudes, aspirations, and sensibilities over a long period."[33] However, the stock of proverbial wisdom fell from the late seventeenth century onwards for a variety of reasons, including the assumed political and social coloring of their "world view," Fox observes:

> Among a generation attempting to define itself as progressive and modern, they seemed intolerably conservative and referential; in an era of increasing individuality they represented the ethics of community; in a climate of optimism and opportunity they were resignedly stoic and hopelessly parochial.[34]

It was, however, a world in which Polwhele, keen, as we have seen, to assert the historic subservience of the Cornish to authority and to lament the rebelliousness of modernity, felt entirely at home.

By some quirk of history, Polwhele appears to us a strangely multifaceted figure, by turns old-fashioned in his tastes and postmodern in his methods; in step with the broadened horizons of eighteenth-century historiography and yet resistant to the interpretative frameworks and narrative structures devised to police and otherwise contain those horizons. His interest in the proverbial; his unwillingness or inability to distinguish in any meaningful sense the oral and the literate, or to refine or otherwise mediate the artifacts of popular culture he presents before us; and his refusal or failure to boil his material down, to shape and select within the frameworks of eighteenth-century historiography, are all symptomatic of the way that his *History of Cornwall* points backwards to the early modern and forward to the postmodern, and stands within an identifiable eighteenth-century type of history and outside of it.

Many of the standard narratives of eighteenth-century antiquarian history, particularly Celtic history, whether they be of noble savages and ideal primitive societies or the undiscovered literary traditions to rival those of the classical world, have a tendency to not only privilege a culture but also to tame and domesticate it, to evacuate it of its true cultural and historical (and maybe political) significance and render it safe for consumption as heritage. This dynamic has been explored in greatest detail in relation to the Highlands of Scotland, where, for example, the ostensive rehabilitation and celebration of Gaelic heroism represented by *The Poems of Ossian* is more than likely now to be seen as an effort "more to anaesthetise than revitalise Gaelic tradition" in an effort to construct "the romanticised basis for cultural tourism."[35] It is a version of this charge that has been laid against the likes of Borlase in Cornwall, or any that, in Payton's useful distinction, mistake change for decline. The pursuit of aboriginal purity leads to the retreat from the lived and, ultimately, from the living. By being unwilling—or unable—to render his material within these kinds of interpretative frameworks, by the very ill-discipline of his method, Polwhele's *History of Cornwall* ultimately resists these distancing critical manoeuvers and narratives and provides a compelling snapshot of Cornwall at the turn of the nineteenth century.

Notes

1. Mark Brayshay, "The Development of Topographical Writing in the South West" in *Topographical Writers in South West England*, Mark Brayshay, editor (Exeter: Exeter Univ. Press, 1996), 14. That said, it should be noted that the doyen of Devon county history, W. G. Hoskins, considered the *History of Devonshire* "3rd rate," patchy in its coverage and in its general history, and exhibiting "a miserable level of performance," as noted in Hoskins' *Local History in England*, 3rd edition (London: Longman, 1984), 23. Certainly

Polwhele's second Devon project was dogged with practical problems, which, while interesting, are not of concern here.

2. Mark Salber Phillips, *Sentiment and Society: Genres of Historical Writing in Britain, 1740–1820* (Princeton: Princeton Univ. Press, 2000), 17. Subsequently referred to as Phillips, *Sentiment and Society.*
3. A. L. Rowse, foreword to Polwhele's *The History of Cornwall* (Dorking: Kohler and Coombes, 1978), n.p.
4. Phillips, *Sentiment and Society*, 343.
5. ibid., 91.
6. As traced for example by Daniel Woolf in his *The Social Circulation of the Past: English Historical Culture 1500–1700* (Oxford: Oxford Univ. Press, 2003).
7. William Borlase, *The Natural History of Cornwall*, with an intro. by F. A. Turk (London: E & W Books Ltd, 1970), 313 (originally published 1758).
8. It is, for example a standard account of the point of Macpherson's *Ossian* as most succinctly explained by Adam Potkay in his "Virtue and Manners in Macpherson's *Poems of Ossian*," *PMLA* 107 (1992), 120–31 and by John Dwyer in "The Melancholy Savage: Text and Context in *The Poems of Ossian* in *Ossian Revisited*, ed. Howard Gaskill (Edinburgh: Edinburgh Univ. Press, 1991), 164–206. But see also Moore, "Heroic Incoherence in James Macpherson's *Poems of Ossian*," in *Eighteenth-Century Studies* 34:1 (Fall 2000), 43–59.
9. Karen O'Brien, *Narratives of Enlightenment: Cosmopolitan History from Voltaire to Gibbon* (Cambridge: Cambridge Univ. Press, 1997), 108.
10. Murray G. H. Pittock, "Scott and the British Tourist" in *English Romanticism and the Celtic World*, eds. Gerard Carruthers and Alan Rawes (Cambridge: Cambridge Univ. Press, 2003), 159.
11. Emma Mitchell, "The Myth of Objectivity: The Cornish Language and the Eighteenth-Century Antiquaries," in *Cornish Studies,* vol. 6, edited by Philip Payton (Exeter: Exeter Univ. Press, 1998), 70–71.
12. Polwhele, *History of Cornwall*, vol. 5, 3. He also prints from MS 12 letters of Lhuyd to Thomas Tonkin of Lambrigian.
13. The Mousehole Fisherwoman, Dolly Pentreath, was held to be the last speaker of Cornish. Danes Barrington's accounts of her were produced for the Society of Antiquaries and are reprinted in Polwhele's *History of Cornwall*, vol. 5, 16–19.
14. In Polwhele, *History of Cornwall*, vol. 5, p.19n. "Ode XXI: To Myself" originally appeared in Peter Pindar's *Lyric Odes for the Year 1785.* Peter Pindar was the pen name of John Wolcot, a friend of the Polwhele family and mentor to Polwhele's since school days, though by this time they had fallen out, no doubt on account of Peter Pindar's anti-ministerial politics.
15. See for example Philip Payton, *Cornwall: A History*, 2nd ed. (Fowey: Cornwall editions, 2004), 176.
16. Polwhele, *History of Cornwall*, vol. 3, 32. Polwhele's *The Idyllia, Epigrams, and Fragments, of Theocritus, Bion, and Moschus, with the Elegies of Tyrtæus* (1786) was pretty much the standard and certainly a highly respected translation of Theocritus through much of the nineteenth century, so he is speaking from a position of knowledge and significant authority.
17. Polwhele cites the politically incongruous combination of Samuel Johnson, John Horne Took, and Archdeacon Robert Nares as his models. Horne Took was exactly the sort of political figure Polwhele spent his life attacking. Nares, on the other

hand, was a correspondent of Polwhele's. Polwhele contributed to *The British Critic,* co-founded by Nares, and in 1824 published "An Epistle to Archdeacon Nares."

18. Payton, *Cornwall: A History*, 179.
19. At the risk of a Polwhelean footnote, it might be worth noting that most British readers (of a certain age at least) will think themselves familiar with the tune of the Helston furry song as the "Floral Dance," popularized in the late 1970s in the United Kingdom by the Brighouse and Rastrick Brass Band and the broadcaster Sir Terry Wogan. "The Floral Dance" is in fact a 20th-century song relating a visit to the Helston Furry by its writer, Katie Moss, with a tune 80% her own. A further confusion is that the "furry song" is today thought of as separate from the "halantow" performance to which Polwhele is presumably referring here, though he terms it the "furry song."
20. Adam Fox, *Oral and Literate Culture in England 1500–1700* (Oxford: Oxford Univ. Press, 2002), 50, 172.
21. Paul Thompson, *The Voice of the Past: Oral History* (Oxford: Oxford Univ. Press, 1978), 28.
22. Polwhele, *History of Cornwall,* vol. 5, 34. Polwhele offers no explanation as to why Cornwall's St. Columb might equate with Warwickshire's Coventry (the conventional explanation for the latter is the frosty reception afforded Cavalier prisoners of war by the staunchly Roundhead city during the English Civil War). He does however note an interesting further usage of the Cornish phrase: a sulky child might be considered to have "gone to St. Columb." I don't think it is the case that sulky children are accused of going to Coventry; this use is not noted in *Brewer's Dictionary of Phrase and Fable,* rev. edition, 1970.
23. Polwhele was to publish his 3-volume *Biographical Sketches in Cornwall* in 1831.
24. Phillips, *Sentiment and Society*, 155. It is perhaps worth wondering whether Phillips's explanation for this in terms of rapid modernization and a "watchful intimacy with a dominant [English] society" applies to provincial Celtic Cornwall as well. In volume 7, Polwhele turns his attention to the people and health of the county in the same way. Nothing is considered either too stomach-churning or too trivial to be included in the discussion of the people, their health, ailments and diets. Feats of strength, strange births, twins with different fathers, the people who seem physiologically incapable of spitting, all find their place.
25. See Polwhele, *Reminiscences, in Prose and Verse; Consisting of the Epistolary Correspondence of Many Distinguished Characters.* 3 volumes in 1 (London: J. B. Nichols and Son, 1836), 75–80, 91. He also corresponded with Sir Walter Scott (see his edited collection, *Letters of Sir Walter Scott, Addressed to the Rev. R. Polwhele; D. Gilbert, Esq.; Francis Douce, Esq.* (London: J. B. Nichols, 1832).
26. In Polwhele's *Biographical Sketches* and *Reminiscences in Prose and Verse,* mentioned above, and also in his *Traditions and Recollections: Domestic, Clerical and Literary,* 2 vols. (London: John Nichols and Son, 1826).
27. Daniel Woolf, *The Social Circulation of the Past: English Historical Culture 1500–1730* (Oxford: Oxford Univ. Press, 2003), 399.
28. Michael Frisch, "Oral History and the Digital Revolution: Towards a Post-Documentary Sensibility" in *The Oral History Reader*, 2nd ed., edited by Robert

Perks and Alistair Thomson (New York and London: Routledge, 2006), 102–114, p. 110.

29. Alessandro Portelli, "What Makes Oral History Different?" in *The Oral History Reader*, 2nd ed., edited by Robert Perks and Alistair Thomson, 33–42, p. 33.
30. William Wordsworth, preface to *Lyrical Ballads* (1802), in *The Oxford Author's William Wordsworth*, edited by Stephen Gill (Oxford: Oxford Univ. Press, 1990) 596–97.
31. See Polwhele, *Reminiscences*, vol. 2, 27–36 for his account of this latter episode in a letter to the Bishop of Exeter of 31 March 1832.
32. Phillips, *Sentiment and Society*, 139; Thompson, *The Voice of the Past*, x.
33. Fox, *Oral and Literate Culture*, 141.
34. Fox, *Oral and Literate Culture*, 168.
35. Allan Macinnes, *Clanship, Commerce and the House of Stuart, 1603–1788* (East Linton: Tuckwell Press, 1996), 220.

CHAPTER 3

Printed Voices: Dialect and Diversity in Mid-Nineteenth-Century Lancashire

Sue Edney

This chapter examines how printing accommodates local voices and whether this affects writing about place and the wider reception of a locality. The discussion will focus on some urban and rural laboring-class poetry from the Manchester area around the mid-nineteenth century to illustrate some of the problems arising from writing in dialect and how its use influences our perception of place and community. Dialect writing had a strong following among urban and rural communities, including establishment audiences, in the early Victorian period. For many local writers and readers, using dialect offered a medium for the expression of ownership of place and also of their own creative productions that was not available, or was diluted, in Standard English. The expansion of printing also ensured that oral forms could be translated into readable material and quickly disseminated among strangers as well as friends. What was particular to a locality might be lost or devalued by a shifting community, producing stereotypical images of identity; it could also be revalued in new varieties of language. Any reduction of language diversity, however it comes about, affects attitudes to its place of origin: differences in language offer different perspectives and enrich stories about locality. Peter Mühlhäusler considers the "repository of past experience" available to future generations through the study of apparently uncongenial systems such as the grammar and syntax of individual dialects: "Linguistic diversity is a diversity of knowledge, philosophies and perspectives, and... this diversity came about precisely because different words are needed to live in different environments."[1]

In the nineteenth century, laboring-class writing chronicled the instability of laborers' lives; at least if they could write down a particular story, even if it had always been a varying tale by word of mouth, they could establish a certain permanent presence. "Seeing" themselves in print was a literal revelation, showing their position in a much wider social and cultural context as well as exposing them to more immediate comment from family and neighbors. As writing became a more complex engagement with personal and public versions of representation, self-taught writers learnt to negotiate their partial or embroidered picture in print. In fact, David Vincent notes that "getting into print... was much the easiest stage in the journey, and adds, "The provincial press provided an obvious outlet for aspiring poets, at once a nursery and a shop window for literary talent. The confines of their columns matched the limited time and energy of their contributors. They had just enough space to publish the short poems which tired working men could manage to set down at the end of a working day."[2]

The first and more arduous task was learning to read and write. Everyday experience was bound up in survival: keeping the fire alight, getting enough to eat, raising children—there was little time or energy to do much else. Formal education was still an optional luxury for most impoverished families in the early nineteenth century, and dislocation in the rapidly expanding towns did little to stabilize it. W. B. Stephens discusses the different levels of literacy across parishes and occupations, showing that the relationships between occupations, place and literacy appear to be strong although the connections are complex.[3] Rural Lancashire children might have had greater access to schooling, especially in the early nineteenth century, however, David Vincent has pointed out that greater pressure in the cities encouraged industrial workers' "reliance on their own efforts... through thick and thin."[4] There were Sunday schools, mechanics' institutes, and there was also endless eye-straining labor over the few books that a family could gather. But the existence of stable "dame" schools in birthplace villages contributed to a belief that there had once been a secure, rural, or semirural "place" that could be used as an authentic original from which to develop stories of stability that supported precarious urban laboring life.

In either case, the cottages and terraces were dark, filled with smoke from poor-quality candles and fires, and noisy with family life. Having learned to write, people wrote about themselves; the condition of their lives, folktales, where they had come from if they had migrated from rural to urban living or from another town, and what they wished for—especially the possibilities of change in circumstances through writing itself. Vincent suggests there was fear in establishment authority that "the newly literate would subvert the distinctions upon which the divide between polite and popular culture was based." Fortunately for the establishment, the tools of literacy had been rendered so "strange to handle and difficult to employ for any but the most mundane tasks" that the majority of so-called "literate" working families saw little reason to extend their knowledge outside their limited access to education.[5] Yet, as Ivan Kreilkamp points out, the definition of literacy was "restrictive" and many working-class English people would never be considered fully "literate" if, for example, they *spoke* with a regional accent. Kreilkamp continues: "The figure of the speaking worker marked, then, a point where two competing or contradictory concepts of literacy collided. An illiterate worker's speech offered the promise of future education, the possibility of improvement, and even the liberal utopia of a fully educated, middle-class England."[6]

These apparent contradictions were especially important to the vernacular poet, searching for an uneasy balance between mass-printed media and the hearthside song.

Brian Maidment has usefully proposed three groupings of self-taught and working-class poetry: radical, Parnassian, and homely rhymers.[7] My intention in this chapter is to examine how some of the homely rhymers depicted their localities on behalf of a wider, fluctuating readership, concentrating on Lancashire weavers. Lancashire was the home of both dialect poetry and cotton production in the middle period of the nineteenth century, culminating (in poetic terms) with the Cotton Famine poets of the 1860s. Maidment takes his phrase "homely rhyming" from titles such as "Radical Weaver" Samuel Bamford's *Homely Rhymes, Poems and Reminiscences* (1864), and Bamford's writing career covers all three of Maidment's categories, from radical to Parnassian to local descriptions. At the time of his birth in 1788, Bamford's home village of Middleton was a community of farmers who were also weavers, rather than weavers who kept a cow or two, but it rapidly became a block-printing and weaving center specializing in silk and later cotton, with handlooms and, eventually, steam-powered machines. Manchester was the draw for manufacturers and their employees: Bamford writes in *Walks in South Lancashire* how weaving "houses" were leaving the small towns to set up steam-powered factories in Manchester—"crape-weaving from the district of Chadderton," for example.[8] Writing about Milnrow, the place where "Tim Bobbin," dialect writer John Collier, had been born in 1708, Bamford describes the farmer-weaver of the mid-eighteenth century, when "such a thing as a cotton or woollen factory was not in existence. . . . A farmer would generally have three or four looms in his house, and thus, what with the farming, easily and leisurely though it was performed, what with the house work, and what with the carding, spinning, and weaving, there was ample employment for the family."[9]

Farming and weaving were carried out on a large scale, primarily because pastoral farming, common in upland and lowland Lancashire districts, was amenable to hours profitably spent doing something else.[10] But increasing demand for fabrics, specialist looms requiring technical assistance, and a generally better income led to weaving families becoming largely divorced from the land. In the earlier years of weaving industrialization, the moves were gradual, more shifts in emphasis than wholesale "flitting." Bamford was still describing the homes of handloom weavers in 1841. Handloom weaving for a range of textiles—silk, wool, fustian, calico, assorted cottons—was at its height during the 1820s and 1830s, the same period when agricultural and industrial disturbance was increasing. The "high earning potential" of hand weaving, together with "low entry costs," as Geoffrey Timmins has explained, were attractive to agricultural workers.[11]

Although many rural weavers set up their looms in existing cottages, others developed small working clusters, as many as 50 or 60 houses in terraces devoted to varieties of textiles. Timmins comments that "colonisation by hand weavers could have a profound effect," especially on small rural hamlets where the weaving "shops" could dominate the village.[12] As the cotton industry expanded, and agents, warehouses, traders, printers, and finishers were increasingly attracted to towns like Manchester, these same rural clusters were often abandoned, leaving desolate villages behind. The speed and character of change was marked: in 1841 Bamford describes "a place called Gravel Hole" near Thornham, including a settlement of some fifty weavers' houses: "About twelve or fourteen years since, these houses were all inhabited by fustian hand-loom weavers; they are now occupied, one or two excepted, by fustian cutters. The old inhabitants have gone down into the vallies to work at the factories, and the present residents are new-comers from many parts of the country."[13]

Where there was a "remnant of the old fustian weavers" left, making cloth to be made up into mackintoshes, "several houses were unoccupied; others in a state of partial dilapidation; garden fences were broken down, and the gardens had become grass plats." In Middleton, however, there were still specialist calico and silk hand weavers reasonably well occupied, and at Shaw, Bamford describes the houses of some "power-loom weavers of cords and velveteens" employed in a small factory as "uniformly neat and clean . . . they generally had flowers and green shrubs in the windows, and before the doors were small gardens."[14] Construction of a home, therefore, instead of just somewhere to subsist—and there also are plenty of examples of desperately poor weavers' cottages—depended on occupation, the type of textile produced, and the conditions of production as well as the place.

As hand weaving declined—more in the cities than in rural areas, partly due to the ease of access to factories—and then as the cotton industry itself fell victim to war, recession, and increased imports, these dwellings often became prisons to their unemployed inhabitants; this was acutely obvious in the new cotton towns such as Manchester, Blackburn, and Oldham.

It can be seen from this brief overview of the pattern and type of settlement among weavers that notions of place and ownership of place, in the sense of a permanent or persistent dwelling in the landscape, were probably not the same as the sense of belonging to the landscape felt by farming families. A sense of place in the city was constructed as much from the communities that dwelt in it as from the bricks and paving surrounding them. How they lived defined where they lived, clearly demonstrated by the homely rhymers; for example, in the proud lists of plants and possessions gathered together or relinquished in time of need. The reciprocal relationship of place to people, and the re-creation of place by and for people, was expressed through varieties of language, demonstrated in Lancashire vernacular poetry, as we shall see.

Brian Hollingworth writes of the golden age of Lancashire dialect poetry, beginning around 1850 and subsiding into insignificance by 1870, and refers to the "rapid and transient movement" of dialect writing in this period (and we must emphasize *writing*)—the "fixing" of speech patterns in print that were related to ordinary experience, which had once been sung on street corners or told in the local pub.[15] It offers a "printed voice" that attempts to bridge place, time, and class while remaining recognizably spoken.[16] Larry McCauley cautions against losing sight of the literariness of much of this poetry, however, and notes: "Dialect and dialect poetry are different things and…as the latter developed, its distance from the former increased."[17] Further, texts were no longer solely directed at dialect-speaking audiences. Writing and print began to take on their own kinds of dialects, which both mingled with and differed from the spoken (and heard) varieties.

One reason for writing down oral tales lay in the general nineteenth-century interest in personal history and collections of all kinds. Interest in philological discovery and language preservation was as keen as the widespread enthusiasm for botany and archaeology. Classification was part of the armory of control; control over nature, but also over one's environment, marking the benefits of book-learning and the disadvantages of illiteracy. Edwin Waugh, probably the best-known of golden age Lancashire poets, portrays the autodidactic tendencies of "honest" working family and community life with particular skill and precision in "Fawr Folk":

> Er Johnny gi's his mind to books;
> Er Abram studies plants,–
> He caps the dule for moss an' ferns,
> An' grooin' polyants;
> For aught abeawt mechanikin',
> Er Ned's the very lad;
> My uncle Jamie roots i' th' stars,
> Enough to drive him mad.
> …
> Er Matty helps my mother, an'

Hoo sews, an' tents er Joe;
At doin' sums, an sich as that,
My feyther licks them o';
Er Charley,–well,–there connot be
Another pate like his,–
It's o' crom-full o' ancientry,
An' Roman haw-pennies![18]

In his poetry, Waugh did not write about the workplaces of the majority—the cotton mills and weaving sheds—although some of his prose portrays the condition of cotton workers, in Preston and Wigan, for example, during the layoffs caused by the American Civil War and the blockade of raw cotton from the southern states—the Cotton Famine of 1861–1865. In "Eawr Folk," Waugh extends the range of working-class potential probably further than most families ever achieved in a desire to portray life skills that *transcend* circumstance, and even place. "The variety of the family's pursuits—scholarly, agricultural, mechanical, and domestic—suggests not a clearly stratified society but a society in flux," writes McCauley.[19]

Waugh was not a weaver, being the son of a shoemaker and born in Rochdale, which was not as oppressive a city as Manchester. In his writing, he grafted his own rural Rochdale memories onto contemporary Manchester urban dialect. He was a typesetter and then assistant secretary to the Lancashire Public School Association in Manchester, working towards the "freedom" of full-time writing: "I have nothing for it but my labour" he writes in his diary for 1847, "'tis for the bare life."[20] He disliked his work and he disliked Manchester, but was determined to celebrate much of working-class life, not merely lament its miseries. Above all, he valued *cultivation* in life—Patrick Joyce refers to it as "the cult of the heart."[21] This is more than cultural aspiration, although that is certainly part of it: Waugh deliberately seeks out the communitarian impulse in humankind—a practical and visible working out of "the brotherhood of man."[22] For Waugh, dialect poetry could "stir the heart" of the working community, like music.

My uncle Sam's a fiddler; an'
Aw fain could yer him play
Fro' set o' sun till winter neet
Had melted into day;
For eh – sich glee – sich tenderness!
Through every changin' part,
It's th' heart that stirs his fiddle,–
An' his fiddle stirs his heart.

It was his wish that such dialect music should stimulate glee and tenderness "through every changin' part" of the working community's diverse fortunes, when

> Sometimes, th' wayter in his e'en,
> 'At fun has made to flow,
> Can hardly roll away, afore
> It's blent wi' drops o' woe.[23]

In Lancashire dialect poetry's golden age, there were genuine attempts to prevent the loss of diversity in language, custom and, through these, locality by encouraging the strong relationships between past place and present place. McCauley points to Waugh's ability to place folk in historical and national contexts:

> "Eawr folk" applies obviously first to the family group described, then to the working people of Lancashire and to a broader English working class. But if we read the dialect as ultimately a sign of what the English people thought they were, we can construe a much broader reference—the "folk" as a mythic, trans-historical, classless construct by which the English people understand themselves.[24]

Waugh's use of a simple ballad structure is combined with differing levels of lexical sophistication: much of it is standard English, but the force of local speech, where it is used, acts as a balance to set against the aspirations of the poem's characters. In this way Waugh encourages his audience to "root[s] i' th' stars," but only insofar as it will bring them real benefits and not take them beyond their communities, which risked driving them as "mad" as Uncle Jamie. Importantly, these poems were also songs, set to printed music for public-house back rooms and mill owners' polite parlors. Bringing cultivation to street level while maintaining the virtues of learning was at the heart of the autodidact poet's mission: to improve through entertainment.

All the dialect writers of this period were attempting to feed a voracious and expanding audience with cultural basics—elements of life skills their local readers had never expected to use, let alone to enjoy and to crave. Popular oral ballads were still the most likely entertainment for working families; they covered every situation a listener might find familiar: injustice, infidelity, drunkenness, fun and games, and trouble at work. They also acted as voices of protest and exhortation, giving a sense of communal solidarity to working groups. The mid-century dialect writers had to juggle several spinning plates—entertainment, protest and encouragement, personal aspiration, and poetic skill itself, the ultimate subject of poetry. Crucially, as a means of binding persons together, threads across time and place had to be woven effectively in order to rebuild a sense of communal place that was feared to have been obscured by industrial smog.

Writers from impoverished, ill-educated backgrounds, working in factories, mills, mines, and as builders of the new industrial towns, needed to establish their knowledge of family and place in localities that were changing more rapidly than their predecessors could have imagined. As a typesetter and a popular poet, Waugh represented the connection between industry and leisure; as a dialect writer, he believed he could reinvigorate the links between a rural past—however mythical—and an urban present, in order to create a beloved place called home. Incorporating an abundance of dialect detail was one of Waugh's characteristic methods, best exhibited in a widely anthologized poem "Come whoam to thi childer an' me" (1856), in which the repetition of homely terms helps to reinforce the connection of home to occupants.[25] Local words can develop a metonymic relationship with fragile communities, helping to reinforce their significance. Regional "listing" (the "bacon-collops" or "ale posset i' th' oon [oven]" in this poem are samples) acts as a signal of authentic local identity that has a link to a named place.[26] Joan Beal comments on how the "linguistic repertoire" of dialect "provides models for the *performance* of local identity" [my emphasis]. In some measure, this includes the performance of *place* by using language closely connected to it.[27]

In this period, there were certain types of vernacular Lancashire poetry about place: they included the contained interior of the cottage, urban or rural; a landscape of escape and consolation in the immediate countryside outside the cities; and cities as sites of communal activity and celebration. A print of Manchester viewed from nearby Kersal Moor in 1857 shows innumerable smoking chimneys in the background, while the foreground is as picturesque a scene as any William Gilpin had painted. James Winter, in a note to the reproduction of this print, adds that the contrast "suggests two things: that most areas of pollution and industrial detritus were concentrated and closely ringed with greenery and that city dwellers were within walking distance of the countryside."[28] Joseph Ramsbottom, a "shadowy figure in the Manchester literary scene," as Brian Maidment remarks, writes particularly sensitively about the connection between town and country for the weaver.[29] In "Coaxin'," first printed in *Country Words* (1866), Ramsbottom illustrates the tender and spontaneous intimacy available to young hand-loom weavers who controlled their own time and were not bound to factory hours or inner city grime.

Hi thi, Jenny, lyev thi loom,
Ther's a bonny sky above;
Eawt o' th' days we wortch to live,
We may tak a day to love
. . .

Fling thi clogs an brat aside;
Let thi treddles rest to-day;
Tee thi napkin o'er thi yead;
Don thi shoon an' come away,
Everlastin' tugg un teighl,
If eawr lives mun so be spent,
What's the good o' whistlin' brids?
Why wur posies ever sent?[30]

Almost nothing is known about Joseph Ramsbottom. John Whittaker, his friend, and editor of Ramsbottom's poems, *Phases of Distress,* remarks in his preface that they had both been "lads toiling in the same dyehouse," and that now both had "escaped from our former uncongenial life." However, "Coaxin'" harks back to a place difficult to find in 1866—the rural, independent weaver's cottage and the family fortunes, past and future, bound to its persistence in the landscape—or if it does not, it *wishes* to do so, which for many locally placed poems amounted to the same thing. The poem continues with an evocation of a domestic idyll:

Deawn bi th' well, at th' hollow oak
Under th' hawthorn blossom sweet.
Wheer a linet sings above,
An' a rindle runs at th'feet;
An' the red rimm'd daisies look
Wi' their gowden een int' heaven.
And eawr gronnies used to tell
Ut the little fairies liven.
There we'll sit, an' talk o' th' time
Ut we so mich wish ud come,
When we'st find it reet to wed;
When we'st have a tidy whoam,
Wi' sich lots o' babby smocks,
An' sich rows o' clogs an' shoon,
An' sich breeches, skirts, an' frocks:
Why – it conno come too soon.

The repetitive simplicity of the poem, emphasizing the dreamlike, fairytale of happy-ever-after, and the gentle rhythm and homely detail of smocks and clogs were all intended to appeal through the twin themes of solace and hope—solace in the natural, timeless world away from weaving, but hope in *future* weaving whether by hand or power-loom, the everyday business of father "eawt t' mi wark" and children "prattlin' reawnd" with "pattherin' feet." Detail expressed in dialect helps to undercut sentiment while keeping the local audience's emotional attention. Ramsbottom frequently juxtaposes images of natural beauty with urban industrial reality. In "Sorrowin'," Ramsbottom's speaker is a mother comforting her young son after the death of his father, struck down by "little rest, heavy care, an' great need." She draws him away from their present grief by reminding the boy of a life outside distress—outside the city. The description is both sentimental and pragmatic at the same time.

> Then he sometimes 'ud hugg thi i' th' fields,
> An' he'd get thi a nice hazel bough;
> An' a posy bunch tee thi o' th' eend,
> Made o' daisies an' primroses too.
> An' he'd bridneeses show thi an o,
> An' he'd put th' little eggs i' thi brat;
> Bo he'd noa let thi break 'em, aw know,
> He wur noane so hard-hearted as that.[31]

In "Preawd Tum's Prayer," Tum walks out into the fields for a different reason; to pray, even to complain like Job that, finally, he feels rejected even by those who are supposed to help the poor. God's compassion is in nature: "here, among o' th' whistlin' brids [...] Ther's summat i' mi breast ut bids / Me neaw to speak witheawt a fear [...] Alone wi' God's things, an' wi God." In the city "They'd crush us wi' a Bible text." An imposed language of orthodoxy is contrasted with the simple honesty of local speech, which is also associated with nature. Dialect as a natural expression of authentic purity was often cited in its defense. In the fields, Tum speaks God's language among God's things.[32]

The contrast between the "sun's great cheerin' leet" in the countryside around Manchester, Preston, and Rochdale and the gloom of the city is a feature of these poems. But where *is* the city? The construction of the city as a force opposing country life is rarely expressed, and is often an unspoken, looming presence. Standard English poets regularly comment on the nature of city dwelling, especially in the second half of the century, when the majority lived and worked away from the countryside and had less access to family memories—real or created—of rural life. Brian Maidment notes the absence of "city-observed" poems: "The subject matter of self-taught writers remained resolutely abstract, rural, or domestic."[33] One Manchester poet, John Owen, explains why cities have no need of proclamations—you can't ignore them, you can only alleviate their effects. Poetry and song are among the reliefs of city life; "manna to the city":

> Broadcast it scatters life, and love, and pity,
> And e'en the reapers cannot tell the yield.[34]

Country dwellers, "calm sitting where the brook and river meet" know little of how the city functions—"know[s] nothing of its intermittent fever"—seeing only distant chimneys. The cohesiveness of oral and literate creativity (poetry *and* song) is not only more necessary in the city, it can even be better directed to general and personal benefit, as Owen goes on to suggest:

> In this strange world's wild hurry and confusion
> A song becomes a sermon if it saves,
> And teaches that which is not all delusion
> But which may brighten e'en the brink of graves.

John Harland even includes a plea on behalf of chimneys in his edition of *Ballads and Songs of Lancashire* (1865), "The Smokeless Chimney," written in order to raise money for poor relief during factory shutdowns; the ballads were printed on cards and sold mainly at railway stations.[35] The disinterested passenger on the Northern Railway, itself a displacer of persons and customs, wonders why he is not wreathed in smoke:

> "How much prettier is this county!"
> Says the careless passer-by;
> "Clouds of smoke we see no longer,
> What's the reason?—tell me why."

To the industrial worker, however,

> ... each smokeless chimney
> Is a signal of despair;
> They see hunger, sickness, ruin,
> Written in that pure, bright air.

The city worker's peculiar preference for soot and dust, also purveyors of sickness and ruin, passes without comment, in spite of the fact that the majority of working-class poets wrote with yearning for pure, bright air. These well-intended verses encapsulate the paradox contained in industrial development: without the smoke, there is no one on the railway to ignore it, nor even any railway for him to whisk along. The city and industrial voice inevitably sounded ambivalent, although there were a few urban vernacular poems, such as the anonymous "Rambles in Owdham," that are relatively positive in their portrayal of urban life:

> When I geet to Coppy Nook
> It pleos'd me reet well,

I seed all the town ofore me,
O' which I'm goin' to tell;
Their wur coaches, carts, an' coal-pits,
As throng as you'd desire,
An' coal enough they'rn gettin' up
To set th' whole town o' fire.[36]

Brian Hollingworth adds in a note: "A feature of the poem is the confidence and optimism which the new discoveries were bringing to working people." This confidence was expressed with new linguistic authority in songs and poems that celebrated their trades, their families and their festivities in various urban districts, "Tinker's [Vauxhall] Gardens" in Manchester, "Karsy [Kersal] Moor Races," "Warikin [Warrington] Fair" among them.[37] Using the locally owned name created a feeling of embeddedness, tying place to people through language.

In the cities, dialect writers create a sense of community-in-place, which arises from the structure of the crowded courtyards, crammed close to the factory, foundry, or mill walls. Samuel Laycock's "Bowton's Yard" lists the characters and how they live, creating a landscape of activity rather than physical elements. The buildings are incidental, and the details picked out: "number three, reet facin' th' pump," or "next door to us, an' close to the side' o' th' speawt" tell us only that the yard was typical in having houses terraced around a courtyard where there was a water pump—and that the houses had guttering (not always the case).[38] Laycock has little need to describe the place to local people, as they all lived in similar houses. However, the proximity of his neighbors makes the speaker slightly more circumspect than he might be in a more scattered community. Widow Burns, "hoo weshes clooas for folk" might be courting with "Sam-o'-Ned's 'at lives at number three"—"It may be so, aw conno tell, it matters nowt to me." Laycock was originally from Yorkshire (house number eight contains "Yawshur folk," and he comments "aw ne'er seed nicer folk nor these i'o mi loife!"), his family moving to Stalybridge (1837) in Lancashire to work with cotton instead of wool. Out of work in the 1860s, Laycock wrote a highly successful series of *Cotton Famine Lyrics,* all of which emphasize the spirited resistance of the working family to the degradation of unemployment.

Hollingworth notes that Bolton's Yard in Stalybridge "was still standing in 1993."[39] Laycock is writing about real places—in fact, there is an early twentieth-century photograph of the yard, in which the small terraces with their large weavers' windows can clearly be seen.[40] In "Mi Gronfeyther," Laycock employs what Martha Vicinus terms "an appropriate voice" in the most appropriate way, to investigate the loss of a rural past and place and the strength of community and family relationships, written with homely good humor.[41]

Aw've just bin havin' a peep at th' farm-heawse
Wheer mi gronfeyther lived at so long;

So aw'll draw eawt a bit ov a sketch o' th'owd spot,
And work it up into a song.
An fust let me tell yo' aw'm sorry to foind
'At th' place isn't same as it wur;
For th' di'mond-shaped windows han o bin pood eawt,
An they'n ta'en th' wooden latch off o'th' dur.[42]

Laycock is writing about Marsden in the Pennines, where he was born in 1826 and where his father had been a hand-loom weaver. His family's tale is typical of Bamford's 1841 portrayal of rural dislocation, in which the "old inhabitants have gone... to work at the factories, and the present residents are new-comers." Laycock has been having a snoop round to see what "they"—the strangers—have done, without any rancor, only sorrow for the shift in stability. In the second verse, Laycock uses domestic detail to build his picture of place then and now as one of difference in levels of familiar knowledge and security.

They'n shifted that seeat wheer mi gronfeyther sat
Ov a neet when her'n readin' th' Owd Book.
An' aw couldn't foind th' nail wheer he hung up his hat,
Though aw bother'd an' seech'd for't i' th' nook.
There's th' dog-kennel yonder, an' th' hencote aw see,
An' th' clooas-prop just stonds as it did;
There's a brid-cage hangs up wheer mi gronfeyther's wur,
But aw couldn't see owt ov a brid.

"They" haven't shifted *the* seat but *that* seat—"the one that was there, look, where it isn't now." The book his grandfather sat reading was the family Bible, symbol of stability, authority, and continuity. As possibly the only printed book in every cottage, it carried the prestige of printing, which could then be translated into homely oral wisdom.[43] The bird cage without a bird mirrors the old house without its occupants; new ones would likely have made many changes described in present-day weaving localities—hand-loom weavers' houses were quickly turned to other uses from the 1850s onwards, making it difficult to establish the full spread of purpose-built cottage construction for weavers. "Ashton Binn," the farmhouse, and "Instaff Head" the poet's birthplace, were typical of these, with long windows under the eaves, characteristic of both wool and cotton weaving.[44]

We should note the dialect form in Laycock's poem "her'n readin'" for "he read" (as in "was wont to read"). Hollingworth used an early version of this poem in his collection *Songs of the People,* which he considered "much more effective than the limp version of the *Collected Writings,*" in which the dialect is diluted.[45] The later version also has "An' th' pot-shelf wur gone eawt o' th' nook" at the fourth line of the same verse, which replaces a rhythmically awkward but powerful image of a displaced adult searching fruitlessly for the beloved continuity of childhood in the simplicity of a nail. Like William Barnes, Laycock rewrote his poems for a more middle-class audience and, like Barnes, he may well have seen the dilutions as poetically stronger while remaining "free of slang and vice," as Barnes put it.[46] Laycock's writing was probably the closest of Lancashire dialect poets to the actual form of speech he heard around him—possibly because he was a Yorkshireman—linking his personal past to his personal present, thereby avoiding some of the rural/urban generalizations indulged in by some other poets. Like Barnes, Laycock used vernacular language for the benefit of the local laborer, "not to show up the simplicity of rural life as an object of sport" or to "lower the dignity of his self-esteem" but to encourage his or her love of the local environment and community.[47] Edwin Waugh, with a self-conscious ear for poetic effect, sometimes misses the authentic local note in his understandable desire to reach the widest audience. One of his popular Lancashire songs was "I've worn my bits o' shoon away,"

> Wi' roving up an' deawn,
> To see yon morlan' valleys, an'
> Yon little country teawn.[48]

The song is modeled on Robert Burns's ballad style with much of his swinging rhythm, and it was certainly true that Waugh longed for the countryside above Rochdale, eventually settling, ironically enough, for Kersal Moor, with its chimney view. But what comes across is the stereotypical countryman's lament for the hills, rather than Waugh's own distress at remaining in Manchester.

> Last neet I laft the city throng,
> An' climbed yon hillock green;
> An' turned my face to th' moorlan' hills
> Wi' th' wayter i' my e'en;
> Wi' th' wayter wellin' i' my e'en;—
> I'll bundle up, an' go,
> An' I'll live an' dee i' my own countrie,
> Where the moorlan' breezes blow!

A song like this was accurately aimed at middle and working classes alike—it could not fail to please. There are some distinctively Lancashire terms, such as "My heart feels hutchin'-fain," a Waugh favorite; his heart is itching with pleasure at the thought of the "little country teawn." Translating "hutchin'-fain" into Standard English, as above, shows the limits of orthodox speech in this type of poetry. When included with the dynamic alliteration of the vernacular, as in a description of his fellows as "wick an' warm at wark an' fun," it explains why dialect was an artistic choice for so many writers who wanted to establish a sense of place and community—with two poetic languages on board, there was more scope to say what was important to both audiences—mill workers and owners alike. Waugh has written an affective, classless, pro-rural song in a Lancashire accent with a few county-based lexical and grammatical features, some of which, "yon" and "e'en" for example, are more probably poetic archaisms applicable to many Victorian ballads.[49] What it lacks in distinctive local flavor, it gains in appealing, rustic Northern-ness. Patrick Joyce points out that the urban/rural dialect community was made up of several social layers, and that linguistic traditions could cross class boundaries:

> Neither the activity of labour nor the identity of being working class provided a complete definition of what such communities were. They were made up of different social elements and of varied cultural traditions, not least linguistic ones... language might cross social boundaries as well as accentuate them.[50]

Moreover, the majority of factory owners themselves had relatively informal rather than public school educations, even until the end of the nineteenth century: they "thought in dialect" because it was their language.[51] However, in the schools, and in government policy, the facts of language use were overridden in an effort to control culture and the acquisition of knowledge.[52] Joyce notes that "Lancashire workers inhabited at least two language worlds at the same time—in this regard there is nothing so revealing as the appearance in dialect books and pamphlets of advertisements for guides to how to speak and write in the 'correct' standard way."[53]

Recollection and celebration of a specific locality, including the association of place with an emotional, spiritual, or moral impulse in poetry, leveled class differences in the production of vernacular poetry, even as the local language itself was stirred up by dislocation, industrialization, and education. Joyce also notes the potential for the dilution of class identity in the greater merit of adherence to place (or lesser merit, depending on the degree of militancy of writer and audience): "It is also true that the very rootedness of language in the local and the particular might at all times tell against the larger solidarities of class."[54]

Dialect authors relied on mass circulation of their writing in newspapers and periodicals, supplementing "penny readings" at local institutes with cheap pamphlets of their poems.[55] In Lancashire, one of the most successful dialect journals was *Ben Brierley's Journal* (1869–1891), "rather like a Lancashire working man's *Punch*," comments Martha Vicinus.[56] Brierley had assisted Charles Hardwick in editing *Country Words*, where Joseph Ramsbottom's poetry had appeared, but it was too much like every other aspiring middle-class magazine. Produced in Manchester, the title was misleading, an aspiration rather than a reality and confirming the general view that vernacular writing had more relationship with "pure" country air than Manchester grime and Manchester speech. Brierley's own journal was unashamedly populist and featured his unique voice in the comic prose creation "Ab-o'-th'-Yate," a sort of literary forerunner of 1950s radio comedian Al Read, with a "canny wife," his "better-three-quarters."[57]

Brierley had been a hand-loom velvet weaver in Manchester, and it is probably his voice (out of easily accessible writers) that establishes the city of Manchester as a dialect place more than any other. Waugh was desperate to get away from Manchester; Laycock was based at Stalybridge; Ramsbottom was not as ubiquitous or ambitious a writer as Ben Brierley. He was "a one-man industry as dialect poet, storyteller, travel-writer, dramatist, journalist and editor," writes John Goodridge, adding "one has for the first time the sense that a labouring-class poet might exert real influence in the literary and cultural scene of his home city."[58] Although a better prose writer than a poet, Brierley had a keen ear for local tales and ways of telling them. His best known poem was a riposte to Waugh's archetypal picture of cottage harmony, entitled "Go, tak the ragged childer an' flit."[59] It is the reverse side of the picture to "Come whoam to thi childer an' me," and a sharp reminder that honesty is one of the working-class virtues most celebrated in vernacular writing; hypocrisy was for the others.

Brierley could make good use of printing technology and improving literacy to advance other writers, to increase access to material, and to raise the status of working-class literature. However, his writing also presents some contradictions that are fairly typical of the second half of the Victorian period. As social and economic pressures moved away from the establishment's fears of mass revolution and economic catastrophe (although there was still room for huge variations in the "condition of England"), education became the main focus as a means of stabilizing local and national inequalities. Dialect writing was no longer considered a useful asset, or even, as J. H. Wylie, an inspector of schools in Rochdale in 1890 suggested, a literature that "might profitably be taught in school to preserve its distinctive characteristics."[60] Dialect literature's success and the key to its popularity—its ability to straddle past and present, oral and print forms, urban and rural—had been overtaken by the means that brought success about: printing, industrialization, and shifting population. Brierley defended the use of dialect robustly in his own journal, while simultaneously conceding defeat in that Lancashire language had not only lost the literary power that it once enjoyed, but also in some measure "deserved" to lose it, as a mark of "the necessities of the age." In an editorial in 1871, written "in standard English of editorial purity and refinement," as Maidment notes, Brierley offers some reasons for promoting dialect as a kind of halfway house towards linguistic emancipation:

> Our object in making use of the humbler method of speech has been to get at a stratum of society to which no other class of journal can carry so potent an

> influence and by degrees lift our readers out of their present "barbarism" and lead them to the pursuit of a higher class of literature.[61]

In this there is no mention of the original benefits of using vernacular language—its relationship to locality, and the place's connection with past and present communities. Joseph Ramsbottom, in an article for *Country Words* (1866), was quite clear about the cultural value of dialect: "None but those who have lived it, or lived with it, and are able to describe that which they have seen, can show us the life of an honest, striving poor man." "National" English was hardly under threat from the vernacular, squashed and hedged round as it was by grammarians and social reformers; "and the reason, perhaps, that we have more [dialect] today than hitherto, is that there is more to be said of, and for our country populations; that they have more to say for themselves." [62]

Samuel Bamford was particular about the specific qualities of South Lancashire speech in much the same way that William Barnes, also writing in the 1840s, insisted that Blackmore Vale speech was different from other Dorset varieties. Bamford produced his own edition of Tim Bobbin's' *Tummus and Meary,* with a revised glossary emphasizing the specificity of language to locality: "the country extending from Blakeley to Littleborough easterly; and from Bury, or Bolton, to Oldham, south easterly"—this was the place-holder of "pure" form. Bamford is more dismissive of Manchester: "Manchester could not be included, inasmuch as its inhabitants having always been a more mixed people, have never spoken the dialect of the country folks around them."[63]

Prescriptions for dialect use were almost as common as those for orthodox English, both part of a discourse of anxiety surrounding the status of Englishness itself. In this case, more authoritarian enthusiasts intended prescription to act as a bulwark against dialect leveling, which was seen as part of linguistic and social disintegration. However, Bamford's remarks expose discomfort in the ranks of vernacular writers themselves. John Trafford Clegg, a later and, sadly, short-lived poet, also a printer, wrote in answer to J. H. Wylie's suggestion that Lancashire language should be taught in schools—disagreeing; because "most on us han getten' a mongrel sort o' talk, 'at's noather good Lanky nor gradely English," partly, it was thought, because of urban distortion.[64] It was and still is a commonly held view that only *rural* dialects, like country living, could represent a "natural," uncontaminated way of life: Asif Agha notes that present-day linguistic surveys still show that "distinctively urban accents are among the lowest ranked" in social value.[65] J. K. Chambers and Peter Trudgill point out "there is probably no such thing as a 'pure' dialect, since most varieties of language appear to be variable and to show signs of influence from other varieties."[66]

For the self-taught poet, local *and* standard languages helped to create his or her sense of identity, and this identity was also bound to place and circumstance, constructed through varieties of language. Thus, to describe weaving in Standard

English is to promote a potentially different experience from the same activity written down, or spoken, in dialect. But it is only understood as different by the "bi-dialectal" poet-weaver—the Standard English reader knows no other, any more than a dialect-speaking but illiterate listener. Local self-awareness increased the recognition of difference in speech that could be incorporated into stories of place and occupation. The construction of people-in-place discourses allowed some aspects of cultural value to gain national status. "Gradely," for example, was and still is the classic epithet applied to Lancashire (and Yorkshire) good qualities, epitomizing the bluff character Edwin Waugh displayed in his public readings, wearing "thick tweeds . . . evoking an image of the traditional countryman" in the middle of Manchester.[67] "Gradely" becomes, therefore, a term expressing the *culture* of Yorkshire or Lancashire, a local term "standing in" for a value perceived as specifically applicable to the area.[68]

Although it might be supposed that the audience for vernacular poetry was limited, Standard English aspiring poets were all too common: the boundaries of locality acted in favor of dialect—at least for a while. Turning speech into printing, though, involves dilution: it must conform in presentation. Distinctly local speech differences, minutely observed by natives, can remain impenetrable to outsiders—even in the poets discussed here, there are subtle orthographic differences deriving from different accents—not different dialects. As writing can never fully express speech, the literary language of these dialect poets is, inevitably, a "mongrel" variety—but is this necessarily detrimental to place or people? The ability to read/hear familiar "voices" establishes references for memories still lingering in diasporas, often stimulated by local poetry. Becoming literate, and then being exposed to mass-produced printed texts, often necessitated dislocation from immediate, familiar surroundings in order to engage with the wider world. Often, the experience of dislocation triggered the attempt to reconnect through writing, in spite of literacy's discomfort.

The hybrid literary dialect of nineteenth-century poets puts forward a controlled local language of place, one that responds to the constraints of vernacular, remaining adaptable and expressive in order to promote active engagement with places. Even in this "mongrel" form, dialect writers carry a bit of home with them on their travels: place-specific language can become an expression of dwelling. In mid-nineteenth-century Manchester, "we do not find the faithful recreation of a dying idiom but rather a sense of the linguistic ferment" that parallels the social and economic ferment of industrial places, Larry McCauley noted.[69]

Literary dialect is not oral history, although it might contain many similar features, as these poems demonstrate. In oral history, change is part of what is being recorded; the nature of speech is that it is ephemeral and dialect-monitoring records what is transitory as well as constant. Studying vernacular writing, we might be witnessing one of Wordsworth's "spots of time"; a determined attempt to "enshrine the spirit of the past / For future restoration."[70] When Laycock revised his poem, "Mi Gronfeyther," in order to make it more accessible or consciously poetic, he reduced its immediacy—maybe even its efficacy in giving "a substance and a life" (line 341) to what he felt when revisiting his childhood home. However, Laycock and Wordsworth had a wider audience to consider. Linda Shopes phrases the dilemma in a less poetic but similar vein: the spot of time becomes "a storied account of the past recounted in the present, an act of memory shaped as much by the moment of telling as by the history being told."[71] Shopes argues for sensitive editorial management of perceived divergences in accuracy, even to the extent of recording dates and the presence of given narrators.

> Narrators turn history inside out, demanding to be understood as purposeful actors in the past, talking about their lives in ways that do not easily fit into preexisting categories of analysis.[72]

On the other hand, Susan Allen points out the dangers of "compulsive laundering of oral history"; it "inevitably causes fading, stretching out of shape, and possibly loss of material."[73] There is a fine balance between storytelling for the public, historical record, and, especially for the poets discussed here, the dialect community: How will they be received and how can they maintain their family histories' integrity in the middle of "deeply constraining circumstances," as Shopes remarks?[74] Dialect poets, if they are to see themselves in print, have to negotiate a form that is stable and representative of a community and a place that has already become history. As Sarah Houghton has suggested, with reference to John Clare's apparently "unpolished" poetic language "in the very act of picking up a pencil . . . Clare is ensuring that his description must be of an ideal, [not] a true state of affairs."[75]

For the historian, then, dialect poetry presents a limited if useful snapshot of what was potentially of central importance to mid-Victorian dialect-speaking communities, without any certainty—in fact, there is no certainty even in the nature of transcription, as I have shown, since there was no standard orthography and each writer used a variety of accents as well as vocabularies. The poems were made by communities as much as by individuals, for they relied on the community's approval—they represent a dialogue, although there was often disagreement between the poets and disagreement with their audiences about details of places, people, or the language.[76] And, arguably, for some literary scholars, dialect poetry is again of limited value. It rarely meets unrealistic expectations that dialect writers should write "authentic" local speech *and* should also be great writers. In this period, probably only William Barnes hits both targets, even with all his inconsistencies. There is, moreover, a tendency to dismiss a writer who is perceived as less than accurate in his or her attention to linguistic authenticity. For the oral historian, on the other hand, the slipshod and haphazard accumulation of words representing localities, customs, work, and family life is of greater value as it shows up the likely sociolinguistic creep of everyday flux in impoverished and unstable communities. "It is history already written on the wind," writes Susan Allen on the precarious preservation of taped interviews at the mercy of the injudicious transcriber.[77] Victorian poets cleaned up their speech acts in order to create texts: it is in orthographic vagaries that we can hear the printed voice, not in the ordered precision of standardized dialect representation; it is the "minute fossils," as Allen calls them, which "some scholar may . . . be after" and "which you have scraped off and swept away."[78] Our attention to these fossils, to the minute particulars of dialect, can give us insights into the affective attachment to place and community *because* of their instability, not in spite of it.

Notes

1. Peter Mühlhäusler, *Language of Environment, Environment of Language* (London: Battlebridge, 2003), 120.
2. David Vincent, *Literacy and Popular Culture, England 1750–1914* (Cambridge: Cambridge Univ. Press, 1993), 214.
3. W. B. Stephens, *Education, Literacy and Society: 1830–1870* (Manchester: Manchester Univ. Press, 1987), 10-11. See also Chapter 2, "Schooling and Literacy: Regional Characteristics and Influences," 15–48. "Existing school facilities were swamped," writes Stephens, adding that increased child labor, at home and in factories, "militated against formal schooling."
4. Vincent, *Literacy,* 101.
5. Vincent, *Literacy,* 279.
6. Ivan Kreilkamp, *Voice and the Victorian Storyteller* (Cambridge: Cambridge University Press), 41.
7. Brian Maidment, *The Poorhouse Fugitives* (Manchester: Carcanet, 1987), 14–15. Maidment's categories are as follows: "Chartist and radical writing linked specifically with other forms of political activism"; Parnassian writing, representing "a conscious cultural attempt to join in literary discourse at the highest possible level [. . .] in cultural and philosophical debates of the time"; and "deliberately homely rhyming, often carried out in an entirely local manner," which "sought to articulate common feeling within the working and artisan classes." Then again, Maidment cautions that using such terms "carries the further danger of institutionalizing artificially imposed, retrospective perceptions of literary traditions" (16).
8. Samuel Bamford, *Walks in South Lancashire* (1844), in *Society and the Victorians* reprints series, edited by John Spiers and Cecil Ballantine (Brighton: Harvester, 1972), 232.
9. Samuel Bamford, *Dialect of South Lancashire, or Tim Bobbin's Tummus and Meary* (Manchester: 1850), iii–iv.
10. Geoffrey Timmins, *The Last Shift: The Decline of Handloom Weaving in Nineteenth-Century Lancashire* (Manchester: Manchester Univ. Press, 1993), 71–77.

11. Timmins, *Last Shift,* 31, 25.
12. Timmins, *Last Shift,* 75–76. Timmins points out that whether rural weavers had access to land is debatable; some cottages had nothing. Richard Arkwright, though, built a weaving cluster close to his first mill at Cromford in Derbyshire that had gardens with pig-pens and access to a communal area for pigs, and possibly other livestock. "He especially asked for large families to come and join the work force and a whole town was constructed to house them, rows of cottages, a school, a chapel and a hotel. The pattern for later industrial towns had emerged. North Street in Cromford was built in 1776 and still to this day consists of terraced 3 storey buildings which were used to house the mill workers. A school was built at its far end, as Arkwright had insisted that children who came to work in the mill could read and write." This model community was not often repeated, either by Arkwright or by other cotton industrialists, as it proved expensive. http://www.derbyshireuk.net/cromford.html Accessed 01/14/2010.
13. Bamford, *Walks in South Lancashire,* 28–30.
14. Bamford, *Walks in South Lancashire,* 32–33.
15. Brian Hollingworth, *Songs of the People: Lancashire Dialect Poetry of the Industrial Revolution* (Manchester: Manchester Univ. Press, 1977; repr. 1982), 3. Henceforth referred to as Hollingsworth, *Songs.*
16. Eric Griffiths, *The Printed Voice of Victorian Poetry* (Oxford: Clarendon Press, 1989). Griffiths's title comes from Robert Browning's *The Ring and the* Book (1868–69), in which during a trial the plaintiff "only spoke in print / The printed voice of him lives now as then." (vol. 1, lines 166–167).
17. Larry McCauley, "'Eawr Folk': Language, Class, and English Identity in Victorian Dialect Poetry," *Victorian Poetry,* 39 (2001), 287–301, (296). Henceforth referred to as McCauley, "Eawr Folk."
18. Edwin Waugh, "Eawr Folk" (1866) in *Poems and Songs of Old Lancashire* (Bury: Printwise reprints, 1992), 137–39. Originally published 1889. Book henceforth referred to as Waugh, *Poems and Songs.* Also in *Nineteenth-Century Labouring-Class Poets, 1800–1900,* 3 vols., edited by Scott McEathron, Kaye Kossick, and John Goodridge (London: Pickering and Chatto, 2006); vol. 2 (1830–1860), edited by Kaye Kossick, 323–34; see also Hollingworth, *Songs,* 15–16.
19. McCauley, "Eawr Folk," 297–98.
20. From Edwin Waugh's *Diaries,* September 1847, quoted by Patrick Joyce in *Democratic Subjects: The Self and the Social in Nineteenth-Century England* (Cambridge: Cambridge Univ. Press, 1994), 56. Joyce interprets Waugh's poetic impulse through the vagaries of Waugh's life as evidenced in his diaries. Book henceforth referred to as Joyce, *Democratic.*
21. Joyce, *Democratic,* 56.
22. Joyce, *Democratic,* 64.
23. Waugh, "Eawr Folk," in Waugh, *Poems and Songs,* 137–39.
24. McCauley, "Eawr Folk," 299.
25. "Come Whoam to the Children," in Waugh, *Poems and Songs,* 106-08.
26. Joan C. Beal, "Enregisterment, Commodification, and Historical Context: 'Geordie' versus 'Sheffieldish,'" *American Speech,* 84 (2009), 138–156, p. 141. Henceforth referred to as Beal, "Enregisterment." Beal discusses a range of research that examines how the use of local terms, even in nondialect speakers, "can be

used to project localness," including Asif Agha's influential study, "The Social Life of Cultural Value," *Language and Communication*, 23 (2003), 231–73.

27. Beal, "Enregisterment," 140.
28. James Winter, *"Secure from Rash Assault": Sustaining the Victorian Environment* (Berkeley, CA: Univ. of California Press, 1999), 154.
29. Maidment, *Poorhouse,* 261.
30. Joseph Ramsbottom, "Coaxin'," in Maidment, *Poorhouse,* 263–65, and Hollingworth, *Songs,* 51–52. "Brat" means "apron."
31. Ramsbottom, "Sorrowin,'" in *Country Words* (1866); also in Maidment, *Poorhouse,* 261–63.
32. Ramsbottom, "Preawd Tum's Prayer," In Ramsbottom, *Phases of Distress: Lancashire Rhymes*, edited by John Whittaker (Manchester: John Heywood, 1864), 59–69. Also in Maidment, *Poorhouse,* 86–90.
33. Maidment, *Poorhouse,* 150.
34. John L. Owen, "The City Singers," in *Ben Brierley's Journal* (1873), 241; also in Maidment, *Poorhouse,* 158–59. Maidment adds in a note: "Number III in a series called "Manchester Idylls."
35. Mrs E. J. Bellasis, "The Smokeless Chimney," *Ballads and Songs of Lancashire,* edited by John Harland (London: Whittaker and Co, 1865), 289–92. "The authoress is the wife of Mr Serjeant Bellasis, and the only daughter of the late William Garnett, Esq. of Quernmore Park and Bleasdale, Lancashire."
36. Traditional, "Rambles in Owdham, and peep into the workshops," in Hollingworth, *Songs,* 83–85; note, 142.
37. All poem titles in Hollingworth, *Songs:* Alexander Wilson, "Johnny Green's description of Tinker's Gardens," 33–35; Michael Wilson, "Jone's ramble fro' Owdam to Karsy Moor races," 31–33; Traditional, "Warikin Fair," 29–30. Michael, Thomas, and Alexander Wilson, father and two sons, were important collectors and composers of popular Lancashire songs and poems from well before 1840 (Hollingworth, 3–4).
38. Samuel Laycock, "Bowton's Yard" (1864), in Samuel Laycock, *Warblin's Fro' an Owd Songster* (Oldham: W. E. Clegg, 1894), 3–5. Book henceforth referred to as Laycock, *Warblin's.* Also in Hollingworth, *Songs,* 20–21.
39. Hollingworth, *Songs,*131.
40. *Minor Victorian Poets and Authors,* Ian Petticrew (webmaster) www.gerald-massey .org.uk, http://www.gerald-massey.org.uk/laycock/b_biographical.htm accessed 01/09/2010.
41. Martha Vicinus, "An appropriate voice: dialect literature of the industrial North," chapter 5 in Vicinus, *The Industrial Muse: A Study of Nineteenth Century British Working-Class Literature* (London: Croom Helm, 1974), 185. Henceforth referred to as Vicinus, *Industrial.*
42. Laycock, "Mi Gronfeyther," (n.d., probably 1860s, although Laycock's poetry was appearing in local newspapers as early as 1856); in Laycock, *Warblin's*; also in Hollingworth, *Songs,* 21–22.
43. This is different from the enforced "Bible text" crushing of charitable authorities. For an example of the "family" status of the Bible, see John Clare, "The Cottager" in *Major Works*, edited by Eric Robinson and David Powell (Oxford: Oxford Univ. Press, 1984; revised 2004), 133–35.

44. See http://www.gerald-massey.org.uk/laycock/c_warblins_5.htm#226 (accessed January 9th 2010).
45. Hollingworth, *Songs,* 131. The late version I have referred to is in *Warblin's,* 1894.
46. William Barnes, Preface to *Poems of Rural Life in the Dorset Dialect,* 2nd ed. (London: John Russell Smith, 1847), 48. Henceforth referred to as Barnes, Preface.
47. Barnes, Preface, 48.
48. Edwin Waugh, "I've worn my bits o' shoon away" (1876), in Waugh, *Poems and Songs*, 152–53; also in Maidment, *Poorhouse,* 252–53.
49. J. K. Chambers and Peter Trudgill clarify popular distinctions between accent and dialect as follows: Although "we are used to talking of accents and dialects as if they were well-defined…this is actually not the case. Dialects and accents frequently merge into one another without any discrete break." For the purposes of this discussion I am using a general interpretation of "accent" and "dialect": *Accent* refers to the way in which a speaker pronounces; *dialect* refers to varieties which are grammatically (and perhaps lexically) as well as phonologically different from other varieties. *Dialectology*, 2nd edition (Cambridge: Cambridge Univ. Press, 2005), 5.
50. Patrick Joyce, *Visions of the People: Industrial England and the Question of Class 1848–1914* (Cambridge: Cambridge Univ. Press, 1991), 199. Henceforth referred to as Joyce, *Visions.*
51. Joyce, *Visions,* 201–02.
52. See Vincent, *Literacy,* 156–195 (p. 183), on oral and literate "knowledge."
53. Joyce, *Visions,* 201.
54. Joyce, *Visions,* 199.
55. Vicinus, *Industrial,* 195.
56. Vicinus, *Industrial,* 202.
57. Al Read (1909–1987) was born in Salford, Manchester, the son of a sausage maker. He was known during the 1950s for his domestic comedy radio monologues for the BBC, in which he provided all the voices and several popular catch phrases. Vicinus discusses and reproduces some of Brierley's "Ab-o'-th'-Yate" adventures (200–203).
58. John Goodridge, headnote to Ben Brierley, *Nineteenth-Century Labouring-Class Poets*, Vol. 3 (1860–1900); edited by John Goodridge, 363–364.
59. Ben Brierley, "Go, tak the ragged childer an' flit," in *Nineteenth-Century Labouring-Class Poets*, Vol. 2 (1830–1860); edited by Kaye Kossick, 331–333. "The Reverse Side of the Picture" is Brierley's own title. In the poem, his sharp-tongued wife remarks "Theau thinks, 'cose theau plaguet *t'other wife*, / Theau'll ha *me* at th' same rate as theau'd *her*." Waugh was known to be living with another woman and separated from his wife, who was, so Bamford reported, "in the Marland workhouse" at the time. Vicinus (*Industrial*) comments: "Bamford is not a totally reliable informant," (235n). Hollingworth (*Songs*) notes that Waugh's ideal, which was probably common to a number of working men, was "[a]n industrious woman, a working husband, a spick-and-span home, a new baby, real affection between man and wife, and a meal to come home to" (139). See also Susan Zlotnick, "'A thousand times I'd be a factory girl': Dialect, Domesticity, and Working-Class Women's Poetry in Victorian Britain," *Victorian Studies*, 35 (1991), 7–27.

60. Vicinus, *Industrial,* 226.
61. Ben Brierley, "The Lancashire Dialect," editorial, in *Ben Brierley's Journal* (1871), 308; in Maidment, 364–366.
62. Joseph Ramsbottom, "Writing in the Dialect," in *Country Words* (1866), 104–105; in Maidment 362–64.
63. Bamford, *Dialect of South Lancashire,* xvii.
64. Vicinus, *Industrial,* 225–26.
65. Asif Agha, "The Social Life of Cultural Value," *Language and Communication* 23 (2003), 240.
66. Chambers and Trudgill, *Dialectology,* 2nd ed., 46.
67. Vicinus, *Industrial,* 194.
68. Asif Agha expresses the connection of place, people, and language in terms of cultural value as follows: "cultural value is not a static property of things or people but a precipitate of sociohistorically locatable practices, including discursive practices, which imbue cultural forms with recognizable sign-values and bring these values into circulation along identifiable trajectories in social space." Agha, "Social Life," 232.
69. McCauley, "Eawr Folk," 297.
70. William Wordsworth, *The Prelude,* XI: ll. 258, 342–33, in *William Wordsworth: The Major Works,* edited by Stephen Gill (Oxford: Oxford Univ. Press, 1984; revised 2000).
71. Linda Shopes, "What Is Oral History?" in *Making Sense of Evidence* series on *History Matters: The U.S. Survey on the Web,* 1–23 (10); http://historymatters.gmu.edu; accessed 10th March 2011.
72. Shopes, "Oral," 4.
73. Susan Emily Allen, "Resisting the Editorial Ego: Editing Oral History," *The Oral History Review,* 10 (1982), 33–45, p. 45.
74. Shopes, "Oral," 3.
75. Sarah Houghton, "The 'Community' of John Clare's Helpston," *Studies in English Literature, 1500–1900,* 46 (2006), 781–802, p. 800.
76. See, for example, Leeds writer John Eccles, "Deein' be inches," in Vicinus, *Industrial,* 212–13; Vicinus comments: "Eccles was frequently criticised by the Yorkshire Dialect Society."
77. Allen, "Resisting," 35.
78. Allen, "Resisting," 44.

PART 2

Introduction: Oral History and Local Environments

Part 1 considered the translation of local oral traditions and languages into print; part 2 shows how oral history can reestablish the connection between the local and oral in new ways and with new relevance in a relatively global context. Each chapter looks closely at experiences, views, and understandings of people living and working in the localities in question, as expressed in oral history interviews. Chapter 4 continues to trace differences between how local voices and written texts engage with locality, focusing on the oral histories of people living and working in a specific postindustrial locality and on how these histories contrast with the romanticization of this locality in literature. This develops and interrogates the argument that written texts have tended to embody a certain middle-class distance from locality (put forward by Fulford in chapter 1; Moore and Edney in chapters 2 and 3 explore alternatives), but rather than attempting nostalgically to recapture or regenerate oral traditions and dialects, the chapters in part 2 explore how oral history can be used to engage with locality in new ways in relation to contemporary issues, especially concerning environmental damage on both local and global scales.

Chapter 4 explores literary and oral accounts of a distinctive landscape in mid-Cornwall, a landscape marked by the shapes of white pyramids as a result of the china clay industry that dominated the economy in the twentieth century. It first considers the romanticization of the landscape in literature by authors including Daphne du Maurier and Rowena Summers (a pseudonym of Jean Saunders). But as well as comparing the clay country to other spectacular, even exotic landscapes like the Alps, authors describe this landscape as polluted and damaged. The chapter goes on to consider how people living in this locality describe the landscape and their relation to it, using oral history interviews carried out as part of a community-based project in 2008. Interviewees were asked for their views of the industrial landscape and also about recent developments such as the Eden Project, with its huge greenhouses in a disused clay pit—a tourist attraction that emphasizes global environmental issues. The interviews reveal how people involved in the clay industry tend to view and to value the landscape in terms of function and income, in contrast to literary descriptions of the landscape by writers who have rarely if ever worked in the industry. The interviews also contrast with narratives produced by the Eden Project, which describe the clay landscape as damaged and ugly in order to emphasize Eden's own role in transforming it into an environmentally friendly, visionary, and beautiful part of the world to *visit*. Moving beyond conventional ideas of landscape as a view from a distance, oral history allows us to consider everyday and bodily experiences of landscape through work, revealing a local perspective that is very different from that of environmentalists, writers, and filmmakers, whose global concerns and visions are spelled out for visitors in books and films that themselves circulate on a relatively global scale.

In chapter 5, Paul Thompson similarly engages with the historical decline of a specific local industry and the repurposing of landscape for tourism and leisure. As in chapter 4, oral accounts by local people become an important resource for considering changing attitudes to the environment. Thompson's chapter draws on memories covering the last seventy years, collected through a community oral history project in the village of Wivenhoe, Essex. Although now mainly a residential town, Wivenhoe, which lies at the head of the Colne estuary, has a maritime history of fishing, shipbuilding, and yachting that goes back centuries. The Essex coast has rarely been celebrated as a landscape of romantic beauty, but has long been valued by locals in terms of both work and play, and some of those most passionate about local natural history came together, including both working-class and middle-class residents, in an ultimately successful battle to save Wivenhoe Wood from housing developments in the 1970s. (This battle can be seen as a kind of localized version of far more widespread concerns about trees and forests, concerns that are also reflected in the Eden Project's rainforest biome, with its aim to educate about the destruction of rainforests on a massive scale and its effects on the climate.[1]) Over the last twenty years, however, the perceptions of all local people have been affected by the economic transformation of the river, which has led to a different kind of engagement with the natural environment. The neighboring city of Colchester no longer operates as a port, only a handful of fishermen survive, and all but one of the Colne shipyards have closed. The soundscapes have changed considerably; where the "banging" of the shipyards once accompanied daily life, and the riverside redounded with the noise of riveters, today the river is almost silent. The only common activity is sailing in the summer season. Sailing also has a long history and continues to be linked with another perception of the local environment, that of the natural history of the lower estuary, and especially the migrant seabirds, which for some provide a much-valued experience of contact with the wild, which certainly is romantic.

In chapter 6, Andrew Holmes demonstrates how oral history can be used to develop an innovative perspective on local environments, again involving historical changes in land use, in this case by combining oral history interviews with ecological research in the field of environmental studies. The Ouse Project uses an interdisciplinary approach to provide the information needed to link biodiversity objectives for meadow grassland to flood-alleviation measures in the catchment floodplain areas of the Sussex Ouse, where the management of streamside meadows has become an important issue, following the floods of 2000. The project combines historical research into past agricultural methods and land use with ecological research into present-day habitats in order to show how land use might be managed around the river in the future. An innovative feature of the Ouse Project has been the use of oral history interviews with key respondents, who can recall details of changes in management of streamside meadows that are not available through written archive sources. By developing feedback loops between farmers in the Upper Ouse catchment area and the three disciplines within the project (oral history, historical geography, and ecology), a method has been developed in which data gathered in layers of detail can be used to inform decision-making about land use. Each interview is discussed with members of the project team, who then propose further questions to be followed up in subsequent interviews. This layered approach to oral history interviewing builds up trust between the researcher and the researched, allowing details of past land management and the related ecology to emerge that would otherwise have remained unknown. This knowledge not only steers the direction of the project and subsequent research, but will also inform recommendations about future land management.

Environmentalists are seeing the value of oral history, as both Holmes's chapter and chapter 7 by Leslie McCartney illustrate. Its ability to gather detailed information from people who work in and with different environments also makes oral history a useful tool in detecting signs of climate change. Over the past several years, scientists have come to realize that particular localities are early barometers that indicate future changes on a wider scale, such as the polar regions where the effects of climate change and pollution have a significant impact on the animals, plants, humans, and the local environment. Drawing on material generated in an oral history project with Gwich'in Elders in the Northwest Territories in Canada, whose ancestors have lived for thousands of years in the region, McCartney's chapter explores how traditional or indigenous knowledge and oral history can be used in developing an understanding of how a land and climate have changed over the past few generations. Looking also at other projects, including the Iglooik Oral History Project and King's Cross Voices in London, chapter 7 points out that stories collected now and also years before in a life-story genre, although collected for other reasons, can be used to examine climate change.

Like the other chapters in this part of the collection, McCartney's looks in some detail at how interviewees describe their surrounding locality and its history in terms of wider concerns about the environment and its future. Perceptions of the environment on a local scale—from the damaged industrial clayscapes in South West Britain to the melting polar regions of northwest Canada—are considered in relation to a much wider context, from the global vision of the Eden Project to widespread concerns about global warming. Each chapter in part 2 explores different ways in which local people engage (or don't engage) with environmental problems. People whose incomes have depended on the clay industry seem to some extent to have accepted its destructive effect on the landscape and to resist the "global garden" of the Eden Project, while people in the polar regions are forced to acknowledge the environmental changes that threaten their livelihood.

I see this middle part of the book, then, as contributing in part to recent oral history studies on environmental consciousness that do not simply endorse environmental projects, but also explore peoples' reasons for becoming involved or otherwise. Holmes's and McCartney's chapters also strongly emphasize the importance of listening to local experts who have specialized knowledge.[2] Holmes's chapter, in particular, demonstrates how oral history can itself have a potentially active role in environmental management. Orality is sometimes associated with some kind of special, even spiritual connection to place or to preindustrial harmony with nature, but much as I believe that industrialism, capitalism, and consumerism are among the main causes of irreparable damage to the environment, none of the chapters here would wish to endorse some nostalgic idea of returning to an imagined age of such spiritual or natural harmony.[3] Rather, these chapters illustrate how oral history can be used as a practical tool to investigate human relationships with and experiences of local environments with respect to a wider context and how oral history might even be employed to actively inform and intervene in future land management. As Holmes demonstrates, oral history has much potential when we think carefully about our methodologies.

CHAPTER 4

Regional Writing and Oral History, from China Clay to Eden

Shelley Trower

The landscape shaped by the china clay industry in Cornwall, in the far south-west of Britain, is represented in strikingly different ways in written and spoken communication. It appears alternately as beautiful, as bleak, as horribly polluted, as a source of wealth, and as a space for future development. This chapter focuses on how this landscape—marked in the nineteenth and twentieth centuries by white pyramid shaped tips, and pits filled with greenish blue water—is seen in a multiplicity of ways by both visitors and inhabitants, and how their different modes of communication, both written and oral, shape the way the landscape is represented. It builds on work in geography that has emphasized subjective narratives of landscapes as an alternative to objectivizing views from above and outside. To do this, it incorporates oral history interviews, in order to compare and contrast written descriptions of landscape, often (but not always) produced by the social and political elites on which geographers have tended to focus (from professional writers like Daphne du Maurier to the environmentalist entrepreneur Tim Smit), with oral accounts by inhabitants who have worked in the clay industry, or at least whose parents and grandparents have. As Mark Riley and David Harvey have observed, historical and cultural geographers interested in the meaning of landscape have mainly concentrated on "the exploration of the writings (and artwork) of specific, and often privileged, individuals, leaving the methodological approach of oral history as a fairly neglected toolkit within such studies."[4] That oral history selects interviewees among groups of people who might otherwise have been "hidden from history" is often considered its most important contribution.[5] By considering oral history interviews alongside written texts, this chapter reveals some of the differences between these two forms of narrative about landscapes, reflecting differences but also complications and overlaps between elite and working-class histories, and views about local and global issues—especially about environmental sustainability. The transformation of a part of this landscape—a disused clay pit that has been turned into a site for the cultivation of plant life from other parts of the world—brings these questions of sustainability in both local and global contexts directly into the material reality of the clay country.

The oral history interviews discussed here were carried out as part of a project funded by the Heritage Lottery in mid-Cornwall in 2008, the main purpose of which was to involve local communities in exploring the history of this area, partly through the use of oral history. An Internet resource with much of this data is available.[6] Interviewees consisted mainly of volunteers who were encouraged to sign up at a series of local "roadshows" or who responded to requests in the local papers and radio. Most of the interviewees, of whom there were 30 in total, had worked in the clay industry before its decline, which started in the 1980s. As in the work of Riley and Harvey, though their focus was on farming practices rather than on the extractive industries, an oral history approach helped to show how understandings of landscape are bound up with personal working histories.[7]

Interviewees were asked for their views of the local landscape as it was in the past, before the decline of the clay industry, and also about present developments such as the Eden Project. The Eden Project opened to the public in 2000 and consists primarily of huge biomes (dome-shaped greenhouses) that contain a wide range of plants from different parts of the world. As a visitor attraction, it presents its primary purpose as being to raise awareness of and knowledge about global environmental issues.

The interviews reveal how people living in the locality tend to view and to value the landscape in terms of function and income, in contrast to literary descriptions of the landscape by writers who have rarely if ever worked in the industry, and who tend to view the landscape in terms of its aesthetic value (as either beautiful or unattractively damaged). The interviews also contrast with written and visual presentations produced by the Eden Project, which represent the clay landscape as damaged and ugly as part of a narrative that emphasizes Eden's own role in transforming the landscape into an environmentally friendly and beautiful part of the world to *visit*. Oral history allows us to consider a local perspective which is very different from that of authors and environmentalists whose global concerns and visions are spelled out for visitors in novels and books such as *Eden,* by Tim Smit (2001). It is to written representations of the landscape that the chapter now turns, before presenting the challenge to these representations that is produced by the material derived from the oral history project.

"This strange white world"

Writers tend to describe the landscape of the clay country[8] in terms of its strangeness or foreignness. They either emphasize its strange beauty or dwell on it as evidence of the destructive impact of the clay industry on the environment. This section will first consider how the landscape is described by romance novelists who offer the strongest examples of its representation as otherworldly beauty, and will then move on to autobiographical accounts by writers who have grown up in the area or worked in the clay industry, in order to examine their more ambivalent perspectives.

Countless romance novels are set in Cornwall, usually deploying landscapes as backdrop, setting their dramatic action against the "wild" coastline, the moors, or the tin and copper mining districts.[9] Fewer are set in the china clay region, although, as Alan Kent has observed, recent years have seen the romantic tradition increasingly move into this newer industrial landscape.[10] Daphne du Maurier typically set novels like *Jamaica Inn* (first published in 1936) on the Cornish moors and thus involved the dangers of the sea and the smuggling industry, but she did go on to include the industrial landscape of mid-Cornwall in her two descriptive guides, *Vanishing Cornwall* (1967) and *Enchanted Cornwall* (1989). In *Vanishing Cornwall,* after mentioning that William Cookworthy founded the clay industry in Cornwall (in 1748 he found chinastone in tin mines) and briefly explaining the process of mining china clay, Du Maurier moves on to the view of the "layman" and the "casual wanderer," who is witness to "the strange, almost fantastic beauty of the landscape, where spoil-heaps of waste matter shaped like pyramids point to the sky, great quarries formed about their base descending into pits filled with water, icy green like arctic pools."[11] So although Du Maurier spent most of her life in Cornwall, she still represents this particular locality as unfamiliar, as "fantastic" and foreign, describing the shape of the tips as "like pyramids" and the water in the pits as "like arctic pools." This locality, it seems, is not quite part of Cornwall, but distinct, separate, a world of its own: a kind of polar Egypt of the mind. A couple of paragraphs later, she goes further in describing the landscape as lunar, and finally otherworldly:

> A stranger set down upon this spot today, or closer still amongst the slag and shale, white hills on either side of him, would think himself a thousand miles from Cornwall, in the canyons of Colorado, perhaps, or the volcanic craters on

> the moon. Sense of orientation goes awry [...] and there seems no way out, no means of escape from this fantastic world...the clay-worker will continue to blast and excavate, the wanderer to stare in fascination upon this strange white world of pyramid and pool.[12]

Du Maurier sets up an opposition here between the clay-worker, who physically affects the land, and the visitor, who stares from a distance at "this strange white world." In *Enchanted Cornwall,* she condenses this account of the beauty and foreignness of the landscape where she again, though more briefly, describes the clay tips as having a "strange, almost fantastic beauty; if you go up there it is like another world."[13]

Rowena Summers (one of the pseudonyms of Jean Saunders), who has written a series of nine novels set in the clay region (1987–2000), also presents the landscape as beautiful. The earlier novels focus on the families involved in the clay industry, especially those of the owners, whereas the final novel makes a decisive shift toward the tourist industry, presumably reflecting the actual decline of the clay industry in recent years and the search for new forms of income. *A Brighter Tomorrow* (2000) thus takes up the view of the visitor, and describes the landscape as both beautiful and unearthly. The central character, Skye, the middle-aged granddaughter of the heroine of the first novel, invests in an enterprise to attract visitors, a museum about the clay industry, for which the landscape appears to be a definite asset:

> The soaring white hills of the sky tips didn't change, though, she thought stoutly, and nor did the milky green clay pools that looked so serene and beautiful in the sunlight. No visitor to Cornwall could fail to be affected by the wild, futuristic, moonscape appearance of it all.[14]

The extent to which the landscape of the clay country, both past and present, may be represented as alien and unearthly is perhaps most vividly demonstrated by its use in the *Doctor Who* episode "Colony in Space" (1971) in which a china clay quarry is used as the setting for the planet Uxarieus, and by a recent James Bond film, *Die Another Day* (2002), in which the Eden Project appears as an exotic headquarters for the film's chief villain. An analysis of this Bond film will be developed later in this chapter as a way of exploring relations between locality and global processes. For now it is sufficient to note that two kinds of "strangeness" are in play. One: the lunar landscape of the pits and pools (the planet Uxarieus) is alien only to its visitors. The other, the futuristic domes of Eden, are alien to the landscape itself and to its regular inhabitants.

The idea of the landscape as foreign to its own inhabitants may also be detected in literary accounts of the industrial clay country. Jack Clemo, a poet and novelist who grew up in and spent most of his adult life in the area, also described the landscape as foreign or alien, in a way that I would now like to contrast to the images produced by non-local writers and television and film producers. Clemo rarely describes the landscape as beautiful; it is far more often dangerous, destructive, and disturbing. For Clemo, the landscape becomes foreign, but as he was a long-term resident of the area himself, it does so in ways that are different to the foreignness evoked by Du Maurier and Summers. The landscape is not foreign at first sight, but tends to become so, as part of some process of transformation, as in his poem "Drought on a Clay Ridge." The changed landscape is caused by what Clemo perceives as a "freak tropic climate":

> The slopes look drained and old, passive as Egypt,
> Though the hot pyramids are white mineral waste
> And the insects are still English.[15]

What interests me here is that this is a landscape with which Clemo is usually familiar, but which has now become uncannily foreign, strange, unrecognizable. The next verse begins: "I can't recognise my own garden hedge" (36). The poet has become newly alienated from his own landscape, has become a visitor, a "wanderer" or "stranger," as Du Maurier put it. The final two lines of Clemo's poem state that

> The native feels himself a foreigner
> When the climate disregards his roots (37).

Clemo's ambivalent view of the clay landscape as foreign but also as home is reflected in many of the characters of his novels, who either see the landscape as strange, or who are depicted as being almost part of the landscape themselves. This may be attributed to the function that landscape typically plays in the novel. Like Thomas Hardy, Clemo uses the landscape as a way of materializing in vivid and pervasive form the psychology of his characters and the direction of his dramatic action.[16] Thus we might understand the transformation wrought upon the familiar landscape as an action performed upon it by the process of literary production. It is writing itself that renders the familiar strange. The relationship between landscape and psychology can be readily identified in passages where bodies, minds, and faces all seem to echo or receive echoes from the environment they inhabit. Clemo's novel *The Shadowed Bed* (first drafted in 1938 but revised in 1985) opens with Joe Gool looking at an old clay dump that has collapsed in rain, which is again to show the landscape as unreliable, as unstable, though this time due to an excess rather than lack of rain. But this does not alienate Joe from his home landscape; he wishes to become a clay worker and is later given a job. Rather, "His pale face had something of the wrenched, warped perversity of the landscape; he seemed to commune with the coldly volcanic clay-world, knowing its vagaries and loving them."[17] In contrast, a little later, the vicar's loathing for the clayscape is described. He had spent ten years in Essex before moving to the clay country, a place which he blames for destroying his sexual relations with his wife.

> He had loathed the clay landscape from the first moment he glimpsed it, and his deepening knowledge of it was forcing him into an acute spiritual disharmony. He was beginning to perceive the clay land as a sort of evil parody of the mental climate and texture which he found most odious—the climate and texture of orthodoxy. (52–53)

Whereas Joe seemed to accept and even enjoy the instability of the landscape, the vicar is horrified by the "continuous state of unrest," the "vicious assaults and transformations" inflicted on the soil, "blasted by dynamite, bitten into by excavators, washed under hose-jets and finally shaped by sheer mechanical force into hard white cubes" (53).

Alan Kent has argued that Clemo contributed to the "romancing" of the clay area, along with writers like Rowena Summers.[18] But although Clemo's novels depict romances—Joe Gool and Morwen are one of the couples who come together in *The Shadowed Bed*—the backdrop is far more austere, menacing, disturbing and weird, than in Summers's novels. In his first autobiography, *Confession of a Rebel* (1949), Clemo describes the clay industry as extremely destructive in its continuous, almost relentless transformations of the environment:

> It was a landscape of purgation in which the soil was thrown into tanks and kilns, and it brought to the human spirit more poignantly than anything in the peaceful countryside the sense of insecurity, the sudden pounce of the destroyer. There were no rhythms about it, no recurrences; only a pitiless finality in every change. Buildings were frequently altered or removed, familiar nooks and hollows overrun by the sprawling refuse; paths that had been used for years by lovers as well as workmen were obliterated by dynamite in a moment.[19]

Again, familiarity and strangeness are bound up together, as parts of the local environment that were previously and intimately known suddenly change: "familiar nooks and hollows" are buried and lovers' paths obliterated "in a moment."

Clemo's own family and personal background help to explain his feelings towards the landscape. His *Confession* explains that the houses of his paternal grandparents, and his mother's premarital home, have all been buried under clay tips, for which there seems to have been no compensation for his family in the form of secure employment in the clay industry. Both his paternal grandfather and father worked in the industry, but neither seems to have provided his family with any reliable income. Clemo describes the poverty of his grandparents' lives, caused partly by his grandfather's drunkenness. Strikes and war meant that work in the industry was very insecure in the case of his father, who was called up into the Royal Navy and died at war in December 1917. Clemo describes the clay work as unpleasant, as "heavy and oppressive,"[20] so he might have sought an alternative occupation anyway, but his own disability—he became increasingly deaf and later blind—might also have limited his chances at becoming a clay worker, despite his father's earlier expectations that he would do so. Instead, he became a writer.

That Clemo's views of the landscape, and the clay industry, are written down at all, then, is bound up with his personal and family history. His views of the landscape as both familiar *and* strange, and of the industry as destructive, are bound up with writing itself as a vocational alternative to working in the clay industry. Other viewpoints, like those of clay workers, are much less likely to be written down than those of writers—whether they are romance novelists from further afield or a local author like Clemo. What written descriptions of the clayscape tend to have in common, despite their differences, is their view of it as strange, foreign, or even otherworldly. Thus it is both Clemo's pursuit of writing as work and the way in which writing puts landscape to work at the service of literary production (in the representation of character and action) that produces the representation of the clay country landscape as both alien and familiar.

Like Clemo, the historian A. L. Rowse, who grew up in the same area and also wrote poetry, looked back on his past in his autobiographical *A Cornish Childhood* (1942) as one of poverty and deprivation, and he did not much value the clay industry in which his father worked. His ambivalence comes across in his poem "The Road to Roche," which describes the "hard-bitten country of my birth" as containing both the heights which "rise pure in colour and line" and frightening depths, violently "torn in the earth":

> Higher and higher, mount the last heave of hill
> To where the china-clay country begins:
> The pyramids rise pure in colour and line,
> On the other hand, the chasms torn in the earth
> Vertiginously deep and frightening [. . .].[21]

Rowse values the landscape, not in terms of the clay industry as a source of income, but as a way of exploring his own ambivalent feelings about the childhood that his vocation as a historian and writer enabled him to escape. Rowse's autobiographical writing is novelistic in its use of landscape. Like Clemo, he presents it as strange in order to make tangible a state of psychological dissociation: in this case his own agonized and hostile relation to the society in which he grew up. The contrast between these literary uses of the landscape and the non-literary experience of it that is recorded in forms such as oral history interviews is illustrated by a brief example from the work of another local writer. This is the dialect expert Ken Phillipps, who also grew up in the area, whose family worked in the industry, and who published an autobiography, *Catching Cornwall in Flight* (1994). Like Du Maurier and Summers, Phillipps adopts the view of the visitor or tourist, but does not share the idea of the landscape as beautiful. Like Clemo and Rowse, he sees the industry as destructive. He mentions a guide to Cornwall that describes it as "dreary" and goes on to refer to how the "china clay industry, however prosperous it has been, has had a pretty disastrous effect, scenically, on the neighbourhood. Probably most visitors do not linger long today".[22] But although Phillipps takes up the typically distanced and critical view of the visitor and writer, he mentions here how prosperous it has been, and later returns to the theme of earning a living, to the view of the industry in terms of income rather than aesthetics or its disastrous effect on the scenery:

> I once won a *Spectator* competition about pollution by focussing on the china clay industry. Mother was very angry: "I don't know about the Phillippses," she said, "but we Hawkens would be nowhere without the clay. 'Tis no good to get biggotty while you've still got to earn your living. (49)

"Our life have been in the clay"

Since the 1990s, an increasing number of oral history projects have been carried out with people involved in environmental movements, and with those who may contribute to an understanding of ecological changes and crises, as I mentioned in my introduction. Here, I will explore how long-term inhabitants of industrial regions may tend to accept the destruction and pollution of local environments, and to resist global environmental enterprises. If oral history is to have a role in understanding and promoting environmental practices, and in overcoming obstacles to this, then it may be important to consider reasons why people do not become involved in environmental concerns.

Interviewees who continued to live in the clay district, and whose families had worked in the clay industry, if they had not done so themselves, saw the landscape primarily in terms of the income that china clay had provided. Many readily described how the clay industry destroyed not only "buildings" and "nooks" and "paths" (see Clemo excerpt above) but also moorland and wildlife, as well as roads and entire hamlets and villages; however, they seem to have accepted this as an inevitable part of earning a living. In an interview with Jean and John Harris and Alfy Taylor (interviewed by Shelley Trower, Roche, 15 July 2008), all three iintereviewees contributed to the discussion of places that are "all buried up now. [...] Hamlets and all is gone," and then they went on to answer the following question about the industry in terms of jobs and income, rather than environmental damage:

> *Shelley Trower:* In some ways the clay industry has been really good for the area hasn't it, it brought in a lot of money but in other ways do you think it's been bad, had a bad effect?
>
> *Jean Harris:* Well, I suppose we don't take so much notice of what they've done to our surroundings because it w3as our bread and butter.
>
> *Alfy Taylor:* It was the only thing we had. I mean, we knew that as soon as you left school you had a job in ECLP [a china clay company] [...]. You always had a job.

Jean and John Harris's families had worked in clay for at least two generations before them, and their son continued to work in the industry, though was now faced with the threat of being laid off. Both recognized that final closure of the clay industry in Cornwall might be imminent. Alfy Taylor knew less of his family history than the Harrises did, as both his parents had died by the time he was 18, but his father had worked in the industry before being wounded in the Second World War, and Alfy himself went on to work in it for over forty years. This long-term involvement in the industry of the three interviewees clearly shaped their view of the local environment. Despite the destruction of buildings, roads, and countryside, and the accidents which occurred, which Alfy and John continued to describe during the interview, the view of the clay tips—the landscape—signals home to them:

> *Alfy Taylor:* You come out the other side of the Tamar Bridge [which marks the border between Devon and Cornwall] and start coming towards Cornwall; as soon as you can see they burras [local name for the clay tips] you know you're home. Is that right?
>
> *John and Jean Harris:* That's right. That is right.
>
> *They emphasized this point by rearticulating it three or four more times, with the same rhythms and intonations, almost in chorus.*

This view clearly and unsurprisingly contrasts with the view of visitors, to whom the landscape appears strange and otherworldly. Crucially, it also differs as an oral rather than a literary account. No attempt is being made in these accounts to use the landscape as a means to another communicative (literary) end. These people "use" the landscape directly as a means of earning a living, and while we might also think of the novelistic, autobiographical use of landscape by Clemo and others as a way of making a living out of it too, they do so only indirectly. This is how the same landscape can take two forms, not only across the axis local–visitor, but also as a result of the differing representational effects of writing and voice. Oral accounts produce a landscape that differs from that produced by writing.

It is here also that we can see the tension between local investment in the clay industry as a livelihood and concerns for the landscape as a marker of environmental destruction. One interviewee, Jenny Moore (interviewed by Shelley Trower, Bugle, 2 May 2008), observed that although the industry has been destructive of the environment, it is only now that it is no longer productive of clay that environmental damage has become an important issue:

> I've lived here all my life, so I am used to the landscape, but I still think that it is destructive of the environment really, destructive of the land. And, I felt for a long time that we have to do something about restoring it, and making the land usable... Because if we just leave it as it is, we've got sort of a lot of wasteland, basically, which isn't productive any more and if the china clay goes out of business it'll stop being... In the past you could sort of, perhaps, justify it by the fact that it was providing jobs and wealth for the area and so on, but if it stops being productive in any way... well... people ought to be able to use it in the future.
>
> *A little later in the interview, Jenny reported that her family had for generations worked in the industry, which helps to explain her point of view regarding the landscape:*
>
> My great-great grandfather was one of the early china clay captains. In fact, both sides of my family have always worked [in the industry]... and I've grown up with it. And, it's why in fact it's quite difficult to talk about the landscape, because you know that the landscape has provided your family, and your forbears, with a living, for hundreds of years almost, so the tips and the pits, although they're very destructive of habitat, have provided wealth for the area.

Many critics and theorists within tourist studies, archaeology, and other studies as well as geography have considered and critiqued how landscapes are conventionally seen from a distance, as a "view."[23] Archaeologist Chris Tilley argues that conventional ideas of "landscapes as objects of aesthetic contemplation" are limited; landscapes should instead be conceptualized as "being lived through, mediated, worked on and altered."[24] Further, he observes that the alleged dominance of the visual in Western culture, which contributes to the distanced, disembodied view of landscapes, has been attributed to the dominance of the written word and print media.[25] Thus, he claims, "In virtually all the academic literature it is quite striking how disembodied written landscapes become, [...] It becomes a variable historical or social discourse principally derived from maps, paintings, archives and texts. [...A] matter of visual representation" (27). Unlike Tilley's methodology, mine does not involve explicitly bringing my own bodily experiences of the landscape to bear on this study; listening to oral history interviews with people who themselves work with and experience the landscape on a daily basis, rather than just reading visual, written descriptions, provides another way of moving beyond the idea of landscape as a view from a distance.

The interviewees in this study did not describe the visual features of the landscape except in terms of their involvement in it. As miners and receivers of income, clay workers and their families have had a physical relationship to the landscape, changing it and being changed by it. David Matless and other geographers have observed in relation to agricultural landscapes how work with the land, with the soil, and its productivity, contributes to strong feelings of attachment to and identification with those landscapes, including their geological makeup.[26] Matless turns to the work of a few individual elite writers who value the intactness and the self-supporting, organic fertility of landscapes; the industrial nature of clay work has undermined fertility and has depended on international trade, but there is a comparable sense that as worked landscapes, as productive, if not fertile landscapes, mining landscapes are valued and identified with personally. The closeness of this relationship, the near inseparability between the interviewees' lives and the landscape, was indicated by Jean Harris in response to my observation that different people, including writers, saw the landscape in different ways, sometimes as ugly waste and pollution:

> We don't, because our life, our life have been in the clay. I mean my father, and his father before him. John was in the clay. [. . .] No I don't think that we ever looked at a sandburra and thought t'was ugly.

The use of the phrase "in the clay" here strikingly literalizes the physical relationship that workers had with this substance, having gone down into the pits, where their bodies got covered in it.[27]

Other interviewees very similarly described their view of the landscape in terms of work, and saw it as home, which corresponds with another recurring theme in the interviews, which may further help to explain such a sense of familiarity or closeness with the landscape: how life was very much contained within a particular locality, a village or town. It was rare to travel far beyond one locality, let alone beyond the clay region itself, so other landscapes than those dominated by the clay industry were presumably not often experienced, at least not in person. Margaret and Robert Puttick (interviewed by Anna Cope, Treviscoe, May 5, 2008), for example, referred to the annual events that took place in many of the villages, including the Tea Treats, carnivals, and Sunday school outings to the beach, but they only described or seemed familiar with what happened in their village, Treviscoe. After describing the local carnival, they then moved on to the annual outing, which was the only time most people went to the beach, though it is close (seven miles away). Margaret recalled:

> Everybody went, and the parents and that went, when it was Sunday school outing, which was usually in August I suppose in the school holidays. You'd

> have three coaches down in the village to pick everybody up. The village would be deserted for the day. [...] People had no cars then, so for a lot of people that was the only time you went [to the sea...].

For the most part, as the Putticks continued to emphasize, people stayed within the immediate locality, where "everybody, almost every man in the village here worked for the clay."

Like Jean and John Harris's families, Margaret and Robert Puttick's families had worked in the clay industry, as did Margaret (in the wages section) and Robert (maintenance in the fuel section). They also described how the industry had provided you with "a job for life," with "the highest wages in Cornwall," but noted how it had declined since the 1990s. Accompanying this decline has been the loss of local resources, especially shops, which was another repeated concern in the interviews. Margaret pointed out that there had been a big Co-op and a post office in the village that are now gone, and associated the lack of a sense of community with this, as people no longer spend time with each other in the village, shopping as well as working in the locality. John Harris, as well as talking about the local shops and other businesses in his town, printed out a list of "thirty odd businesses in Bugle" to accompany the interview, pointing out that there is now, in contrast, just one shop. In the past, "Bugle was self-contained."

Interviewees, then, were understandably focused on their localities. Previously, there was no need to travel beyond them for work, or for goods and services, and travel was anyway more restricted than it is today, as few people then had cars. The interviews documented personal perspectives on some of the dramatic changes and losses in individual villages, which together indicate a wider picture. The loss of local facilities is not, of course, restricted to Cornwall. This case study points more generally toward a particular kind of tension between the local and "global," by looking at some of the discrepancies between the perspectives of people who have lived and worked in this particular locality for long periods of time and the views of people from outside it, which are reflected here in views of the landscape, and, specifically, how it stands as a figure for the global environment.

Since the decline of the clay industry, the landscape, as well as life in the villages, has changed, as grass and other plants and trees have begun to grow and animals have begun to inhabit the clay tips and pits. People living in the area have tended to view the landscape in terms of work and income, but now that the industry has largely gone, some of the interviewees affirmed that they valued the landscape positively as a place for wildlife, while others felt that the planting of trees would cause people to forget the industrial past, either for good or for ill. Terry Richards, who worked for most of his life in the industry and was then employed directly in reshaping the landscape—in flattening the clay tips and making them safer[28]—described the more recent changes:

> They're now obviously planting a load of trees, so in twenty years time people won't remember the clay works as clay works. You've got the holes which will be filled for leisure, which is already happening, for canoeing and water-skiing, and all sorts of things. I just accept it [the industrial landscape] as part of what's happened in Cornwall which you have to have to get employment, because Cornwall is so poor for employment and for decent wages.

These tensions around landscape, historical identity, work and environment manifest themselves most clearly around the Eden Project, a combination of postindustrial regeneration, landscape transformation, and environmental project. Here the terms in which the Eden Project represents itself come into conflict with local perceptions communicated in oral history interviews.

"Our global garden"

Shortly after opening in 2001, the Eden Project became Cornwall's most visited and well-known attraction, topping the mythical Celtic birthplace of King Arthur at Tintagel. Its number of annual visitors reached over a million each year. Its transformation of an infertile clay quarry into an imaginative enterprise seems very much of its time (the age of regeneration through cultural industries), or even ahead of it, with its innovative architecture and its technologically realized microclimates, which seem to promise the future preservation of the natural environment.

Oral accounts of the landscape have revealed the ways in which local people view and relate to the landscape differently from visitors and writers. The Eden Project presents another view of the landscape with which local people are unlikely to identify: that of a place rescued from devastation by technology. By presenting the landscape as strange and terribly scarred, Eden can present itself as the heroic savior of the day. Posters along the route leading into the site, images on the website, postcards, the DVD *Eden: The Complete Inside Story*, and the booklet that serves as a guide for visitors present a predictable account of before and after: The old exhausted clay pit named Bodelva is now, amazingly, regenerated—filled with a rich diversity of plant life from different parts of the world.[29] This narrative matches the account offered of the project's origins by Eden's inventor and director, Tim Smit. In his book *Eden* (2001), Smit describes his first visit to the pit that was to become the home of Eden. At first, he saw the "forbidding Soviet-style concrete works buildings, with their grey asbestos roofs and cracked and grimy windows," a "battered and dust-covered" cabin with "chewed lino floors, the smell of instant coffee, a few cheap desks."[30] He describes this environment as dirty, old, broken, unhealthy, and how he had low expectations. Then, the revelation. The landscape is strangely familiar, or familiarly alien:

> It was the strangest thing. The instant my eyes fell on Bodelva Pit I knew it was the one, exactly as it was meant to be. I felt as if I had been there before. Every lump, scar, crevice and cliff face felt familiar. It was a huge, deep, multi-coloured oval, decreasing in depth at its southern end, where one of those extraordinary milky emerald lakes so much a feature of the clay area glinted in the alien landscape.[31]

In contrast to the clay workers, and like writers including Daphne du Maurier and Jack Clemo, Tim Smit describes the landscape as strange, as alien, and as scarred. He describes the industry as a rapist; the land as if it feels pain: "One is struck by the staggering carelessness of the rape, as if the land existed only for the taking, with no consequent duty of care to soften the pain. It has been left to a new generation to heal the terrible scarring created by the old" (40). Smit does so in order to incorporate his project into the emerging narrative of redemption, in which Edenic paradise is to be regained. Smit emphasizes the present spoilation rather than the past potential of the landscape, insists on its non-productivity and its "ever-larger mountains of waste that sterilized increasing amounts of what could have been productive land."[32]

The present Edenic landscape, consisting largely of a huge range of plants from other, exotic parts of the world, which has replaced the sterile and strange clayscape, is itself perceived as alien, not only by its visitors, but also by those who live in the area. Indeed, to be alien might be said to be its very purpose: to simulate the environments of distant places—most prominently a rainforest and the Mediterranean in the two central biomes—about which it can then educate both visitors and locals. In a sense, its strangeness places both on an equal footing. We are all visitors in an alien world. To enter an Eden biome is an experience of leaving behind the environment you were in and suddenly being enveloped in another place. It is an experience that involves all the senses. Entering the rainforest biome, for example, you feel the warm, humid wind blow about your body, and you see and smell the exotic plants. But before one even enters the biomes, the view of them from a distance, as the visitor approaches, is of an alien or science-fictional landscape. It is this aspect of Eden that is exploited in the James Bond film *Die Another Day* (2002), in which it features as part of the strange icy landscape in which the biomes appear as the futuristic structure inhabited by Bond's evil enemy, Gustav Graves.

That the biomes can be superimposed to look like they are part of this strange, foreign landscape indicates both how the clayscape may similarly work as an otherworldly backdrop for Eden itself and also how readily detachable, and thus "non-local," it is. It also offers an ironic reversal of the Eden Project. In the film, Eden appears as the headquarters of an enemy of the environment, whose futuristic technologies permit his own genetic modification and enable him to destroy the entire world through environmental catastrophe. It therefore offers a kind of inverse plot to Eden's own script, in which Eden saves the environment through education about biodiversity, recycling, and so on. Reading the film against Eden's scripting of its own role produces a challenge on at least two different levels: It uses a site, the biomes, that is already foreign to the place in which it is situated, and then transports that site to another part of the world, both within the film and through the dissemination of the film itself. Further, the general focus of the film's content shifts away from any locality, from the local altogether, toward the world as a whole: the threat to it from Gustav Graves. The appearance of Eden in the film opens up a reading of the real Eden in the clay country as part of a global process of alienation and potential destruction, rather than as the savior of the local environment and economy, as it appears in Eden's own literature. Paradoxically, perhaps, the Bond film—which is so outside the life and landscape of the clay country that it does not so much as name it—ends up representing Eden rather as it appears in the eyes of some of the inhabitants of the clay country: as an alien enemy.

When asked about Eden, most of the interviewees expressed critical or hostile or, at best, ambivalent views. Some described it as a project that they did not want to visit; those who had visited remained skeptical about its benefits for the locality, especially in terms of employment and income, as explored in the interview with Alfy Taylor, Jean and John Harris:

> Shelley Trower: What do you think of other recent changes, like the Eden project, do you think that's any good for the area, or?
> Alfy Taylor: Personally I've never been there. I know I like flowers and gardens and all that, but I don't want to go there, I don't want to go . . . I used to live in Gunwithick, I could've walked there, but I've never been in there . . .
> Jean Harris: John and I have been there once, haven't us.
> John Harris: Yeah, we went there once when it was free [*laughter*].
> Shelley Trower: What did you think of it?
> John Harris: Alright, yeah.
> Alfy Taylor: Would you go back again, John?
> John Harris: I don't think so.
> Alfy Taylor: No!

The subject of the Eden Project also was discussed in an interview with Barrie Kent (Foxhole, April 11, 2008), who also worked in the clay industry for his entire working life:

Shelley Trower: Another recent thing is the Eden Centre isn't it?

Barrie Kent: Oh God, Eden.

Shelley Trower: You don't think that's going to help anything?

Barrie Kent: Oh no. No. I don't like Eden really, I been out there three times but – oh it's alright I suppose but—I don't see why they should have so much money from the lottery fund and stuff like that, you know. No. And the wages is not that good, because my neighbor's son used to work out there, and from what he says the wages is poor really.

It was also discussed during the interview with Jenny Moore:

Shelley Trower: What about the Eden Centre?

Jenny Moore: Well, I was very against Eden when it was first proposed, mainly because it involved developing new infrastructure, new roads and that, so I couldn't see how it was environmentally friendly, and I still don't think it is environmentally friendly. It's made out of plastic, it uses fossil fuels, and so on—I could wax lyrical.

Shelley Trower: And lots of tourists come in their cars.

Jenny Moore: Yes, exactly. So it's not environmentally friendly. It can raise awareness, but the project itself isn't environmentally friendly. It's using, I don't know, a lot of mineral resources and all the rest of it. But it is a re-use of a brownfield site, in a way, so it is, if you like, generating employment and all the things I was saying earlier on. [*For earlier info., see above*]

[*At this point the interview was interrupted. When we resumed, Jenny continued:*]

Jenny Moore: Basically, I don't want Cornwall to end up as a theme park. There's a real danger of there not being proper jobs, and proper sort of training and all the rest of it, and that the whole thing just gets pickled in some, in the past, we just sort of concentrate on the past, and think Cornwall was wonderful in the past, and it's got to have a future.

In contrast to Eden's narrative about its own improvement of the locality, Jenny Moore suggests that Eden has in fact damaged the local environment, and that the employment it generates may not include "proper jobs." As is typical of work in the tourist industry, many of the jobs are seasonal, low-skilled and not well paid, as Barrie Kent also observes. Jenny expresses more ambivalence about the Eden project than Barrie, but both describe it—like the industrial landscape—in terms of the income it brings into the area.

Moving beyond conventional ideas of landscape as a view from a distance, then, and in contrast to written narratives and to film and other images, oral history allows us to consider everyday and bodily experiences of landscape through work. Views of landscape are clearly subjective, and this chapter has explored the very different ways in which people see—and think and feel about and relate to—the changing landscape. In doing so, it has used oral history to reveal a tension between local perspectives and the views of writers and visitors, as reflected in oral and visual narratives of the local and global environment. This tension does not simply reflect clearly distinct elite and working-class histories, as the autobiographies of local writers like Clemo and Rowse have revealed,[33] but rather the ways in which the landscape is used for different purposes: whether that is primarily for the extraction of clay, or in the production of literary narratives, or for the creation of a project like Eden and its promotional narratives. The narratives produced by environmental projects such as Eden, with their global visions, may thus be revealed as coming into conflict with local perspectives. In this case, Eden's own story of redemption, of turning unproductive wasteland into fertility, is one that conflicts with the productive history of the clay industry as experienced by workers.

Notes

1. See Stephen Hussey and Paul Thompson for discussion of involvement in tree preservation and destruction both locally and internationally, in the introduction to *Environmental Consciousness: The Roots of a New Political Agenda* (New Brunswick & London: Transaction, 2004), 7–9, 12, 16–17, and in many of the chapters, including especially Thompson's, "The English, the Trees, the Wild and the Green: Two Millennia of Mythological Metamorphoses," 20–54; and Andréa Zhouri, "Pathways to the Amazon: British Campaigners in the Brazilian Rainforest," 174–199. For information about the Eden's Project's rainforest biome, see http://www.edenproject.com/come-and-visit/whats-here/rainforest-biome/index.php(accessed 1/4/2011).
2. Many of the chapters in Stephen Hussey and Paul Thompson's collection *Environmental Consciousness* discuss the importance of listening to local "experts" (see especially Olivia Bennett, "'Our land is our only wealth': Changing relationships with the environment," 91–108) and/or consider peoples' active involvement in environmental causes (such as Zhouri, "Pathways to the Amazon," 174–199), but others use oral history interviews to explore more problematic relationships to nature (including Giovanni Contini's, "Animals, Children and Peasants in Tuscany," 55–62). Elsewhere there are a few studies that also investigate problematic aspects of particular environmental enterprises and/or of public involvement, including three articles in *Landscapes of Memory,* a special issue of *Oral History* 28:1 (2000): Malcolm Chase's investigation of an environmental project, its racist ideas, and links with Nazism, "Heartbreak Hill: Environment, Unemployment and 'Back to the Land' in Inter-War Cleveland," 33–42; Janice Brummond's discussion of her use of oral history to explore why some people remain remain committed to environmental issues in Ukraine, while many Ukrainians resist the work of environmentalists, in "Liquidators, *Chornobylets* and Masonic Ecologists: Ukrainian Environmental Identities," 52–62; and Shelley Egoz's discussion of how the "clean and green" image of New Zealand exists in tension with the "messiness"

of organic farming, in "Clean and Green but Messy: The Contested Landscape of New Zealand's Organic Farms," 63–74.

3. I have already discussed some of the connections made between orality in place in the general introduction of this book (through the ideas of Ong, Evans, and others). For more specific associations between oral cultures and the environment, with which they are said to have a much closer and more spiritual relationship, see for example David Abram, *The Spell of the Sensuous: Perception and Language in a More-Than-Human World* (New York: Vintage, 1997).
4. Mark Riley and David Harvey, "Oral Histories, Farm Practice and Uncovering Meaning in the Countryside," *Social & Cultural Geography* 8:3 (2007), 392. One of their examples of this approach is David Matless, *Landscape and Englishness* (London: Reaktion, 1997). A further example, which focuses on Cornwall, on the poet Arthur Caddick and artist Peter Lanyon, is Catherine Brace, "Landscape and Identity," in *Studying Cultural Landscapes,* edited by Iain Robertson and Penny Richards (London: Hodder Arnold, 2003), 121–140.
5. See, for example, *The Oral History Reader*, 2nd edition, edited by Robert Perks and Alistair Thomson (London & New York: Routledge, 1998), ix.
6. One outcome of the project is an Internet resource made up of contributions from volunteers about the clay industry, landscape, and life outside work, which incorporates extracts from oral history interviews and other multimedia, see www.sense-of-place.co.uk/Rescorla (accessed 31/3/2011).
7. Riley and Harvey, "Oral Histories," 391–414.
8. "Clay country" is how the area is often referred to by people living outside the area, as indicated by Rowena Summers's novel *Clay Country* (London: Sphere, 1996).
9. Many of Daphne du Maurier's novels, for example, involve the moors and coastline. Winston Graham and E. V. Thompson are among the better-known novelists to have set many of their novels in the tin and copper mining regions. Countless other authors have continued to set romances in Cornwall, including, among the more recent, Jane Johnson with *Crossed Bones* (2008).
10. Alan Kent, "The Cornish Alps: Resisting Romance in the Clay Country," in *Cornwall: The Cultural Construction of Place*, edited by Ella Westland (Penzance: Patten Press, 1997), 53–67. Ronald Perry and Charles Thurlow point to an earlier romanticization that began in the 1910s, but this seems to have been mainly limited to artists. See Perry and Thurlow's "Historical Development and Sustainable Development," in Philip Payton and Shelley Trower, editors, *Cornish Studies* 17 (2009), 108.
11. Daphne du Maurier, *Vanishing Cornwall* (Harmondsworth: Penguin, 1972), 152.
12. Ibid., 153, 155.
13. Daphne du Maurier, *Enchanted Cornwall* (London: Penguin, 1989), 59.
14. Rowena Summers, *A Brighter Tomorrow* (London: Pan Macmillan, 2000), 20.
15. Jack Clemo, "Drought on a Clay Ridge," in *A Different Drummer: Poems by Jack Clemo* (Padstow, Cornwall: Tabb House, 1986), 36.
16. For discussion of the various ways Hardy uses landscape for literary ends, and especially in relation to character and plot, see Andrew Enstice, *Thomas Hardy: Landscapes of the Mind* (London & Basingstoke: Macmillan, 1979), and Michael Irwin, *Reading Hardy's Landscapes* (Hampshire & London: Macmillan, 2000). For

specific discussion of how Hardy uses physical landscape to exteriorize mood, for example, see *Reading Hardy's Landscapes*, 17–18.

17. Jack Clemo, *The Shadowed Bed* (Tring, Batavia & Sydney: Lion Publishing, 1986), 11.
18. Kent, "The Cornish Alps," 61.
19. Jack Clemo, *Confession of a Rebel* (London: Hodder & Stoughton, 1988), 5–6.
20. Ibid., 17.
21. A. L. Rowse, "The Road to Roche," in A. L. Rowse, *A Life: Collected Poems* (Edinburgh: William Blackwood, 1981), 273.
22. Ken Phillipps, *Catching Cornwall in Flight, or, the Bettermost Class of People* (St. Austell: Cornish Hillside Publications, 1994), 4.
23. See for example John Urry, *The Tourist Gaze: Leisure and Travel in Contemporary Societies* (London, Thousand Oaks, & New Delhi: Sage, 1990) and Christopher Tilley, *The Materiality of Stone: Explorations in Landscape Phenomenology* (Oxford & New York: Berg, 2004).
24. Tilley, *Materiality*, 25.
25. Tilley is referring to Marshall McLuhan's book, *The Gutenberg Galaxy: The Making of Typographic Man* (1962), discussed in Tilley, *Materiality*, 15.
26. David Matless, *Landscape and Englishness* (London: Reaktion, 1998).
27. For images of workers covered in the white clay, click on the photograph and film clip at http://www.sense-of-place.co.uk/Rescorla/worked.htm (accessed December 17, 2008).
28. For more information on this landscape change see www.sense-of-place.co.uk/Rescorla/changing.htm (accessed December 17, 2008).
29. See *Eden Project, Our History* http://www.edenproject.com/behind-the-scenes/our-history/index.php (accessed December 17, 2008). [this image has since been removed]. For information about the DVD see http://www.edenproject.com/shop/Eden-Project-The-Complete-Inside-Story-DVD.aspx (accessed March 31, 2011). The most recent visitor guide at the time of writing reprints the before-and-after pictures again, with the caption underneath explaining: "Eden was built in an old clay pit to show that degraded environments can be fixed. It is a symbol of hope, showing what can be achieved when people put their minds to something," *Eden Project, the Guide 2008/9*, 3.
30. Tim Smit, *Eden* (London: Corgi, 2001), 39.
31. Ibid., 40.
32. Ibid., 45.
33. Clemo, Rowse, and Phillipps all had working-class family histories, as I've discussed, and Clemo in particular struggled financially in his quest to become a professional writer throughout much of his life.

CHAPTER 5

Wivenhoe Landscapes Remembered: From a Working River to Romanticized Nature

Paul Thompson

"The Essex shoreline is especially memorable for its obstinate refusal to conform to conventional notions of what is beautiful or picturesque," write Jason Orton and Ken Worpole in introducing their recent book, *350 Miles: An Essex Journey* (2007), vividly illustrated by stark photographs of oozing mud; flat, dyke-fringed fields; and wrecked buildings and piers. Nevertheless, they declare, "This landscape is singularly rich in history, and full of layered meanings and visual pleasures to those who give it the time and attention it deserves."[1] And for Essex University biologist Jules Pretty, who has walked the whole East Anglian coast for his 2011 book, *This Luminous Coast*, right along the coastline there is a constant tug between the beauty of nature and wildness on the one hand, and human folly, which is leading to climatic change on the other: for "this is a coast about to be lost." Nowhere is this more obvious than along the Essex coast, with its succession of derelict abandoned industries. Yet historically, this is precisely what makes it fascinating.[2] We agree. But we want to suggest in this interpretation of memories from the north Essex village of Wivenhoe, on the banks of the Colne estuary, that here at least the last layer of meaning includes a revival of romantic attitudes to landscape, and, for some, even a touch of the sublime.

Community Change and Romanticization of Lost Pasts

The former industrial coastal village we examine here makes an interesting comparison with Shelley Trower's discussion of the Cornish clay country in this volume. In Cornish clay country, a romantic literary tradition had already begun to develop while the china clay industry was still active, but local people involved in the industry "tend to view and to value the landscape in terms of function and income, in contrast to literary descriptions." In Wivenhoe, on the other hand, the industrial phase is clearly finished. A number of other oral history studies have shown how, with the loss of a working community, some form of romanticization of memories can ensue, celebrating a place now lost or changed beyond recognition. Examples of this include former workers at a closed railway junction in New Zealand, and slum-cleared shantytown dwellers in South Africa.[3]

A different type of romanticization can occur when change is more gradual and many people stay on in the community. In "Born and Bred," a notable community study of the former Lancashire textile town of Bacup that was done in 2000, the anthropologist Jeanette Edwards has shown how possession of local and family history has become crucial to community belonging. This belonging can come from simply being "Bacup born and bred," and therefore having personally experienced the town's history, but it also may come through membership and activity in the thriving local history society, the Bacup Natural History Society. A celebration of shared knowledge of the past that dwells proudly on some of the pain of it, such as the discomforts of back-to-back slum housing and the grinding work conditions in the mills, but also relishes stories of "th'owd characters," has become part of a shared identity for the Bacup people who have stayed on, rather than move in the face of the town's industrial decline.[4]

On the other hand, yet another kind of romanticization has been found among migrants who have left their original communities, whether Bulgarians moving from the countryside to the towns or Jamaicans moving to Britain and North America. Thus those who stay talk about the land in terms of the crops it will bear and the fruit on the trees, while by contrast the migrants dwell on the beauty of the land, the nectar of flowers, and the sound of birds: glimpses of a paradise they would like to recapture.[5]

Classic Perspectives of Landscape

In referring to "the picturesque" and "the sublime," we have already hinted at another frame through which to view the memories of Essex landscape that follow. We can trace these concepts in literary discussions of landscape back at least to the eighteenth century, and especially to two major seminal works, William

Hogarth's *The Analysis of Beauty* (1753) and Edmund Burke's *Inquiry into the Origin of our Ideas on the Sublime and Beautiful* (1756). Theories of landscape were immensely influential with the cultured elites—particularly with painters, architects, gardeners, park designers, and aristocratic travelers and landowners. They also had practical local consequences, as in the landscaping of Wivenhoe Park in the 1770s. But these earlier discussions had no direct influence on the older Wivenhoe generations, since they had no contact with such writings. On the other hand, it does seem likely that recent attitudes to wilderness, evolving from the sublime, have been more directly influenced by the printed concepts of landscape, especially through the popularization of green and environmental ideas.[6]

The basic concept of the picturesque was that its aesthetic appeal lay in surprise, evoking curiosity, typically through variety and irregularity, asymmetry, and rough textures. The sublime evoked wonder and terror—for example, a bottomless chasm, through vast height or length, evoking a sense of power or the infinite vastness of cliffs or mountain peaks. Thus Arthur Young, agricultural reformer, in 1770 rowed out into Derwent Water in the Lake District "for catching the varieties of the prospect," taking a clear delight in the awesome scenery with which he was confronted:

> A dreadful shore of fragments, which time has broken from the towering rocks, many of them of terrible size, through a path of desolation, sweeping rocks, trees, hillocks, everything, to the water; the very idea of a small shiver against the boat strikes with horror.[7]

Not surprisingly, nothing in the Wivenhoe landscape rises to this level of terror. But Wivenhoe was still more rarely described in living memory in terms of the picturesque, despite the nearby example of picturesque landscaping in Wivenhoe Park, and the efforts of some nineteenth-century artists to make a picturesque scene by broadening the river and raising the height of the ships' masts and the hill behind the village. Yet, remarkably, we will find in these memories some definite resonances of the sublime—especially if we take into account some of the developments of the concept of the sublime in the nineteenth century.

These developments take two forms. The first is the landscape of industry: the vast mills, high chimneys, flaming furnaces of William Blake's "dark Satanic mills," the celebration of steam power in the hiss and fire of Turner's wonderful painting of 1844, "Rain, Steam, and Speed" (now in the National Gallery in London), and the mad but prescient warnings of environmental destruction in John Ruskin's lecture, "The Storm-Cloud of the Nineteenth Century" (1884), his lament against the "plague wind" and the new industrial cloud, "one loathsome mass of sultry and foul fog, like smoke.'[8] The landscape of industry was both awful and awesome. In a small way, the memories of the power of local industry in Wivenhoe have a touch of this.

The second development was the landscape of American wilderness. There were American landscapes that were unquestionably sublime: the Rockies, Niagara Falls, the Grand Canyon. But much American landscape was relatively flat, and originally was too thickly wooded to give dramatic vistas. So at first it was little appreciated. The early American settlers saw the wilderness in which they had landed with dismay. William Bradford of the *Mayflower* wrote of Cape Cod in 1620 that "the whole countrye, full of woods and thickets, represented a wild and savage heiw" from which they could find "little solace of content in respect of any outward objects."[9] Through the nineteenth century, by contrast, the remains of these unfarmed hills and forests became increasingly valued, to the point that wilderness became seen "as an end in its own right and as an endangered species in need of preservation."

In this shift, important roles were played by American landscape painters and especially by Walt Whitman's poetry. However, the two most powerful voices were those of John Muir and Henry David Thoreau. John Muir, a pantheist who equated nature with divinity, was father of the American conservation movement and the campaign to set up national parks, an outstanding popularizer, and a sage of the American wilderness. Henry David Thoreau, one of America's outstanding writers, set a personal example by choosing to live the simple life in the woods of Maine. For him wilderness was "savage and awful, but beautiful." He felt in it the power of creation, before man's interference, "the unhandseled globe... It was the fresh and natural surface of the planet Earth, as it was made forever and ever." The wilderness has become the sublime.[10]

There might seem to be little connection between the vast forests and rough peaks of the American wilderness and the mud flats of the Colne estuary. But as we shall see, Wivenhoe people were prepared to fight for their own woods, and more remarkably, both in terms of ideas and choice of words, it was of the sublime of the wilderness that they chose to speak of the estuary itself.

Sea-change in Wivenhoe

Wivenhoe lies on the estuary of the river Colne, just at the point where it broadens out towards the North Sea and the Thames estuary. Behind the village, the land rises a hundred feet, with Wivenhoe Wood on one side, masking the slope. Upstream, the narrowing tidal river continues as far as Hythe, Colchester's former port, at full tide an impressive sweep of water, but each low tide shrinking to a narrow channel edged by steep slopes of purple-gray mud. Downstream the Colne is edged by flowering tidal mudflats with grazing marshes behind the sea dykes, while the river curves and widens quickly, until, beyond the final islands and creeks, the open sea is visible.

The Colne at Wivenhoe has been a working river for centuries, and it was above all the riverside that made the village such a busy and distinctive place. Fishing, shipbuilding, and also, less continuously, the port can all be traced back to the late Middle Ages. There were similar activities in Rowhedge village across the river, reached by ferry, and in the somewhat larger town of Brightlingsea six miles downstream, connected by a branch railway line. Besides the ferries across to Rowhedge, there were sailing barges and cargo boats heading up to Colchester's Hythe. Wivenhoe was also a key center for laying up and crewing the great steam yachts, with up to forty laying downstream for early twentieth-century winters. The skipper of George V's *Britannia*, Captain Albert Turner, was a Wivenhoe man; his handsome white house in the High Street now singled out by a blue plaque, and many of the crews of these prestigious yachts were from the village too.

In the last fifty years nearly all that has gone. The era of the great yachts ended with the Second World War. Wivenhoe's two shipyards had had little work in the 1930s, and then they strongly revived during the Second World War, only to struggle again from the 1950s. Both shipbuilding and the port finally ended in the 1980s. The regular ferries ceased by 1961, and the Brightlingsea branch railway closed soon after. A century ago, there were more than 200 fishermen in Wivenhoe; today there are under 5. With the closing of the Hythe port in 2005, you no longer see great cargo ships slip silently upstream. Industrial Wivenhoe's population in the 1950s was just above 2,000; new housing estates have brought the village population to some 10,000 today, and the Colne lives primarily as a pleasure river.

The memories cited here are all drawn from the community oral history project, Remembering Wivenhoe, for which some 190 local residents were recorded in 2004–2006 by a team of over 30 local volunteers. The project was supported by the Heritage Lottery Fund, and its outcomes included workshops in local schools, a summer exhibition, a DVD, and a book, *Sea-change: Wivenhoe Remembered*; the DVD and book have both sold several hundred copies in the Wivenhoe Bookshop. There has been remarkable local enthusiasm for the project, and we are grateful to all who contributed to it.[11]

The Landscape of a Working River

The Wivenhoe landscape was not wholly unappreciated in the past. Indeed, John Constable, the most famous of Essex artists, painted in Wivenhoe Park, and there are several engravings by less-well-known hands of the river with shipping that attempt to make the estuary landscape look more picturesque by broadening the river, steepening the hill behind the church, and mooring very large ships below it. Moreover, since the 1950s, Wivenhoe has had its own colony of artists; several find local themes, from clinker-built smacks and dinghies and the village Regatta Day, to the sea-marsh flowers. But older inhabitants certainly do not look back on the village as having been picturesque. On the contrary, they celebrate its industry, the skills of its workforce, and the noise and bustle of a working town. They especially recall this through the landscape of sound, a harsh audio equivalent to the old northern adage, "Where there's muck, there's brass." Thus local novelist Olive Whaley (pen name, Elizabeth Jeffrey), whose father worked in the shipyards, enthusiastically recalls the wartime shipyard revival in Wivenhoe:

> It was a thriving place then! When the hooter went at half past twelve, the High Street was full of bikes, with the men coming home to lunch. And there was always the noise of the shipyards, the banging, and it wasn't so much the riveters, because they were soon taken over by the welders, but my grandfather was a riveter, but there was always banging going on. The noise—it was just something that accompanied life—that noise. It's quite sad, isn't it, that it's gone now.

Martin Newell, local poet and musician, feels similarly:

> Changes? This was a working town when I was first here. As late as the mid-eighties it was still a working town... This place had a working port and a working shipyard and I can remember coming home from my job, washing up or wherever I'd been, at five o'clock, down East Street, the motorbikes and the bicycles and the battered old cars of the shipyard workers would come roaring out, coming out like out of any factory or shipyard—that was the Shipyard emptying out. And if you walked across it there'd be welders and men building ships and, the light from acetylene welders, and the bang of rivets. It was a working town...
>
> I think Wivenhoe's become a bit more middle class, you see people jogging along the path. You see people wearing Walkmans and sports clothes, puffing and panting along the cycle path and assiduously doing their exercise in the morning, and that's very kind of London parks and gardens, that, it's not really Wivenhoe. What are they doing? But it's still possible for me to go into Wivenhoe Wood and spend three-quarters of an hour there and maybe not see another soul.

John Bines, who was a plater at Cook's until this last shipyard closed, and remains a great enthusiast for the history of the yard, spoke similarly:

> The constant noise, I mean, people in Wivenhoe... must have had horrendous lives when the riveters were going, and the caulkers were going. It was noisy and

> dirty. I think Wivenhoe was controlled by the hooters in the two shipyards. The hooter went at five and twenty past seven, and again at half past seven in the morning. It was a loud hooter.

These memories do give an important sense of the harsh power of local industry: the continuous and invasive noise, and above all of its power in controlling the village people. In this especially there are some echoes of the industrial sublime. And while it is very unlikely that shipyard workers would know of Burke's theories of the sublime, it is highly probable that a good many of them were familiar with William Blake's "dark satanic mills;" "Jerusalem" was a well-known hymn both for Christians and for Socialists.

Perhaps not surprisingly, given their work context, much of it carried out indoors, former shipyard workers rarely gave us memories of landscape or the environment. They spoke vividly about their work, but focused on work skills, the processes in building a ship, the launching of ships into the river, and relationships among workers, the trade unions, and management. John Bines, for example, gives a plater's view of other workers:

> The labourers always got an earful if they didn't move the bar smoothly enough, or that stopped. No, you got your ear bashed, or your arse kicked, or hit with a two-foot rule, it was nothing to see boys and labourers get smacked because they didn't. They were perfectionists, these old boys, it had to be right, and it had to look right.
>
> The riveter was using a mechanical gun, which weighed 10 lbs, the gun itself, and you think, holding a 10-lb. gun up for nine hours a day, just without a 100-lb airline going into it, so the pressure was 100-lb. push, which you've got to keep... The muscles and the veins used to stick out on their arms. They were solid. And their knees, when they were under the bottom of the ship, most bottoms of the ship were about three foot high, so you would sit, and your right knee, was where you put the machine, so they used to have a series of blocks that they could put their foot on, so their knee always took the weight of that machine. They were jammed under there, had a hat on, so that their head used to be jammed up under the bottom of the boat all the time. Yes, I was glad I was a plater!

One might expect fishermen's memories, by contrast, to be more environmentally sensitive. Certainly they celebrate being outdoors in the open seascape. As Rodney Bowes, still an active fisherman, puts it:

> I think, once you've got the [fishing] bug—I don't know whether that's the freedom of it, you know, we work all silly hours because of the tides, and my wife will ask me what I'm doing tomorrow, the next day, I never know, I've had, like, 24 years of can't give her a straight answer, because you don't know, you

> don't know whether the weather's going to be all right or not. When you can go, you've got to go and earn money while you can. Every day is different. And I think that's quite rare, to really enjoy what you do. Every day is a bit of a challenge. I'm at my happiest when I'm at work, to be honest!

But the environment here is celebrated primarily as a work context, and in that spirit the prevailing themes of fishing memories were about their means of earning. Thus Brian Green recalled how fish were found and fishing nets when he started in 1947:

> That was as primitive as you could get. It was in the winter, it was the November, and we were spratting—no electrical device to find fish with then—you used to watch for a flock of seagulls, and they told you they was working over sprats. You had the old stowboat gear, which you had to lay at anchor to, and you couldn't get your nets back until the tide eased, because there was so much tide you couldn't get them up. Stowboating gear. Well, that's a big net, about 200 foot long, and that's supported by two poles in the front—one drops below the other one, and there's a chain from the top to the bottom. The top one is held on to the boat, and the bottom one drops on its own weight, with a railway sleeper stuck to it for weight. And then a square-fronted net streams out for about 200 feet behind the boat and underneath it, hoping that the shoal of sprats are going to go into it. And quite often they did. You'd get twelve, fourteen ton of sprats would go into that net if you were in the way of the shoal properly.
>
> You hauled all [the gear] up on a windlass with spikes. There was a little winch aboard, but that wasn't much more than pulling the anchor up. But there was no wheelhouse. My father used to put a rope round me and tie me to the tiller, so if I fell over he could pull me back on the bit of rope!

You do get a sense of the seagulls and the tides here in his description, but that is much less important to him than how to catch the shoal of fish. And similarly, when fishermen talk about quotas, their concern is much more likely with to be earning than with long-term ecology. Barry Green (Brian's cousin) complains he is not fishing at the moment because (February 2005),

> We're banned, to catch soles. The ban is crazy...The ban is only on for boats under ten metres. We're only a small fleet. They do what they like with the little boats, don't they? The big people have got people to say why they shouldn't go.

Rodney Bowes is equally disgruntled:

> [The quota system] sickens me...We have to go, like we did a few weeks ago, cap in hand to some politician in London, begging for a few more hundredweights,

> tons hopefully, of Dover sole, to keep under-ten-metre boats, so we can carry on earning a living. And that just sickens me.

Memories of Play Places

The most significant contrast is not between different types of work memories, on land or sea, but between memories of work and play. As we shall see, there are romantic adult memories linked to sailing, and also to Wivenhoe Wood. But a sense of the specialness of place is found most of all in memories of childhood. For the older generation, the whole terrain of the village, its six farms, the wood and the river was used as multiple play spaces. Most boys made soapbox trolleys, which they rode up and down the streets, or in winter homemade sledges (sleds), careering down the steep High Street hill. In late summer they went out on bikes "rabbiting in the harvest fields, with a stick. You couldn't afford luxury meals, the rabbits were quite good fare for all the local folk" (Brian Green). Groups of boys and girls would collect acorns, blackberries, and hips and haws to sell. Up on the hill they played Cowboys and Indians on the Broomie, a small patch of heath with broom and gorse. There were a few who built tree houses in Wivenhoe Wood. But inland, the favorite place for most was Bobbits Hole, or the Pits, a small disused quarry, which evoked many idyllic memories, some with a distinctive sense of a miniature landscape: "It was grassy, gorse bushes, blackberry thickets, lots of rabbits. Wonderful for hide and seek and other wild games, and blackberrying in the summer" (Sue Kerr). "We spent a lovely lot of time there, picnicking. And there was a garden with apple trees and a brook, and the brook was lovely, we used to paddle in it and we used to catch frogs and put them in our mugs and then let them hop" (Hilda Barrell).

Most important of all for children, however, was the river. One pleasure was simply to watch the boats go by. But for both boys and girls, the quay "was our playground." The boys especially were "always on the quay, up to their necks in mud and water and boats" (Freda Annis). Most boys and many girls swam in the river, diving from the boat jetties. Many made makeshift boats, and some made and sailed model boats. Sue Kerr remembers the special fun of climbing into the ruined hulk of the old *Cap Pilar:*

> This three-masted barquentine, which had circumnavigated the world and came back to Wivenhoe to die, was moored a little further downstream, and that was a great game. We used to go on board this old hulk, and the contents, to begin with, were pretty well intact. There were elegant chairs in the saloon, and gilt, with crimson velvet upholstery, which floated as the tide rose up and filled the hulk, and then they all sank down again. And gradually all disintegrated. But we used to pinch bits off that just for the fun of it! But that was very dangerous, playing on an old hulk.

Further away from the quay, some fished in the marsh, grazing behind the sea wall for sticklebacks. Others went two miles downriver to dive off the railway bridge or to camp or picnic at a riverside spot known as the White House. Freda Annis remembered:

> When we went down to the White House for a day there were several families, and you'd have a packet of sandwiches and about a pennyworth of lemonade powder in a bottle of water and you'd paddle around there. We didn't go in the water, not to swim. Some of the boys used to but none of the girls did. But I can remember paddling around there in all little rills and that, where the water came in when the tide came up and we'd be down there as happy as larks!
>
> There had been a house called the White House down there, it was across the railway line but there were apple trees still in the garden and part of the house was there. Well, one family in Anglesea Road, her grandmother had got a big iron kettle, and she used to bring this kettle and a newspaper and some matches, and there was an old fireplace left in this house and there was a well there so you could get some water and fill your kettle, and we used to collect up all the driftwood and light a fire. I wonder we didn't burn. They used to make this smoky old tea, in a blue enamelled teapot she had!

Of all these play places so fondly remembered, the White House, the river and Wivenhoe Wood are all that remain still available for children today. Children's trolleys and sledges have been edged off the streets by motor traffic. Over half of the former farmland is now covered by new housing estates, which have erased all trace of the Broomie and Bobbits Hole. These play places were lost without protest. But it was a different matter when Wivenhoe Wood was threatened by housing development, for the wood was valued as a play place by adults as well as by children. The fight for Wivenhoe Wood became a major local political issue, and a turning point in bringing local environmental consciousness out into the open.

Saving Wivenhoe Wood

The environment had never been an issue in earlier local politics. Despite its small population, from 1898 until 1974 the village was run by Wivenhoe Urban District Council, which provided a range of services, including its own fire station, sewage, and water supply. The councillors were local shopkeepers, builders and farmers. "It was businessmen, completely, which ran Wivenhoe," said Peter Green. Their main interest was to keep the rates low, and protect each other's chances: as Rodney Bowes, grandson of a councillor, put it, "I expect they were all as corrupt as buggery, truth be known." The battle for Wivenhoe Wood came right at the end of the Urban District Council's life, just before Wivenhoe became administratively part of Colchester, retaining only a largely advisory Town Council of its own.

The first sign of changing attitudes came in 1945, when Margery Dean, wife of one of the local doctors, was elected to the Council for Labour, top of the poll. Her daughter, Halcyon Palmer, describes how she came to found the Wivenhoe Society, which initially focused on architectural preservation.

> She was a bit of a champagne Socialist. Somebody on the council suggested that [they should] knock all the houses on the Quay down, and put a row of council houses there. She had a very strong idea of what was aesthetic and what was not, nearly had apoplexy, and certainly put *paid* to that idea. [Later] it was mooted that somebody had bought the old shipyard at the end of West Street, and wanted to have a wood importing factory, and to store wood down there, all over the marshes. And she just thought this was horrendous, and she thought it would be really the end of the nice little village we knew and loved, with lorries charging up and down the street, and not knowing what development there would be on the marshes.
>
> So she started, in conjunction with a well-known journalist called George Gale, who lived here at that time, she had the idea of starting the Wivenhoe Society, to try to prevent this yard coming, or if it did come, at least to contain what was done there. And also, with the view of not just stopping things, but retaining the nice things that we had in Wivenhoe, and being aware of what we had, being aware of the fact that we did have some—perhaps not very important—but some nice old buildings, which would be a great shame to destroy or alter even. So she, with a group of people, started this Society. She was the Secretary, and she was the one who really was the leading light behind it.

The Society's first major success was its campaign in the early 1970s was to save the Falcon Inn. This partly medieval building next to the church had been very significant in local history, and a meeting place for the great yacht owners: subsequently, Elizabeth Jeffrey was to write a whole novel centered on it, *Cassie Jordan* (1990). The Falcon had been bought by the Co-op, which wanted to pull it down and build a supermarket in its place. The Urban District Council (UDC) had voted for its demolition. But as a result of the campaign, the building still stands, now converted into housing. This intervention was not appreciated by the UDC, who had been used to having their own way. It is said that one Councillor, Councillor William Sparrow, who was landlord of the Rose and Crown at the time, was moved to say, "Who are these people who haven't been in the town five minutes, trying to tell us what to do?" (from an interview with David Craze)

The issue of Wivenhoe Wood was still more annoying to the old councillors, because it impeded the ambitions of one of their own, the leading local builder and funeral director, Leslie Kemble. He had bought up land, including the edge of the wood, and had begun building executive houses. It looked as if he would infiltrate much more of the wood unless he was decisively stopped. The Wivenhoe Society led the campaign to save the wood, and at the local election put up candidates against Kemble, who "to his considerable displeasure" was voted off in 1971. Finally the Council bought the disputed part of the wood by Compulsory Purchase Order to preserve access and create a nature reserve. As Halcyon Palmer's husband, Dr. Ted Palmer, local doctor and Wivenhoe Society chairman, summed it up, "We saved the woods, in the end. Some of it went, but not much."

The campaign marked a turning point not only in being around a local environmental and landscape issue, but also because for the first time it brought together old villagers with incomers (newcomers) in such a cause. Perhaps the same might have happened if access to the river itself had been threatened. However, fighting to save the wood certainly showed how there were local working-class people with a passionate belief in the value of the local environment. One was Eunice Baker, a farm worker, who campaigned in her own style:

> Kemble, the builder, wanted to build executive type houses in the woods here. And I said, "Our children go down there for the bluebells and the chestnuts, and bird watching," I said, "No way are we going to let him build in there." There was a Fancy Dress on the Sports Day, on the playing field, and I dressed my girl up all in ferns and leaves and branches, as the woods, "Keep Out the Woods!" Teenage boys come up, "Why do you want us to keep out the woods?" "No dear, we want you to keep the woods. We don't want Mr. Kemble building in it, do we?" So they went and painted his gate that night! We kicked up havoc. Everybody in Wivenhoe, got them all on our side, "We ain't gonna let him build in there. No way!" And we've still got our woods!

Equally striking is the meaning of the woods for Michael Mason, a publican's son, later a groundsman and amateur dog breeder. He told how he had been fascinated by owls and other birds since childhood:

> I've been on owls, since I was a boy. Yes, yes, always. Heard a lot at the Park Hotel, because there was so many large gardens. The other side of the High Street, where the Congregational Church is, that was all large garden. The Nook in Valley Road was all trees and wild ground, and the dawn chorus, in those days, literally woke you up in the Park Hotel. It was all round, there was little woods, little patches here and there, everywhere there was little spinneys, and they were just full of songbirds. They've all gone and so have the birds now. But I remember when I was a boy, it was '45/'46, when we were at the

> Park Hotel, it literally woke you up on a summer's morning, the dawn chorus in Wivenhoe.

The woods had been Michael's most important playground:

> [As a child] I used to get over there a lot on my own in Wivenhoe Woods, and hardly met a soul—that's before the Council houses were built—and I'd be in there all day long, on my own, just watching birds and things. I've always been interested in natural history, and that's why I collected the stuffed birds, so I'd get to know the birds, because I'd got them round me in my bedroom. Yeah, my mother never knew when I was coming home.
>
> We [boys] always walked along the river, to Colchester, to Hythe. Got plenty of exercise in those days, and we made huts up in the trees, and used to drink from—nearly any running water we'd drink from. We used to say, "Oh, that's pure, if it's running."

Now retired, Michael has made his home right next to one of the previously threatened parts of Wivenhoe Wood, a perfect base from which to pursue his love of birds.

> Yes, I walk [in the night]. Sometimes I walk along the cycle path, well, as far as the University, new houses, I don't go right to the Hythe. I think I know my way about there [in the dark] through being in there all my life, and you get acclimatised. Once you've been out there, your eyes sort of—it's not really dark. That's much better on a moonlight night, but there's paths there, and I know what obstructions, where there's things I could fall over or hit.
>
> If there's nothing on [television], I'll go out over my fence into the woods and listen, see how many owls I can hear. I do the same in the spring for the nightingales. I go out early morning, five o'clock in the morning, listening, counting nightingales. But you can hear nightingales nearly all day out there singing. You can't pick out their song so much with the din of traffic, and the other birds singing, but they're singing just as much as they are daytime as they do at night.

Sailing: The new Romantic Landscape

As with the woods, enthusiasm and support for leisure sailing brings together old Wivenhovians and newcomers, both middle class and working class. It also shifts the focus from the village and its immediate hinterland to the flat landscape of marshland and mud as the river twists out towards the sea. Writers in the past had a very ambivalent attitude to these estuarine marshes. Perhaps the most extreme and certainly the best-known instance was in Sabine Baring-Gould's novel *Mehalah* (1881).

Sabine Baring-Gould is best known as a Devon folklorist, but this was only one aspect of his prodigious output. Altogether he published over a hundred books, including fifty novels, and he was a well-known hymn writer, his most famous composition being "Onward Christian soldiers." The son of a Devon landowner, he had no formal education before going to Cambridge and becoming a priest. Sent to a Yorkshire mill town, he fell in love with a local mill girl, Grace, whom he married—after she had been sent to a family member for social training—and with whom he had fifteen children. In 1872 he inherited his father's Devon estate at Lew Trenchard and became its parson as well as squire. He would have stayed there for life but for the controversy brought by his book on *The Origin and Development of Religious Belief* (1869–70), which was vociferously attacked for its evolutionary Darwinian perspectives. But the book was read by Gladstone, who suggested that Sabine might take refuge in the obscure and little-visited parish of East Mersea, at the mouth of the Colne. So Sabine Baring-Gould was rector of East Mersea for ten years, from 1871. Both he and his family seem to have hated the landscape, hated the mud and even—despite his wife being from the working classes—hated the people. In *Mehalah* he wrote:

> A more desolate region can scarce be conceived, and yet it is not without beauty…The sea is not here what it is on other coasts—foaming, colour-shifting, like a peacock's neck; here it is one tone and grey, and never tosses in waves, but creeps like a thief over the shallow mudflat, and babbles like a dotard over the mean shells and clots of weed on our strand.[12]

But if Baring-Gould was ambivalent about the landscape itself, he had no doubt at all of its malevolent impact on local people. "The rustic brain has neither agility not flexibility," he asserted, citing as an example the shepherd Abraham, "a man of small reasoning power…very slow, muddy in mind, only slightly advanced in the scale of beings above the dumb beasts." For Gould, these estuarine rustics were like the oysters, equally fatally sucked into the mud: "When the oyster spat falls on mud in a tidal estuary, it gets buried in mud deeper with every tide…Mind in the rustic is like an oyster spat, unformed, the protoplasm of mind but not mind itself, daily, annually deeper buried in the mud." Today such a characterization seems intolerably patronizing. But *Mehalah* undoubtedly struck a chord with a very wide readership. The novel had sold out fourteen impressions by 1906. Swinburne compared it with *Wuthering Heights*. And indeed, as Sabine's grandson put it, "it has about it a brutality, a savagery, seldom equalled in contemporary literature."[13]

Equally striking is the landscape description by Rider Haggard, Norfolk small landowner, farmer, and novelist, of Dengie Marshes, which come into distant view as a yachtsman leaves the Colne for the open sea. For Rider Haggard in June 1901, this landscape seemed "desolate and strange," but what redeemed for him it was not the intrinsic beauty of wilderness, as many would feel today, but the signs he could see of human activity:

> Behind us lay a vast, drear expanse of land won from the ocean in days bygone...In front, thousands of acres of grey mud where grew dull, unwholesome looking grasses. Far, far away on this waste, two tiny, moving specks, men engaged in seeking for samphire, or some other treasure in the ooze-mud. Then the thin, white lip of the sea and beyond its sapphire edge in the half-distance the gaunt skeleton of a long-wrecked ship. To the north, on the horizon a line of trees; to the west, over the great plain, where stood one or two lonely farms, another line of trees. On the distant deep some sails, and in the middle marsh a barge gliding up a hidden creek as though she moved across the solid land. Then, spread like a golden garment over the vast expanses of earth and ocean, the flood of sunshine...But what must it be like...when the howling easterly winds of spring sweep across its spaces...?[14]

Local sailors understandably have a very different relationship to this landscape, and they see it very differently from such writers. For them, this "desolate" windswept landscape of marsh and mud gleams with a special romantic beauty. Sailing has a long history in Wivenhoe. In the eighteenth century, the village fishermen were already racing their smacks on the Colne for prizes given by the local gentry. By the early twentieth century, the climax of the year's sailing had become racing small dinghies at the annual Town Regatta. For this, a key step was the introduction of the Wivenhoe One-Design dinghies in 1935, designed by the local doctor, Walter Radcliffe. The present Sailing Club was founded in 1925, growing over the decades from a hut on the Quay to its present ample buildings by the flood barrier. It operated on a volunteer basis and it was well-known for its friendliness and its regular parties, including cruising in company down the river: "There was quite a cross-section of people that belonged to the Sailing Club, that weren't sailors at all" (Jan Frostick). Alan Tyne recalls the Sailing Club as "a place where I just fairly instantly found friendship," and it remains a crucial center for Wivenhoe's social life.

A hundred years ago, Wivenhoe was simply the starting point for ambitious voyages to romantic destinations as far away as Egypt or St. Petersburg for the great yachts. Today, the focus is more often local. While the activity of sailing has not changed much, there has, we would suggest, been a romanticization of the way in which people speak about sailing and how it relates to the landscape of the Colne estuary. There are three aspects to this.

The first is the emphasis on how the key skill in sailing is to relate to nature, to the wind, the tides, and the local topography. Stan Fenton, local electrician and racing champion, explains the art of winning dinghy races:

> You have to have a well tuned-up boat with good sails, and you have to have a very good crew and work together as a team, because the helmsman would steer the boat, and use the mainsail, while the crewman would use the jib, and he'd fly the spinnaker. And you have to also work in tandem together to sit the boat out, get the weight right, know when to tack. So good teamwork really, is very important.
>
> A lot of it is you have to know the wind, and look out for wind shifts, especially in the river, like the River Colne, up at Wivenhoe, the conditions can be quite fluky, so I have to judge where the wind shifts are, tack into the wind. One side of the river there could be no wind, the other side could be where the little breeze is. The local conditions, yes, you build up over the years. And also, keeping out of the tide is very important. It's a tidal river, so obviously the mainstream of the tide is in the middle, and it's obviously a lot more advantage to keep to the edges of the river if you can, without going aground. It's a balancing act of how you do it, yes.

The second is the historicization of sail. There have been a series of local projects for restoring old sailing boats, from early Wivenhoe One-Designs to substantial

Figure 1 "Winter Refit," lino cut by Wivenhoe artist James Dodds, 1992.

fishing smacks. Probably the best-known recent instance is the restoration of the deep-sea fishing smack *Pioneer,* originally built in 1864, which was rescued from the mud and rebuilt in the late 1990s, beautifully illustrated by lino cuts by Wivenhoe artist James Dodds (see Figure 1, "Winter Refit," 1992).

As a young man, Dodds was a boatbuilder, and he also paints magnificent colorful oils of old clinker-built wooden boats. But for Tim Denham, teacher and ornithologist, it is not only the boats, but the intrinsic skills of sailing which are historic:

> You should learn in a little dinghy, because then you become aware of wind shifts, you realise that the wind isn't constantly running, it flutters and it either backs or veers a few degrees. And in the creeks and rivers, over the years, you get to know where the little tidal eddies are. You work the wind shifts, the tidal eddies.
>
> I think it's an ancient craft, an ancient skill. I love little clinker boats, because, when I listen to the sound of the water chuckling under the bows, I think that our ancestors, the Vikings, would have heard that very same sound. And the thrill of going from A to B, just using the tides and the wind: it's a prehistoric skill that we can still practice.

Last, there has been a romanticization of the natural life in the estuary. Even for Don Smith, former shipyard worker, there are benefits in the deindustrialization of the Colne:

> The river is much cleaner now. It's gotten better. You see cormorants up here now. And a seal comes up too. Years ago, there used to be a terrible discharge, all the time, from the gasworks at Colchester, used to come down the river. And you've no commercial craft coming up now. Because you used to get oil, too, on the water, with the commercial craft.

But some of those still at work in the estuary are less welcoming of these changes. For example, there is a new conflict between leisure sailors and fishermen over the presence of seals in the estuary. For the sailors, seals are an attraction. For the fishermen, they are mere pests that make it more difficult for them to earn a living But the fishermen feel that their voice is no longer being heard. As Barry Green sums it up:

> The less said about them, the better! You don't get no fish. Yes, they take the herrings out your nets, and they also take the soles out your nets when you're trawling. Their numbers are increasing because of just being protected. There weren't so much talking, in the old days, about it, there was more action. There wasn't so many sailors, was there, about? There was only fishermen, or people doing commercial work. Now it's the other way around, isn't it? There's more people not earning a living, and finding time to report people, and feel sorry for things, which don't really involve them, does it?

These leisure sailors include old Wivenhovians like Joyce Blackwood, retired teacher, whose father was a hand on the royal yacht *Britannia*. Joyce and her partner Pat Ellis especially enjoy sailing just beyond Brightlingsea to Pyefleet Channel, and mooring for the night there.

> There were seven or eight seals up there. The fishermen don't like them very much, but we think they're very nice. At night, I don't sleep! That's why I can hear the birds! Oh, curlews, you hear them, and you hear the oyster catchers, which squeak as they fly, and they seem to be on the go all the time, the oyster catchers. And you definitely hear the rain! Oh God, yes, you hear the rain!

This enthusiasm for nature is perhaps most vividly expressed by Tim Denham. For him, the estuary birds are themselves a romantic landscape.

> I've always loved birds. And sailing, you can get so close. When you're at anchor, they'll come and perch on your boat. When you first see the terns—summer visitors—dropping into the river all round you, catching little shrimps and sand eels, it's just a lovely sight. And then you get magical flocks flying over. Even a bird as ordinary as the starling, they land and take off in large numbers on the marshes, and they fly in formation—when one turns, they all turn. Lots of the little shore birds—the ringed plovers, the sanderlings, the dunlin—they all have this skill of flying in fairly tight flocks and all turning at the same time, and one minute you see them brown, and the next minute you see them white, as they flit off in another direction, and somehow, it is just magical.
>
> Cormorants were very very rare on the river, in fact so rare that when the fishermen went away as yacht crews, they came across them first in the Solent, standing on the end of the groynes, with their wings up drying, they nicknamed them "Isle of Wight Parsons," because of their black plumage and their white throat breathing pads. But now, of course, there are over 500 pairs at Abberton [reservoir], and they're a complete nuisance!
>
> Of course, on the river the one that I longed to see when I was little, was an avocet. The RSPB [Royal Society for the Protection of Birds] emblem is, of course, the avocet. I never saw one on the River Colne. Now we've got flocks of 450, and it's just wonderful to see them. They fly like butterflies, so elegant!

Tim sums up how he feels about the landscape of the Colne as it meets the North Sea:

> When you're out there, midweek, there's nobody else there, and you really are living life to the full, pitting yourself against nature. And when the weather's

> beautiful, it's absolutely heaven on earth, and when the weather's awful, it's very exhilarating, very frightening, but very rewarding when you get safely back. It's the last bit of real wilderness out there.

For centuries the people of Wivenhoe have known the dangers of the Colne and the sea, and many of them have earned their living from it. But with the closing of the shipyards and the port, and the ebbing away of the fishing, the meaning of the river has radically changed. It is no longer a source of earning, but of leisure. It provides a way of escaping from the town, from work and everyday life. So birds, which were once seen as attacking fish, can become rainbow landscapes, and mudflats and marshes the last bit of "real wilderness": a wilderness which, especially in angry weather, can even offer a touch of the sublime.

Notes

I am very grateful to Shelley Trower, Brenda Corti, Janet Turner, and Mark Girouard for their helpful discussions of this paper's themes. The paper draws on the work of the Wivenhoe Oral History Group, and I am especially grateful to all the interviewers and interviewees who contributed to that project, and to the Heritage Lottery Fund for their generous grant of £43,000 in its support.

1. Jason Orton and Ken Worpole, *350 Miles: An Essex Journey*, 2007, self-published (Chelmsford, UK: Essex Development and Regeneration Agency, 2005), 3. Landscape historians have had relatively little to say about coastal landcapes in general: for example the stimulating social historian David Matless has a mere three pages on the coast in his book *Landscape and Englishness* (London: Reaktion, 1998).
2. Jules Pretty, *This Luminous Coast* (Framlingham, UK: Full Circle Editions, 2011).
3. Shelley Trower, "Regional Writing and Oral History, from China Clay to Eden" (chapter 4 of this book). Anna Green, "Coffee and Bun, Sergeant Bonnington and the Tornado: Myth and Place in Frankton Junction," *Oral History* 28:2 (2000), 26–34. Uma Dhupelia-Mesthrie, "Dispossession and Memory: the Black River Community in Cape Town," *Oral History* 28:2 (2000), 35–43.
4. Jeanette Edwards, *Born and Bred: Idioms of Kinship and New Reproductive Technologies in England* (Oxford: Oxford Univ. Press, 2000).
5. Daniela Koleva, "Narrating Nature: Perceptions of the Environment and Attitudes towards It in Life Stories," in *The Roots of Environmental Consciousness; Popular Tradition and Personal Experience,* edited by Stephen Hussey and Paul Thompson (London: Routledge, 2000), 63–75. Elaine Bauer and Paul Thompson, *Jamaican Hands Across the Atlantic* (Kingston, Jamaica: Inan Randle, 2006), 60–65.
6. C. L. V. Meeks, "Picturesque Eclecticism," *Art Bulletin* (1950), 226–35. Christopher Hussey, *The Picturesque* (London: G. P. Putnam, 1927 and 1967).
7. Hussey, *Picturesque,* 104.
8. Denis E. Cosgrove, *Social Formation and Symbolic Landscape* (London: Croom Helm, 1984), 223–53.
9. Ibid., 170.

10. Max Oelschlaeger, *The Idea of Wilderness: from Prehistory to the Age of Ecology* (New Haven: Yale Univ. Press, 1991); see chapter 5, about Thoreau and chapter 6, about Muir.
11. The project was based on the Wivenhoe Oral History Group, with Paul Thompson as director and Brenda Corti as administrator. The interviews are archived with the Colchester Recalled collection in Colchester Castle, Essex.
12. Sabine Baring-Gould, *Mehalah: a Story of the Salt Marshes.* (Leipzig: Bernhard Tauchnitz, 1881), 8, 25–26.
13. Bickford Dickinson, *Sabine Baring-Gould: Squarson, Writer and Folklorist, 1834–1924* (Newton Abbott: David and Charles, 1970), 64.
14. H. Rider Haggard, *Rural England* (London: Longmans, 1902), Vol. 1, 469–70.

Interviewees cited

Freda Annis, born Wivenhoe 1917, shop assistant.
Eunice Baker, born 1923, came to Wivenhoe 1935, farm worker and club steward.
Hilda Barrell, born 1895, came to Wivenhoe 1900; from an old farming and maritime family (earlier interview by Diana Gittins).
John Bines, born 1934, worked in Cook's shipyard, Wivenhoe, 1950–1986.
Joyce Blackwood, born Wivenhoe 1928, daughter of yachtsman; became a teacher and pioneer woman sailor.
Rodney Bowes, born 1960, son of Wivenhoe farmer, fisherman.
David Craze, born 1947, came to Wivenhoe 1970s, teacher.
Tim Denham, born Wivenhoe 1935, teacher, sailor, and ornithologist.
Stan Fenton, born Wivenhoe 1957, electrician.
Jan Frostick, born 1940, hairdressing business in Wivenhoe from 1960s.
Barry Green, born Wivenhoe 1942, shipyard welder and fisherman.
Brian Green, born Wivenhoe 1932, fisherman and then fish-and-chip shop shopkeeper.
Peter Green, born Wivenhoe 1932, fisherman and fish salesman.
Sue Kerr, born 1934, father Wivenhoe butcher; became physiotherapist.
Michael Mason, born Wivenhoe 1937, apprentice shipyard worker, estate groundsman.
Martin Newell, born 1953, came to Wivenhoe 1975, poet and performer.
Halcyon Palmer, born 1934, daughter of Wivenhoe doctor William Dean. Wife of Dr. Ted Palmer.
Dr. Ted Palmer, born 1931, Wivenhoe general practitioner since 1963.
Don Smith, born Wivenhoe 1923, shipyard engineer and water engineer.
Alan Tyne, born 1945, came to Wivenhoe 1973; social worker.
Olive Whaley, born Wivenhoe 1931, novelist under pen name Elizabeth Jeffrey.

CHAPTER 6

The Ouse Project: A Case Study of Applied Oral History

Andrew Holmes

Background: The Emergence of Interdisciplinary Work

In 1998, in the journal *Science,* Jane Lubchenco called for a response to an emergent "century of the environment."[1] In response to the changing world, where human beings were now recast as an additional force of nature, she called for a new social contract for science, one that reflected the broadness of the Environment as a topic. Lubchenco identified the need for research across all disciplines in order to provide the requisite knowledge base that could inform policy and management decisions and reflect an increasingly complex world.

The ensuing years have seen increased interest in interdisciplinary projects, with funding bodies, such as the European Commission, calling for research that crosses disciplinary boundaries. Further, scientists and academics, even when pushed together in new working patterns, have moved towards alternative, more democratic models of scientific research, which emphasize the importance of dialogue between experts and lay people and recognize the existence of multiple forms of knowledge and expertise.[2] Although scientific knowledge remains central, it can no longer be seen as the only authority on which to base decisions, since lay people are not simply consumers but are also participants in thinking about contemporary issues within a system of deliberative democracy.[3] The notion of an active interface for communication between scientific research and the public appears increasingly in recent government initiatives and reports, often under the rubric of "participatory environmental management."

The Beginnings of the Ouse Project

In October 2000, the river Ouse in Sussex flooded, devastating the town of Lewes, which became the worst-affected town in the widespread floods occurring nationally at that time.[4] As a result of these floods and amidst warnings from the Environment Agency that climate change would have a major impact on the extent, depth, and frequency of flooding in the future[5], flood alleviation measures were pushed higher up the agenda in the county. Recognizing a need for creative thinking in the face of the increased flood risk, and recognizing an evident loss of biodiversity in the river catchment area, the initial framework of the Ouse Project was formed in 2006 at Sussex University's Centre for Continuing Education (CCE). The germ of the idea had come from Margaret Pilkington, an ecologist who, in conversations with Will Pilfold, a historical geographer, and Alistair Thomson, an oral historian, had discussed the idea of creating an arcing project that could harness all three disciplines.

The initial idea of using oral history narratives to explore past land use and agricultural methods built on the recent research carried out by oral historian Mark Riley. Of particular interest to the project was Riley's work in the Peak District in Northern England, which he had carried out as part of a project on preserving traditional haymaking practices. His research had led him to suggest that oral histories of farmers—those who had worked in the meadows for a number of years—could provide the most conclusive observations on the cumulative effects of management changes over the decades.[6] Such was the quality of information in this context that Mark Riley and David Harvey in subsequent research contended that oral histories had considerable potential for the way in which the British landscape is managed by means of "destabilizing" the scientifically derived narratives of the landscape.[7] Recognizing this potential, the Ouse Project would attempt to fuse local, oral accounts with research from other disciplines and produce ecologically measurable benefits.

The Ouse Project focused on grassland and woodland habitats in upper inundation areas of the river Ouse in Sussex, where recent theoretical work had suggested that flood alleviation measures could be linked to biodiversity objectives. Many flood alleviation measures depend on managed water storage in ponds or farm reservoirs. Another strategy, however, is to allow land bordering streams to flood and drain over time. Such areas are known as *washlands*.[8] Because the flooding of the latter is of short duration, it makes them ideal for flood alleviation, because the site quickly becomes available to store water again. However, the vegetation of washlands has to be able to withstand long periods of time without standing water, as well as the brief periods of flooding. Conservation efforts, therefore, cannot be directed just towards wetland species of vegetation. Instead, in the Ouse Project, the idea emerged to use meadow wildflowers such as cowslip, birdsfoot trefoil, meadow buttercup, oxeye daisy, common knapweed, and meadow vetchling—species that can tolerate short-duration flooding, provided this is followed by relatively quick drainage of the land. In terms of biodiversity, the importance of meadow wildflowers is vast. For example, they provide a continuing source of nectar and pollen for insects such as bumblebees throughout the long season when these bees are active. Bumblebees are important agricultural crop pollinators, but as a species they are in decline because the flower-rich grassland on which they depend is vanishing from the countryside. As these bees don't store large amounts of pollen and nectar, they are dependent on a continuing supply from a range of wildflowers, which flower at different times of the year. The vegetation of a washland meadow provides this.

By combining historical research into past agricultural methods and land use with ecological research into present-day habitats, the project aimed to demonstrate how land use might be managed around the river in the future. Eventually it was hoped that the results of the project would inform a flood-alleviation strategy for the river Ouse.

Interdisciplinary Research to Meet Environmental Challenges

Although they had initially developed the Ouse Project to address ecological aims, the creators of project knew that the issues connected to any washland flood-alleviation strategy—such as meadow conservation and restoration—would require an array of expertise. So, from the outset, the ecologists brought in historians and geographers—those who could help to provide information on how these landscapes had changed.

Traditionally, ecologists have used the presence of wildflowers of grassland or ancient woodland to make assumptions about past land use, and then have used these assumptions to inform conservation management. For example, the presence of wildflowers such as cowslips and oxeye daisies might lead an ecologist to conclude that the field had not been fertilized or ploughed and that this was archaic grassland with vegetation of similar antiquity to ancient woodland. However, Mark Riley's work, which used the oral narratives of farm workers, had suggested that there might be inconsistencies in this approach. An example of this is in the question of what time of year hay should be cut. Ecologists often set rigid prescriptions on such issues—for example, the field must not be cut before mid-July. This prescription would be based on the timing of the seed set in the meadow plants. Farmers, on the other hand, sometimes step outside of usual patterns and make decisions "on the hoof," rather than following rigid prescriptions. A farmer might look at the grass as it develops under different weather conditions from year to year and assess the situation. Some wildflower species, such as meadow vetchling, rarely set seed before the hay is cut, but as the latter is a long-lived perennial, which also spreads itseld through the grass with long rhizomes, it only needs to set seed every once in a while. Therefore, we felt that assumptions based on an ecological research needed to be tested and redeveloped in association with historical research on the complex and changing relationships between rural land use and wildlife. The Ouse Project planned from the outset to gather oral history narratives *alongside* ecological field surveys, creating an iterative research plan that would lead to the project's various disciplines informing each other as the research progressed. Having decided to utilize oral history accounts, a second factor that affected the design of the Ouse Project was Sussex University's Centre for Community Engagement (CCE) itself—the department where the project began. CCE had existing strong links with local communities and had been the base for the first Ouse Valley Oral History Project (1997–1999). The latter research produced thirty life-history interviews about twentieth-century rural life in the Ouse Valley. Although that project did not focus in detail upon the historical relationship between ecology and land use, and was much more general in its focus, it did generate contextual accounts of twentieth-century farming history. It also resulted in a list of potential contacts, such as farm owners, farm workers, and others involved in land and river management—local people with a rich store of detailed memories about changes in land use and local ecology. As a result, in the CCE at the outset of the Ouse Project, a network of local people, interest groups, and conservation societies were already in place, ready to be utilized.

Oral History and Ecology: Creating a New Relationship

In their 2008 study of farm practices in the Peak District, Riley and Harvey noted that although there had been increased interest in contextualized accounts of the countryside, the methodological approach of oral history remained fairly neglected.[9] Oral histories are often the most conclusive accounts of a given piece of land, providing the landscape expert with access to information that simply wasn't previously there and that would be otherwise lost and unrecorded.[10] In his 2004 study of haymaking, and more specifically of the cutting dates for hay, Riley was able to uncover other sources of information in addition to the oral accounts that led directly from the dialogue that occurs with this method. Riley had noted that biographical events such as family weddings and birthdays acted as signposts for participants as they recalled exact cutting dates for the hay crop but two more unique *aides-mémoires* were also noted: one was a tractor log, which confirmed mowing dates, and the other was a personal diary, which indicated that there was a high level of diverse species in the meadow at the time.[11] The oral history method therefore allows the researcher to uncover other materials, such as diaries, which increase the amount and variety of data and information that flow into the research.

Although Riley's research had shown that oral history narratives were an underutilized resource that could offer previously unknown information, the research done so far had not integrated the work of historians and ecologists. However, from this baseline, the Ouse Project set out to develop important understandings about land use and biodiversity by way of a detailed ecological survey of present-day grassland habitats, combined with the narrative histories of the same sites. We hoped, through this combined approach, to reveal key features about colonization and survival of species, as well as to resolve discrepancies between ecological research and oral history narratives.

A Big Box of Oral Histories

Richard Aspinall, the chief executive of the Macaulay Institute in Scotland, described a communication phase at the outset of interdisciplinary research when the discussions and debates between disciplines generate processes that, in time, become genuinely productive.[12] Reflecting such a phase, the Ouse Project began by testing out different means of disciplinary collaboration. Riley's work had indicated that there was potential ecological information to be sourced from rural communities in the form of local histories, but we were also keen to build on information that had already come out of previous oral history work with farmers and in doing so, to utilize the existing networks between the university and the local communities.

When I joined the Ouse Project as a research assistant in late 2006, I was given a large box of transcripts, clippings, photographs, and cassettes from the Ouse Valley Oral History Project, which had been carried out between 1998 and 2000 and was funded by the Sussex Downs Conservation Board. As well as generating contextual accounts of twentieth-century farming history, this earlier project provided a list of potential informants and key contacts with local workers, who have a wealth of detailed memories about changes in land use and local ecology. During a month spent reading these transcripts and listening to the recordings, I made notes of what I thought were interesting pieces that related in some way to the river and the land around the river. For example, one retired farmer described how he used to "gather water cress from the streams... [and would] swim in river cuts where they were silty and shallow." Another interviewee spoke of how the "brooks were drained in the 1960s," and "more of the river is now under crop."

It seemed, even unprompted, that there were people who had memories of the Ouse as it was and how it had changed. Having found these accounts, the question now was what to do with them. Could they be used in a project that had an ecological goal?

The Experiment Begins

Given the methodological differences between an ecological survey, for example, and an oral history account, it was clear from the outset that there needed to be a method in place which could generate suitable ecological information whilst at the same time creating a relaxing experience for oral history interviewees, allowing them room to speak about their life histories. The Ouse Project was also keen to maintain the good community links that CCE had developed in the region. As Alastair Thomson points out, oral historians "engage in active, human relationships in the course of [their] research."[13] Such relationship-building can have another effect, which goes even further beyond the positivistic goal of mapping out blank areas for the academic, and that is to give what George Ewart Evans describes as "social therapy."[14] Oral historians are unique in being able to question their informants, to ask the questions that might not have been imagined in the past, and to evoke recollections and understandings that were previously silenced or ignored.[15] In the context of the Ouse Project, oral histories would bring hidden communities into a scientific research project. As a result, the Ouse Project was something of an experiment in interdisciplinary methods and at the same time an experiment in public participation. Ultimately, we aimed to take the stocks of local knowledge in the upper Ouse that we knew existed and apply this knowledge practically in an academic research setting.

In an early project meeting, a wish list of ecology-driven questions was provided by the ecologists, including such questions as "What was the frequency of lime and fertilizer application on the land?" and "Can you give any details of seasonal grazing: numbers, stocking density?" These questions were built into a pilot interview guide, which began with a general talk about the respondent's life before moving on to more focused questions on streamside ecology.

Evans described oral history as enabling the older generation who have been "shunted into the scrap-yard" to transmit the skills just as they did in former generations.[16] In order to investigate some of the questions provided by the ecologists, it was clear that the Ouse Project would need the knowledge of older people extensively. Yet, as the oral historians began contacting some of the previous interviewees from the former Ouse Valley Project, the precarious time frame of such research became apparent. For example, many of the interviewees had been very elderly when the Ouse Valley Project had taken place and through contacting them—we were intrigued by accounts that painted a picture of the river as a former source of food and recreation—the Ouse River Project received news that some participants had died in the intervening years. However, some, including an ex-farmer, now aged 98, who had previously worked the land adjacent to the Ouse, were ready and willing to help.

As the oral history contribution began to look promising, a further problem occurred when it appeared that we were "blinding" the respondents with the project terminology. For example, words like "ecology" and even "Sussex University," words that we hadn't thought of as particularly problematic, had the effect of unnerving potential interviewees, who felt that they were "not qualified to comment." In light of this, we had to develop our method by making people feel at ease so that they felt comfortable detailing their experiences of the land whilst at the same time gathering useful data to present back to the project.

The Pilot Interviews: The Wayward Walks

The first pilot interview was with Mrs. Woods, or "Fairwarp resident A," to give her her project title, who, I had established from the earlier interviews, had been walking the tributaries of the river Ouse for fifty years and who had a good knowledge of the local wildflowers and trees. On the telephone she also appeared slightly reluctant to be interviewed. On arrival at her house I found Mrs. Woods was already strapping on her walking boots and fastening her wax jacket—she insisted she would be more comfortable walking the streams than she would be talking about them in her house. After slinging my camera and audio equipment around my neck, I followed Mrs. Woods deep into the Ashdown Forest. We walked and talked for three hours, during which Mrs. Woods pointed out wildflowers, such as wood sage and marsh marigold, as we walked along points at which the stream had flooded during the 1987 hurricane, washing her beehives down stream, she told me.

When I fed back the summary of the pilot interview to the ecologists back at the university, I discovered that my new information was not as relevant as I had at first thought. Closer analysis revealed that, although still very interesting from a historical perspective—Mrs. Woods had been a WREN (Women's Royal Naval Service airplane ferry pilot) in the Second World War and had spent a lot of time traveling and working all over the world—her account of the local area had largely included heathland plant species and not the desired streamside habitat species that the project was particularly interested in. A further problem was that although Mrs. Woods had relaxed into the interview by walking in the familiar paths of her life, we had inadvertently veered out of the project research area and into a different geographical zone. This experience emphasized the importance of keeping the project team close to the information that was coming from the interviewees, and so I decided to develop an iterative process that would start with a general interview and develop over two further interviews (see Figure 1).

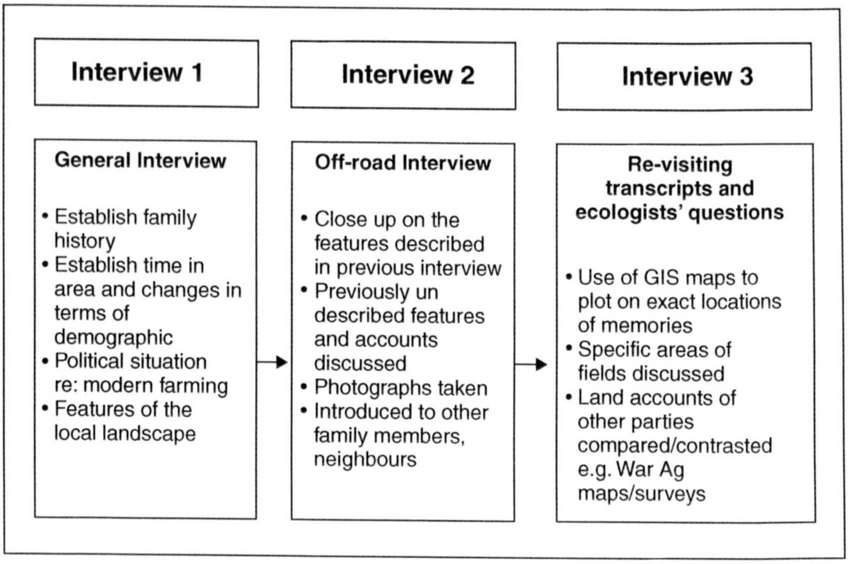

Figure 1 The three-interview process.

Case Study Illustrating the Three-way Interview Process

To best illustrate the iterative process that finally emerged, I will use the example of Nick Gray, or "Horsted Keynes Farmer A," to use the parlance of the Ouse Project. Nick Gray owned a mixed farm of approximately 60 hectares in the upper Ouse catchment. His farm included dense woodland, bogs, and slopes, and a lot of the land was adjacent to the river.

I first interviewed Nick in the summer of 2007. There had been a recent outbreak of foot-and-mouth disease in Surrey, and this latest disaster to affect British farming was perhaps the reason the interview revolved around risk, disease, and politics. Nick showed me around his farm and we discussed previous instances of pestilence, including a gruesome account of the effects of the warble fly:

> You know, one day I was out up the cattle shed with a power-saw and the warble flies were around then and the cattle went berserk! They thought it was the warble fly. Honest and truly, they went mad around the yard—tails in the air. I had to stop it. These warble flies they used to buzz. Bloody flies were horrendous—huge things. It would lay its eggs in the cow's feet and the maggot would travel all the way up [the leg tissue] over the winter and then in springtime, around May, it would appear on top of its back. We used to pop the maggots out of the bumps on the cow's backs—you'd press them and they'd go flying up in the air and you'd put your foot on the maggot, squash them.

Although the interview revolved around the general state of farming, Nick described a change in land ownership that he felt was negatively affecting the local farm land:

> Loads of land around here is just left. In the last eight, nine, ten years a lot of land has been left. Bits of land sold to private people, ten acres, and they've just left it. A lot of people are buying a cushion (barrier) of land between them and their neighbor and just leaving it.

As I interviewed other farmers in the area, similar accounts emerged. This thread greatly interested the ecologists in the Ouse Project and was something the project would later seek to investigate.

During the same interview, Nick also mentioned that his father had preceded him and had worked the land from his years as a youth in the 1930s until his recent retirement. Following our interview, he said he would try and persuade his dad to see if he would be prepared to be interviewed.

Back to the University

At a team meeting back at the university, I was able to present the interview to other project members. Over the course of the meeting, the ecologists identified certain strands of text (see Table 1) that could offer details on the past management of the river and that would need to be followed up.

Based on the interview transcript, the geographers and historians attached to the Ouse Project drew my attention to further records of Nick's land. These included the Environment Agency's records of local engineering work, as well as historical records such as Land Utilisation maps,[18] and the maps and surveys created for the National Farm Survey (1941–1943).[19] The latter documents offered

Table 1 Team meeting; transcript points to follow up on

Farmer Quotations	*Next interview: Discuss*
"We can only get 5–6 months grazing anyway because of the layout of our farm."	The *pattern* of grazing in these streamside meadows would be very interesting—which months of the year are the cattle there for; what sort of stocking densities (how many animals to how much land)?
"At the moment I'm in the stewardship scheme for 10 years. I've been in one year and a half and a lot more yarrow is spreading down there."	Did they ever have cowslips?[17]

a snapshot of life on a farm in the war years; from these accounts, we were able to extract information such as the "infestation" of particular "weeds" on an individual's land at that time.

These maps and accounts had another important function in the Ouse Project, as they could act as a stimulus during oral history interviews, replacing George Ewart Evans's "material object"[20] and fulfilling a similar purpose of establishing rapport. The manner in which the wartime surveys were carried out—often resulting in farms being ordered by the committee to grow certain crops, against the farmers' judgment—meant that the materials were a useful means of starting a discussion on the historic role of farmers in land management decision-making. Although already recognized for their potential for the study of issues such as farm building history, farm size, and farm structure, these documents would also act as a means of deconstructing the very ways in which this history was written.

Interview, Part Two

I returned to interview Nick in September 2007. In the interim, he had successfully persuaded his elderly father, Peter, to join us for the interview. The latter had been very skeptical about being interviewed, and on my arrival at the farm, he mistook me for a trespasser and demanded to know what I was doing there. Initial misgivings aside, we went on to discuss his life of farming the river Ouse pastures from before the Second World War up to the present day. This interview took our accounts back a further generation, providing specific dates of events such as floods and storms that the project could add to a growing picture of these riverside lands. Not only that, but we were also gathering pieces of very specific, field-level information that were of particular use to the ecologists, such as details about a field's drainage. Peter noted:

> We were doing a little bit of draining down there [a field down by the road] and as I was digging one day, funnily enough I came across alder in the ground and it hadn't even rotted. If you use alder on a fence it's rotted in a year, but funnily enough, in the ground they don't rot. You could see water running down the alders where they'd put them in. Amazing. We were putting ordinary pipes in and yet you came across these alders that were draining the fields. Extraordinary, isn't it.

This piece of information meant that we had a picture—via the farmer's excavation—of a specific section of field where the outfall from under-field drains was being carried away from the land and into the streams and rivers. In addition, as the drains had been installed long before the present family had moved into the farm, we were able to take a more distant look at the management of the field.

Farmer–Researcher Knowledge Exchange

By the second interview, Nick had begun to add names to fields that we could not locate through archival searches. These were often names which related to the fields' past usage and the flora it once contained, for example, "Slaughterhouse field" and "Gorse field." In order to create an information exchange, I offered copies of the documents we had gathered in archival searches to the interviewees. These documents served as a way in which—to use terminology from Gill Valentine—the project could "give something back."[21] The oral history interviewers were able to offer unique maps and documents, which often related to a participant's family farm, in exchange for the "time, experiences, thoughts, and emotions" that the participant had offered us.[22]

In the case of some of the more elderly respondents, these archival records—such as the National Farm Survey records—provided a previously unseen document of their farms during their childhoods or even during their early working lives. However, this had to be handled sensitively, as some of the documents—compiled by government officials—often included harsh descriptions of the farm and the farmer. For example, the records relating to the farm of one of our interviewees included the following description of the overall state of the farm in 1941: "This farm could be greatly improved by ploughing up more of the pasture as it has been allowed to get very poor. The owner has no ambition as a farmer."

Having two sources of information—the farmer and the records—allowed us to conduct minor comparative studies that often led to new information coming to light. For example, in the interview extract below, the interviewee elaborates on the 1942 War Agricultural Survey, which included details about his predecessor's management of the same farm:

> *Interviewer:* It says here, for the management section [of the War Agricultural Survey], that the reasons for the farm failing is the "inability of the agent to gain the necessary power and ready cash to farm the home farm properly."
>
> *Farmer:* Yes, that was true, he was always drunk....There were two big fields by the river, one was twenty-seven acres and the other twenty-one acres, and the twenty-one acres the War Agricultural Committee made them plough up, but they made such a mess of it that it didn't produce anything.

With the farmer's descriptions of the "mess" created by applying the War Agricultural Committee's recommendations on ploughing, we were then able to "join up" the period detailed in the survey report to the undocumented proceeding years. This meant that by coupling the archival documents with the oral history accounts, we could create a map of streamside land-change up until the present day. This was developed further during the second interviews, when a degree of trust had developed between the interviewer and interviewee. In some cases, the interviewee recommended us to other family members, adding not only alternative perspectives but also intergenerational perspectives of change.

Off-road Interviewing

During the pilot interview with Mrs. Woods, I had noted the way in which, during our walk through the forest, she had become gradually more relaxed, as if she were more comfortable in the forest and trails that she knew well. At one point, as she traced an old walk she broke out into a verse of "The Brook" by Tennyson, inspired by the sight of the water:

> There's the Brown's brook again, running down. One of my favorite poems is "I come from haunts of coot and hern." Do you know that? Oh, it's wonderful—Tennyson. It describes the stream as it comes down. "And sparkle out among the fern, to bicker down a valley..." And it ends up, "For men may come and men may go, but I go on for ever."

As described above, the trust between the interviewer and interviewee was something that developed as the project proceeded, but in one of the first pilot interviews, Mrs. Woods's initial determination not to answer questions in a formal sense led to a new technique that we subsequently employed in other interviews, namely *off-road interviewing*. After adapting the recording equipment to deal with this outdoor, cross-country interviewing style, we realized that the features of the landscape on the walk acted as a stimulus for the interviewee to talk about other accounts that might not have been described in a more formal interview. Some of these insights again enabled us to build up specific details of specific fields and the reasons for their current state. One example of this came when, during the off-road interview with Nick, we walked through a drainage ditch that had become clogged up over recent years:

> But you see...there's a pipe under here which should be kept free, and in the old days when you had more labor, there were certain times when they were obviously standing round out of season and you'd say "oh, go and dig that old ditch out, and they'd go down with a shovel," but because you're flat out all the time now on your own, you don't, whereas [if] you dig that back from the pipe and then this ditch would keep on running.

Map-building

Prior to the off-road interview, a small Geographic Information System (GIS) map of the area around Nick's house was created by the ecologists and geographers of the team so that during the walk we could note features being described. By interviewing off-road, we were also able to photograph landscape features and link these photographs to sections of text in the transcript for the benefit of the ecologists later on. This further level of detail meant that the ecologists were able to specifically pinpoint areas on the GIS map, such as wildflowers and sections of river, that they wanted to know more about (see Figure 2, The GIS map in development).

Postinterview Meetings

During the course of the three interviews with Nick and Peter Gray, we opened out some of our findings to members of the Ouse Project Steering Group, which included representatives from the Environment Agency, Sussex Wildlife Trust, academics from other universities, and members of local history groups. This enabled two things: first, we were able to get advice on issues that had arisen during interviews and second, we could pass on our findings and the concerns of

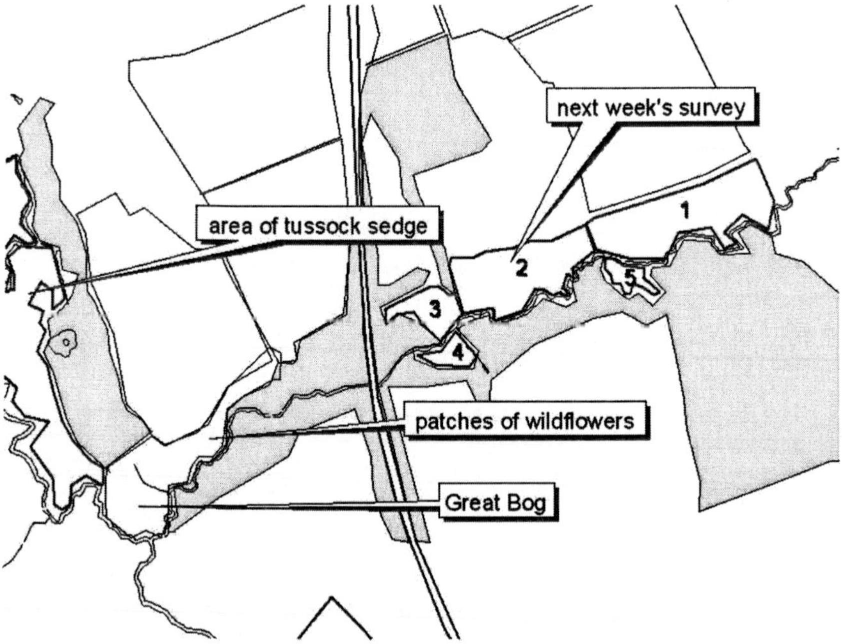

Figure 2 The GIS map in development.

the interviewees. For example, during the off-road interview with Nick, he had pointed out large sections of the river where the banks had collapsed on account of "the River Board dumping spoil from the bottom of the river onto the sides of the bank." By consulting with the latter day "River Board"—the Environment Agency—we could begin to find out whether this had been a regular practice in the wider upper Ouse catchment area. Similar concerns had been expressed by another interviewee—Derek—who described in interviews how his local knowledge of the streams that ran through his farm had been consistently ignored over the years. The result of this had been that on one occasion he had seen a stream running dry on account of poor management of a sluice. As trust was built up between the Ouse Project and the interviewees, we were able to bring forth concerns and address the problem of trust between farmers and experts. One farmer told me in an interview that, prior to my visit, the only time he ever came across people from the university was when they had appeared on his land one time, unannounced:

> I think ecologists and so forth have really antagonized a large section of agriculture by blaming us for reductions in birdlife, etc. but I really don't think it is [our fault]. I was on the hill one day and I saw some chaps in shorts, beards, white coats, etc. sitting down. I said, "What on earth are you doing here?" They'd got papers out and said "Oh, we've come to count the birds."

Interview 3

A copy of the customized GIS map (see Figure 2), which had been populated with information from the first two interviews with Nick, served as a useful document in the development of the Ouse Project in that it enabled the project's disparate disciplines to contribute to the research. Nick was by now familiar with the project and agreed to let the group as a whole walk around his land. By arranging regular project walks based on routes taken during off-road interviews, and by following the populated GIS maps, project members such as geographers and historians were able to add to the oral history and ecology base. In the photograph (Figure 3), for example, the Ouse team attempt to find the location of an old photograph taken by a farmer in the 1950s who had been interviewed earlier in the year (2007).

During the final interview (see Figure 1, Interview 3), the GIS map could finally be checked with the respondents who had originally provided the data. In this way, an exchange of information between academic and local people occurred in a continual loop, with our interpretations of interview data checked by the interviewee and then plotted onto the maps, with changes added.

Figure 3 The Ouse Project team, following details from an oral history transcript.

Results

Using the method detailed above, the Ouse Project produced substantial information about an area that would not have been possible to assemble otherwise. This was achieved by combining new layers of information as it emerged, creating interactions between disciplines and data, and reassembling it, much like overlaying acetates on an overhead projector, or map layers on a GIS map. An important feature of the oral history used in this project was that it gradually narrowed in focus to specific sections of this multilayered picture (see Figure 4). By carrying out oral history interviews in this way, the Ouse Project produced a lot of information about a particular area. Some examples are given below.

Field names

Although archival research, such as tithe maps, had provided names of some individual fields in the upper Ouse, the project has so far been able to add a further layer of geographic information by using the names given to fields by the present farmers. In an interesting example of the exchange of information between the Ouse Project and the farmers, some farmers interviewed have actually started using the names shown on tithe maps, copies of which were provided during oral history interviews.

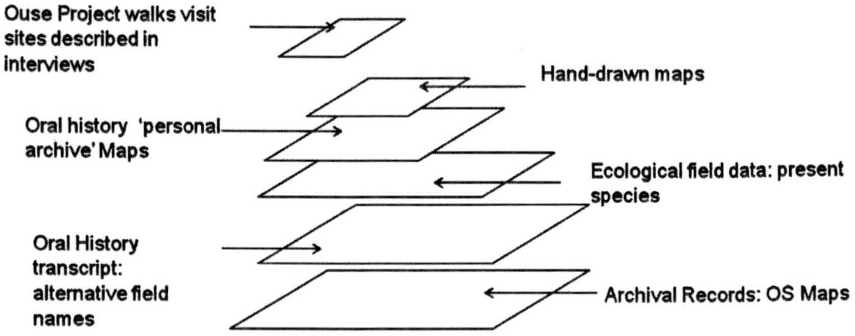

Figure 4 Focusing on smaller areas with the iterative process.

Photographs

Some of the respondents have been happy to share their personal photographs with the project. Some examples show the extent of floods over that person's lifetime, while other photographs show the condition of meadows and fields prior to agricultural "improvement." Both of these can help to build up a picture of the past landscape and can be used as a link to the descriptions given during the interviews.

Personal Maps, Personal Diaries

Some respondents were able to draw maps of their childhood haunts, which provided snapshots of changed environments. These maps have included annotations such as "the boggy area where we used to sink up to our knees in mud" and "the snipe's nest." Such illustrations, when added to interview data from other local respondents and archival data of the parish, create a fairly vivid picture of the past streamside environment. Some of the respondents have also kept more scientific records of their land; one farmer was able to provide temperature and rainfall records on his farm going back to the 1940s.

New Sites Identified via Contacts

By developing relationships over time between the project and the local people of the upper Ouse catchment, we have been able to utilize the family links and working links of some of the respondents. The extent to which farmers and farms in the upper Ouse are still linked by family and friendship was itself an interesting find, and it has led to many sites that had not been previously ecologically surveyed being brought into the project, purely by recommendations that followed oral history interviews.

Species Change

The data gathered in this phase of the project will eventually lead to the development of a grassland enhancement field experiment. This experiment will determine an effective method for increasing the plant biodiversity on the sites identified during the ecological survey work and historical land use research, by using plants that have been identified as being suitable for grassland enhancement and flood alleviation. The local knowledge brought in via the oral history interviews will be utilized by way of the selection of wildflower species to be included in the experiment. This will now include cowslip, a "flagship" species that the oral history narratives have revealed as being part of these streamside meadows until fertilizer was applied in the 1950s. This is illustrated below in two quotations from farmers describing their respective farms:

> When I came here, the Iron Gates was *full* of cowslips, and as soon as I applied some fertilizer, the cowslips disappeared completely and have never come back.
>
> —Farmer, aged 87

> I remember back of [our farm] as a kid, we had a field we called the long field and the cowslips and oxlips that was in that were fantastic. The biggest problem with cowslips though is nitrogen.
>
> —Farmer, aged 59

Farm Methods on Field-to-Field Basis

By interviewing different generations of farmers, for example a father and a son, we have been able to put together a detailed history of land management at the field level. Below are two quotations from different farmers of different ages, describing the same twenty-seven-acre field and how it was used during their respective tenancies:

> The grass [in Iron Gates field] was a very fine grass and made beautiful soft hay, very suitable for feeding to calves... I think the floods in the winter brought a lot of silt down with them which settled on the ground, and made the heavy clay much lighter, and encouraged the finer grasses to grow. I can't think of any other reason.
>
> —Farmer, aged 87

> We actually burnt off the grass [in Iron Gates field]. We didn't disturb the soil; we burnt it off and direct-drilled grass seed in because the productivity of the grass wasn't very great. It made great hay, but I didn't want to make hay, I wanted silage, and we used to make hay or silage down there, and to make better silage we then reseeded it, but without breaking the soil, just drilled in.
>
> —Farmer, aged 55

Farmer's Perceptions of Flooding

During the interviews, we found that the farmers' perceptions of environmental impacts such as flooding were sometimes not quite what we expected. This is illustrated below in a response from a farmer to a question about flooding on his land:

> Because the Ouse floods we've had people say, "Oh well do you mind it flooding?" We bought this farm and it's flooded every year ever since I can remember. I've got nothing against flooding.
>
> —Farmer, aged 59

The responses, as in the example above, showed that flooding was often perfectly acceptable, despite the problems caused to the farmer, mainly because it tends to occur in the winter when the cattle are kept inside. Another finding was that the floods quickly drained away from the streamside land on account of the free-draining soil:

> This [land] drains off very well...I've got one field without any drains at all, and that can have two foot of water on it, three foot of water on it, which it has had at some time perhaps three days. Two days after that, it's gone down and I've drove a tractor over it and you wouldn't see where I've been.
>
> —Farmer, aged 59

A Way Forward

It has been noted by other authors that ecology, as a discipline, has always been broad and outward-looking, as at its center is the relationship between human action and the environment.[23] The success of the Ouse Project has been in recognizing this human element of ecology. This recognition has led to disciplines working alongside each other in new, creative ways. As it has developed connections between disciplines and university departments, the project has also built closer links to environmental policymaking. For example, the project has incorporated advisers from organizations such as the Environment Agency (EA), which has become a project partner, offering advice on hydrology and matters relating to the management of the Ouse. One example of the effectiveness of the iterative process has been the use of accounts of past river-management problems that were provided by farmers in the oral history interviews. One farmer in particular had described occasions where damage occurred to stretches of riverside land on his farm as a result of the management techniques used by the local river authority. Although he had voiced concerns to them at the time, the authority had not taken into account his local knowledge of the river.

By creating an iterative process, the Ouse Project has been able to gather accounts from farmers, augment this information with ecological and other historical data, and present this to organizations such as the Environment Agency. Such an approach fits in with the current vision of the UK Department for the Environment, Food and Rural Affairs (DEFRA), whose recent policy statement on flood and coastal erosion risk management[24] calls for "a greater focus on early engagement with the community."

However, the Ouse Project not only engaged with the local communities; it harnessed their energy. This was achieved by way of the strong ties that existed between CCE and the local communities, and was evident in the numbers of volunteers who helped with the oral history interviewing and ecological survey work. Many of these volunteers were past and present students from the university, who had been helping out with the research since 1997. As most of them lived within the study area, they were also able to provide links to local networks.

Judy Clark and Jonathan Murdoch have drawn attention to the potential of a hybridized scientific knowledge and local-knowledge approach in addressing environmental problems in creative ways.[25] In the Ouse Project, such mutual enhancement was realized, with farmers and local people informing and then steering the direction of this research as a whole. For example, one site, which has been a particularly rich source for oral history and has produced several interviews with four farmers of different ages, has, as a direct result of these interviews, emerged as a potential future location for wildflower meadow re-creation. As the interviewees had farmed the site through different periods, we have been able to gather, from their accounts, the types of wildflowers that have come and gone as farming methods and land uses on the site have changed. Another important finding has been the recurrent theme in interviews of demographic change and its effects on the streamside ecology. According to the accounts of established residents, such as Farmer A, a transformation in land management is happening in the upper Ouse area:

> [Our former] farm land was bought and it's not farmed . . . I do cut the grass off it and there's a neighbor of mine that puts sheep on it in the winter just to keep it tidy, but we've noticed now that because it's not being farmed properly there's the likes of thistles, stinging nettles, docks, are all coming up which quite honestly they come under the, I think it's the 1947 Act of likes of ragwort and things like that that should be taken down, you mustn't let them seed and this sort of thing. And that land is now back up for sale because the chap that bought it has got no farming connections. They moved into the area, wanted a couple of fields to put some ponies in for [their] daughters and when they grow up, that's it.
>
> —Farmer, aged 59

The next aim for the Ouse Project will be to find out the extent of this demographic shift and its effect on the wildflower populations. This will be achieved by seeking out interviews with the "newcomers" that the farmers describe and by applying the methods detailed in the sections above. Thus, the Ouse Project has illustrated not only how oral history narratives can have an important, legitimate role in ecological research, but also how the interviewees who contributed to the original project and helped fulfill its aims have contributed to the future direction of the research.

Notes

1. Jane Lubchenco, "Entering the Century of the Environment: A New Social Contract for Science," *Science* 279 (1998), 491–497.
2. J. Durant, "Participatory Technology Assessment and the Democratic Model of the Public Understanding of Science," *Science and Public Policy* 26: 5 (1999), 313–319.
3. Jurgen Habermas, *Between Facts and Norms: Contributions to a Discourse Theory of Law and Democracy* (Cambridge: Polity Press, 1996).
4. Source: East Sussex County Council, http://www.eastsussex.gov.uk/NR/rdonlyres/00016FE4–50D0-4AD8–99BB–BB06D7BEEF22/0/lewesflood.pdf (accessed March 28, 2011).
5. Environment Agency, "River Ouse Catchment Flood Management Plan Consultation Draft Plan" (2008). Available at: http://www.grdp.org/static/documents/Research/1_es_and_int_2020599.pdf (accessed March 28, 2011).
6. Mark Riley, "Ask the Fellows Who Cut The Hay: Farm Practices, Oral History and Nature Conservation," *Oral History* 32 (2004), 42–51. Henceforth referred to as Riley, "Hay."
7. Mark Riley and David Harvey, "Landscape Archaeology, Heritage and the Community in Devon: An Oral History Approach." *International Journal of Heritage Studies* 11:4 (2005), 269–288.
8. J. Morris, T. M. Hess, D. J. Gowing, P. B. Leeds-Harrison, N. Bannister, M. Wade, R. M. Vivash, *Integrated Washland Management for Flood Defences and Biodiversity*. English Nature Report No. 598 (2004).
9. Mark Riley and David Harvey, "Oral Histories, Farm Practice and Uncovering Meaning in the Countryside," *Social & Cultural Geography* 8 (2007), 391–415, p. 392.
10. Riley, "Hay," 47.
11. Riley, "Hay," 50.
12. Cited in A. Holt and T. Webb, "Interdisciplinary Research: Leading Ecologists Down the Route to Sustainability?" *Bulletin of the British Ecological Society* 38 (2007), 2–13 (3).
13. Alistair Thomson, "Making the Most of Memories: The Empirical and Subjective Value of Oral History," *Transactions of the Royal Historical Society* 9 (1999), 291–301 (291).
14. George Ewart Evans, "Approaches to Interviewing," *The Journal of The Oral History Society* 1:4 (1970), 56–71 (71).
15. Thomson, "Memories," 291.
16. Evans, "Approaches to Interviewing," 70.
17. Cowslips had been mentioned in an other oral history interview as being a former species on a riverside meadow in the upper Ouse, sparking the interest of the Ouse team's ecologists.
18. The Land Utilisation Survey of Great Britain was compiled during the 1930s by schoolchildren throughout the country under the direction of Professor Sir L. Dudley Stamp and his team, based at the London School of Economics (LSE). The maps, which are held at the LSE, illustrate how individual fields were being used at that time by denoting what was forest and woodland, meadow land, and arable.

19. The National Farm Survey was commissioned to assist the work of the County War Agricultural Executive Committees by assessing the extent to which Britain could feed itself during wartime. The survey produced a record per farm that covered farm type, cropping, stocking, machinery, labor, farm size, and land ownership. The boundary of the farm during the survey was also plotted on a separate map.
20. George Ewart Evans wrote: "Before I go to [an interviewee] I have a fair idea of his background and I know what his work was, the chief thing in his life, and I take along a material object connected with his work which I think will light him up" (56).
21. G. Valentine, "At the Drawing Board: Developing a Research Design," in *Qualitative Methodologies for Geographers,* edited by M. Limb, and C. Dwyer (London: Arnold, 2001), 41–54.
22. Ibid., 50.
23. See A. Holt and T. Webb, "Interdisciplinary Research: Leading Ecologists Down the Route to Sustainability?" *Bulletin of the British Ecological Society* 38: 3 (2007), 2–13.
24. Source: DEFRA, http://www.defra.gov.uk/environment/flooding/policy/guidance/project-appraisal.htm
25. J. Clark, and J. Murdoch, "Local Knowledge and the Precarious Extension of Scientific Networks: A Reflection on Three Case Studies," *Sociologia Ruralis* 37 (1997), 38–60.

CHAPTER 7

Witnesses to a Changing Landscape: From the Circumpolar to Central London

Leslie McCartney

Over the past several years, scientists have come to realize that the polar regions of the world are early barometers to the rest of the planet. We have been made aware that the increasingly rapid rate of climate change is magnified in the polar regions, where not only is the permafrost melting earlier and deeper each year, but water and air pollution, coupled with ultraviolet radiation due to ozone depletion, have made a significant impact on the animals, plants, humans, and the local environment.

Today, people continue to inhabit the polar regions of the northern hemisphere of this planet, as they have done for many millennia. Their intimate knowledge of the land and environment comes from their ancestors, who lived and traveled the regions for generations. In this chapter, I argue that the usually unheard local voice of people living in a particular environment can inform on matters of global importance such as climate change. I will provide examples of the changes that inhabitants of the polar regions witness in their local environment, due to climate change on a much wider scale. Through their traditional knowledge and lived and embodied experiences, they can discuss the rising temperatures and accompanying changes they are witnessing. I will also argue that there is a wealth of untapped sources in the form of stories and oral history that can be used for this purpose, although when they were originally collected, climate change was not the focus of the work.

Traditional Knowledge/Oral History

In Canada, in recent years it has been recognized that many First Nations peoples possess an intimate knowledge about the land and animals. This knowledge has been termed "traditional knowledge" or "traditional ecological knowledge" and is mainly seen by scientists as a means of learning about the land and animals in order to help them mange wildlife populations or other resources such as forestry and fisheries.[1] Such terms as *traditional knowledge, traditional ecological knowledge,* and *indigenous knowledge,* are used to describe the knowledge of indigenous people about their physical and cultural landscapes. It is a knowledge that is passed down orally through generations and it incorporates learned experiences, spiritual teachings and empirical observations of the local environment.[2]

Today there is a blurring of lines among traditional knowledge (knowledge gained through the experiences of generations living in a particular environment),[3] oral tradition (a community's historical and cultural traditions passed down from one generation to the next by word of mouth), and oral history. For indigenous people who are now recording their oral history, many of their life stories include their traditional knowledge. Thus, much traditional knowledge, now that it is being recorded, has entered the realm of oral history, making details of the past available that did not previously exist in written or printed forms. It is only quite recently, however, that oral history/indigenous knowledge has been acknowledged by outside groups such as scientists or governments as a valid way of knowing, one that is as valid as, or even more valid than, written texts.

What story is being told, or what history is being told, whether oral or written, it is always told for a purpose, usually a social purpose.[4] As I will discuss later, many indigenous groups of people have requested that their traditional knowledge be recorded for a variety of reasons: so that future generations can benefit from their knowledge; so that their language, today threatened with extinction, can be recorded and preserved; as a document of their changing landscape and society; and as part of their peoples' social history.

Although many projects do not have climate change as their central focus, indicators of climate change can be found in the narratives recorded. I would like to illustrate these points by reviewing six projects, some in more detail than others: four in the northern Arctic areas of the globe and two in England, to demonstrate that indicators of climate change can be discovered, although they may not have been the direct reason for the oral history interview. By reviewing what has already been recorded in other projects where observations of the environment are mentioned, and by collecting new recordings and combining them with the scientific data collected over the past hundred years or so, a more holistic picture can be developed.

A perfect example of this is the Exchange for Local Observations and Knowledge of the Arctic (ELOKA) program. This organization advocates and supports the efforts of the indigenous peoples in the Arctic to collect, preserve, and use local observations and knowledge.[5] The communities involved have already made significant contributions to understanding recent environmental changes, changes such as those in the melting polar ice cap, which can also be monitored daily from satellites in space.[6] All the types of data collected, be they scientific measurements from space or local observations and traditional knowledge, work together in creating a more complete picture of what is actually occurring at a rapid pace in the Arctic.

One Instance of Gwich'in Involvement in the Mackenzie Gas Pipeline Project

From 2002 to 2004, I was employed as the executive director of the Gwich'in Social and Cultural Institute (GSCI) in the Northwest Territories of Canada. My colleague, Ingrid Kritsch, was and continues to be the research director of the Institute. We advocated that the GSCI should be the lead organization in the Environmental Assessment Act/Regulatory Requirement Studies that were being made of the area for the proposed Mackenzie Gas Project.[7] The GSCI was the perfect organization to conduct this study. Founded by the Gwich'in people in 1993, it had been carrying out its mandate "to document, preserve, and promote the practice of Gwich'in culture, language, traditional knowledge and values," and therefore it had already collected a large archive of traditional knowledge and oral history. The GSCI also had a bevy of Elders who worked with it on its various projects. We argued that ethnographically the study needed to be holistic in its approach and it needed to take into consideration the entire cultural landscape of the area and not compartmentalize knowledges of specific topics, for example.[8] We believed that scientific knowledge and traditional knowledge could be linked together to produce this more holistic approach to the Gwich'in landscape.

Save for the Inuit, the Gwich'in are the most northerly aboriginal people in North America. The traditional Gwich'in lands extend from the Mackenzie Valley in the Northwest Territories in Canada to the interior of Alaska. Originally Athapaskan speakers who now speak predominately English, the Gwich'in, who live at the northerly limit of the boreal forest of the Northwest Territories, number approximately 2,400.[9] In 1992, the Canadian Federal Government and the Gwich'in signed a comprehensive Land Claim Agreement and the Gwich'in Settlement Region, as shown in Figure 1, was formed.[10] It was from the signing of this agreement that the Gwich'in Social and Cultural Institute was created.

The Gwich'in Traditional Knowledge Study of the Mackenzie Gas Project Area was initiated by a conglomerate of proponents of this project.[11] They commissioned the work to meet a requirement that meaningful community participation

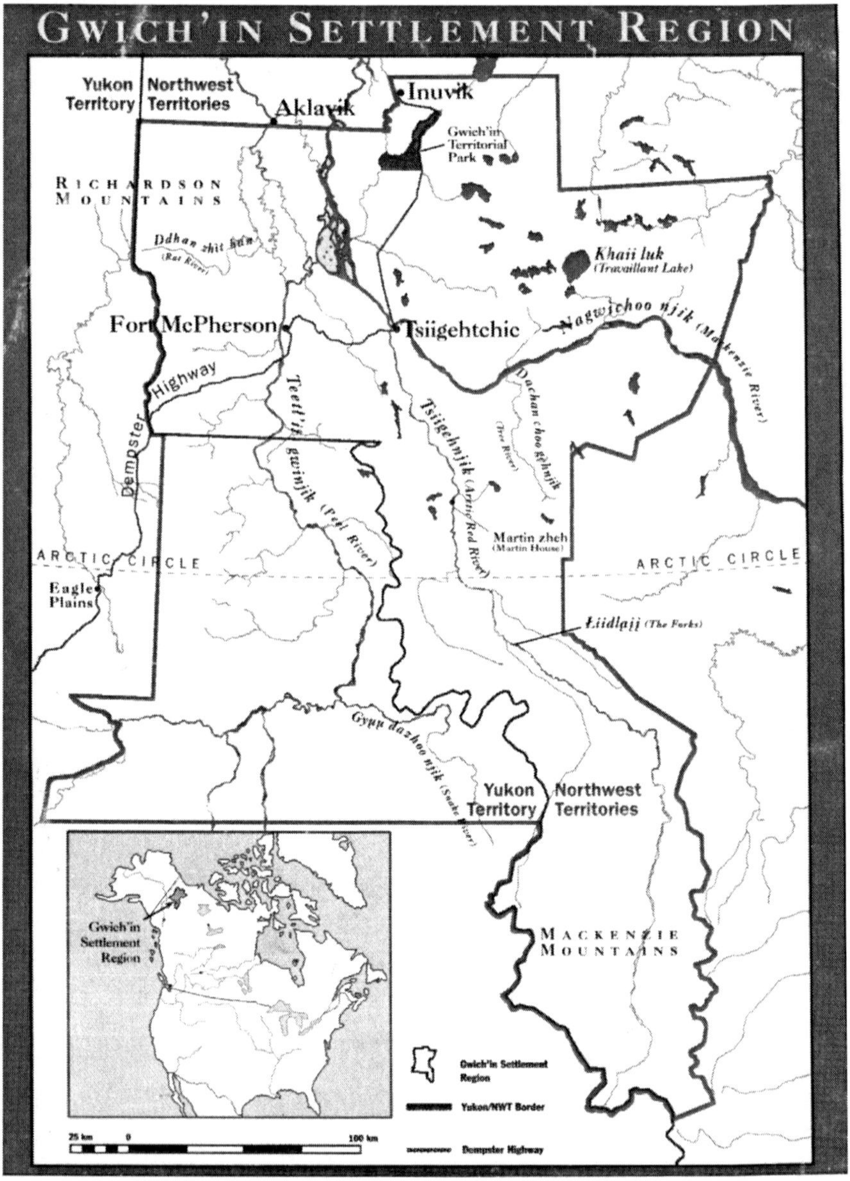

Figure 1 Gwich'in Settlement Region (source: Gwich'in Social and Cultural Institute).

and traditional knowledge collection be carried out in the environment and that socioeconomic impact be included in the assessment process.[12] The entire study hoped that by using traditional knowledge of the area, important cultural and natural areas, as well as flora and fauna lying within the area near to the proposed pipeline right-of-way or near to potential construction areas along the route, would be protected. They also hoped that damage to the fragile environment and to cultural practices and traditional livelihood on the land would be minimized.[13] The study area was composed of 18,000 square kilometres (6950 square miles), a portion of which lies within the Gwich'in Settlement Area (GSA).

We envisaged two phases to the project, the first of which began in 2004, with the hiring of a traditional knowledge coordinator/researcher and a geographic information system (GIS) analyst, who would construct a GIS map of the entire area, beginning with a review of existing data.[14] Phase two involved hiring local researchers to interview 51 local individuals about their knowledge of various topics including: plants, animals, fish, weather, birds, cultural retention concerns, and traditional knowledge.[15] The length and depth of the interviews was substantial, and workshops were set up with all Elders to explore in greater detail their specific knowledge of heritage issues and natural systems, as relevant to the proposed pipeline corridor.[16] Concurrent to this, a working group composed of Elders Councils, Band Councils, (the local government or administration arm in the aboriginal communities), and Renewable Resource Councils of the four Gwich'in communities, Aklavik, Fort McPherson, Inuvik, and Tsiigehtchic, was set up with a view to directing the project in terms of the workshop process, making a list of possible interviewees, and mapping information such as caribou migration routes, heritage sites and trails.[17] Hence, the community was actively involved with the direction of the project, and what they felt was important and should be included was listened to; and their discussions, remarks, and experiences were recorded in the report in the hope that it would be acted upon when the Mackenzie Gas Project commences construction of the pipeline.

The land is at the core of Gwich'in culture. It serves as the source of Gwich'in identity through the emotional, spiritual, and economic gifts it provides. The study area encompassed two eco-regions: the boreal and the Arctic.[18] Animals that inhabit the land include moose, caribou, black and grizzly bears, small furbearing animals, and over two hundred species of migratory waterfowl, which travel thousands of miles to nest in the massive delta of the Mackenzie River.[19]

In describing the environment and the migratory routes of many of the animals, what began to emerge were continuing references to how things were changing and at a rapid rate. For example, when discussing the types of flora, many Elders started to discuss how the willows were more plentiful now along the waterways and noted that they were growing faster and stronger in places they never used to grow. This led to observations that spring breakup of the ice was happening earlier, freeze-up was coming later, and ice conditions were longer in duration than they used to be.[20] Water levels were noted now as being unusually low for the entire summer; cracks in the ice were still visible in January; sandbars were shifting and hindering navigation; the water was warmer, but this meant the fish died faster in nets; the fish were staying longer than before and they were being fished in waters further upstream than previously known. Many

Elders noted how the weather was now less predictable, the summers were hotter, the winters not so cold. When they were young, traveling on the land with their families, temperatures of –50 °F to –60 °F were not uncommon. Today such temperatures are rarer. The Elders observed that several species of plants and animals that normally lived further south were coming north, and polar bears were venturing further south. Everyone agreed that all of these changes were having a huge impact on the local diet, leading to an increase in the reliance on store-purchased food, which in turn is seen to decrease the cultural identity of the group.[21]

During the interviews and workshops, the Elders traced the proposed route of the pipeline and commented on each section, noting at times that it would be a good place, or alternatively noting problems. Khau luk, or Travaillant Lake in English, is an important Gwich'in area that includes archaeological sites, a multitude of traditional trails, fish lakes, and important hunting grounds. The participants were active in pointing out areas that the proposed pipeline should not go through and, in so doing, this led to their telling stories of the dangers of overflows, of the depth of water in various areas, and of how some of these things were changing over time.[22] (An overflow happens when the river is frozen over, but the water may start to melt at the sides and therefore surges up from below, covering the ice with water; this is very dangerous. It can also happen when small patches in the ice thin or melt and water bubbles up from underneath.)

The stories of the seasonal rounds that the Gwich'in Elders experienced in their earlier life were thick descriptions of where people traveled and what they ate. This led to discussions of how the climate was changing; the most common change noted was in the spring breakup of the ice and flooding. James Andre described one of the changes: "Usually in the spring you have north wind . . . That would help the ice, you know, to move, to break up, smash up. But now you're getting south wind. So instead of your ice really moving, it's sort of melting."[23] Andre, born in Aklavik in 1949, originally from Tsiigehtchic, is now a community member in Fort McPherson, but was very familiar with the Nagwichoonjik and Khaii luk areas and was a participant in the Gwich'in Traditional Knowledge Study of the Mackenzie Gas Project Area report. His parents were Caroline and Antoine (Tony) Andre, who were interviewed in the Gwich'in Elders Biographies Project. The usually dramatic breakup of ice breaking, tumbling, and being pushed down the river has been reduced in its show.[24] Peter Ross, former Chief of the Tsiigehtchic, mentioned that breakup would previously be completed in late June but now it is usually done by the end of May.[25] But, as in all oral history, versions are contested. Some interviewers felt that breakup wasn't that different. Bob Norman, an Elder in Tsiigehtchic, indicated that breakup was the same as years before, the ice leaves around mid-June and it varies from year to year, just as it did in previous years. The knowledge of an Elder depends in part on his or her age, as the knowledge is built on the variability of the climate experienced in his or her own lifetime. A younger generation, who are now on the land more than their Elders are able to be, today insist that things are changing.[26]

Many Elders discussed the melting of the permafrost and how there were more slumps on south-facing hills and inland than previously seen. Ellen Firth described how in only two years, the ice on the Nagwichoonjik (Mackenzie River) was eroding the bank and how the river bank, once far back from the house, was now only a feet from her father-in-law's cabin door.[27]

One section of the report deals primarily with the melting permafrost, a very strong indicator of a changing climate. Slumping and sinkholes are caused along the rivers or inland when the permafrost melts. Many of the interviewees were concerned about the increasing numbers of slumps and sinkholes, which have substantially changed the river banks and dramatically altered the channels in the Mackenzie River Delta. Inland, these observations are critical knowledge to those planning the route of a large pipeline.[28] This knowledge will assist the engineers designing the route to avoid these areas or, alternatively, the knowledge may affect the way the pipeline is constructed to compensate for them. Lessons have already been learned by large companies entering the area and working on the land. Seismic work was carried out in the area in the 1960s, the scars of which are still visible on the landscape today. Poorly cleaned-up brush from when the seismic lines were cut, coupled with the type of machinery used to cut the lines, affected the spring thaws, causing melting to the permafrost to occur; large-scale slumping resulted. Companies have since learned that they need to use "mushroom shoes," not the regular caterpillar tracks on the machinery, to avoid damaging the fragile frozen earth, and they have put this learning into practice.[29]

Most interviewees agreed that it was the ice breakup and spring weather that had most substantially changed.[30] The weather was warmer earlier, the ice broke up more quickly, and there was less water to push the ice down the river, so flooding was less, which is of utmost importance in the replenishing of a delta environment. As Peter Ross, born in 1938, described it,

> We used to get a lot . . . of big storms in the summer too. We don't get that anymore. So that, that's the big change I seen over my lifetime of, you know, being out on the land and of today, today's a lot, a lot of difference in the time when I was brought up . . . Oh rain, August used to be a bad month, we used to get a lot, a lot of rain and a lot of, a lot of northwest wind, and [it would be stormy for] 2 or 3 days at a time.[31]

Using the 240-page report that was based on traditional knowledge and was recorded for this project, and using the oral history already residing in the GSCI archives, which was very important, as well as other oral history projects of the area accessed through archives, the Gwich'in people made a series of recommendations about how the developers could reduce their impacts on the area. They gave suggestions as to where forest should be cleared, suggested that any changes in the proposed route should come back to the communities for approval, noted that extra vigilance was needed in some areas and that monitors should be put in place to ensure that the Gwich'in portion of the route was treated with respect, and suggested that the data gathered should be used as a baseline for change. Because of the changing climate, the Elders argued that every five to ten years, changes needed to be assessed, as some of these changes could affect pipeline stability.[32]

In addition to the work done by the GSCI in the preparation of the report, the opportunity to do the project has substantially increased the realization of their mandate. It has provided another archive of traditional knowledge and oral history, which can be revisited as years go by. This one particular project illustrates how the topic of climate change emerged unintentionally within another project, but there are also indicators of a changing climate in many of the Gwich'in Elders' personal narratives, which are lodged with the oral narratives of another project completed by the GSCI.

Gwich'in Elders Biographies Research Project

In the summers of 1999, 2000, and 2001, with the assistance of several local people, we recorded the life stories of twenty-three Gwich'in Elders as part of the GSCI's Gwich'in Elders Biographies Research Project. This substantial work resulted in over 58 hours of audio recordings being collected. The Elders' life stories and personal narratives read more like travelogues as they describe their travels over the Gwich'in landscape. The stories are peppered with traditional place names, mythical tales, genealogical information, songs, and prayers. The youngest Elder interviewed was born in 1935 and was 66 years of age when interviewed in 2001. The eldest was born in 1901 and was 100 years of age when interviewed.

This generation of Gwich'in people witnessed phenomenal changes in their lifetime. The fundamental change has been from living on the land and traveling in seasonal rounds to living in sedentary communities. These twenty-three Elders are probably the last generation to live most of their life on the land, a way of life that for many Gwich'in people today has disappeared. They went from hearing and having Gwich'in names to hearing and having Christian names, (from "Vishriinintsi Tryl," meaning *Red Leggings,* to "John," as named by the missionaries; from "Tziatchadh" to "Charlie"), from their marriages being arranged, to choosing their own partners, to couples today, who, as Elder Pierre Benoit says, "just borrow each other for a while." They have seen their people's lives change from one of hunting and trapping to purchasing food in the store. In their stories, many of the Elders, such as Jim Vittrewka, quoted below, discuss and reflect on their lives and what they have witnessed and experienced in their lifetime, including observations about the changing climate and resulting changes in the landscape.

> To me, this was not a hard life. It was a good life. No matter if we work hard, I never look at it as hard work. I remember that life was great. Nobody can tell me it was a hard life. I was happy then. In those days sometimes I walk with snowshoes all day. I never look at it as hard life. I like it. At that time, sometimes it was very cold. It used to be fifty or sixty [°F] below. But you never think it's cold. You were used to this type of weather and this type of life. So, it is just like everyday. I remember as far as I can remember I had lived a good life. Today the weather has changed from then to now and because of that the animals change too.

These life stories were recorded to meet several needs. The vision was that by collecting the Elders' stories, it would be a step in bridging the generations. Recording of individual histories is of course not just telling stories about certain people; when several stories are collected in one place, they tell a collective history. Oral tradition, in the form of stories, songs, and prayers, has been the vehicle in which culture and important lessons for the next generation have been transmitted. Through storytelling, people learn their identity, create a sense of selfhood and community, and become connected to their past. We were faced with the decline of a generational oral tradition; by orally recording and writing down these stories, we hoped to achieve the same thing that the oral tradition had given. Buried within the hours of recording are references to the changes in animals and in their migratory routes, and references to the weather, how it isn't as cold as it used to be, and how the tree line is moving further north and with it, various birds and species of other animals not seen before. Kernels of climate change information can be found within the threads of the Elders' stories, and they can be used as starting places for scientific research or combined with scientific experience.

Snowchange Cooperative

When working with the GSCI, we were approached in 2002 by Tero Mustonen from Finland, who introduced to us the Snowchange Cooperative, which defines itself as: "an independent educational, scientific and environmental non-profit organisation, where all members are stakeholders... it follows the ancient method of consensus-based käräjäpiiri [governance] of traditional Finns. This allows all members of the cooperative to have a voice."[33]

The scientific priority of Snowchange is currently the lands of the countries to the north or just to the south of the Arctic Circle.[34] Tero and his two Finnish student researchers arrived in Inuvik on the North American portion of their project, to interview Gwich'in Elders on their observations of the weather and what changes they had or had not experienced during their lifetimes. Their goal was not unlike that of the previous Gwich'in Traditional Knowledge Study of the Mackenzie Gas Project: to link scientific and indigenous observations of change together as well as to provide a platform for community-based indigenous voices to be heard internationally, and from this to present both scientific and indigenous voices in a meaningful dialogue.[35]

Their circumpolar work with indigenous people culminated in a wonderful and highly detailed book published in 2004, entitled *Snowscapes, Dreamscapes—A Snowchange Community Book on Community Voices in Change.*[36] This publication was produced as another way of showing change, beyond assessment reports per se. The Snowchange Cooperative acknowledged that the Arctic Climate Impact Assessment (ACIA) 2004 report did contain a small chapter on the importance of including indigenous observations and perspectives, but felt the report did not go far enough. With their view that climate impacts are already being felt by people in northern climates, *Snowscapes* proceeds to present local and indigenous viewpoints and argues that indigenous assessment, through traditional knowledge and oral history, should be a primary tool in documenting climate change. A holistic approach is advocated, which should include geographic knowledge such as place names, events connected to place, weather lore, star lore, and traditional navigation, as well as natural calendars, ethnobotany, ethnomedicine, communications, hunting, fishing, reindeer-herding, and the changing roles of women and gender in indigenous societies.[37]

The Igloolik Oral History Project

It is through one of the chapters in the *Snowchange* book that we enter into a discussion of another project in the Canadian Arctic, which has combined traditional knowledge and oral history to form an invaluable archive for future generations.[38] The Igloolik Oral History Project was begun in 1986 by the Elders of the community and the Igloolik Research Centre.[39] Similar to the Gwich'in Elders, the Inuit Elders of Igoolik were concerned about the loss of their language, cultural skills, values, and traditions; they wanted to record their experiences, family history, contact history, knowledge, and teachings for the benefit of their youth.[40]

Igloolik (see Figure 2) is located in Canada's newest northern territory, Nunavut, on the small island of Foxe Basin just off the Melville Peninsula. The community was formally established in the 1950s, as the Canadian government's administrative interest in the Arctic grew during that time. The Anglican Mission arrived in 1959 and a school, a Royal Canadian Mounted Police (RCMP) detachment, and a nursing station, followed in the 1960s. The community grew quite quickly when Inuit families living in surrounding tundra camps moved into the community.

Figure 2 Igloolik. Photo: Patricia Veltman.

Since the beginning of the Igloolik Oral History Project, over 500 interviews have been conducted, on topics ranging from cultural and traditional skills, legends, and hunting to navigation and social control. As in any culture where the land is paramount and at the center of a people's cultural identity, the Igloolik land and weather are woven inextricably into the tapestry of the story being told. As in the Gwich'in studies, the details to questions asked were found embedded within the stories the Elders told. For instance, the Elders spoke about the respect for the spirit of *Sila,* the weather embodied within a spirit. In doing this, they talked of the cold, and of actions that could create good or bad weather. In almost all the stories they told, topics related to the weather crept into the story. This is unsurprising, considering the environment they lived in. Life and survival depended on knowledge of the weather conditions and environment. The stories taken together are a great resource for people to review, to get a glimpse of the weather conditions experienced in the past, and to compare them to those being experienced now. They are, as it were, a barometer of the weather that enables an understanding of its changes.

Southern Climes

I do not wish to exoticize or idealize northern or aboriginal peoples or say that they are the only people we should look to for information about climate change or changes to the landscape, either changes caused by by human forces or by natural forces. I would like to advocate that anyone who is involved with the land in any way and in varying degrees has a contribution to make, or has possibly already made it, a point I will come back to shortly. Recent studies by cultural geographers who have incorporated the oral history of farmers, for example, in Devon and the Lake Districts in England, illustrate this point well. Mark Riley and David Harvey argue the point that it is through oral history—and the interface that it generates between scientists and farmers and their relationship with the land—that a nuanced understanding of the agricultural landscape can be gained, whereby one can understand its transformations and develop new understandings of landscape management and conservation. (For more about this and a similar project developed on the river Ouse, see chapter 6 of this book, by Andrew Holmes.)[41]

Evidence of a changing climate can also be found buried within collected urban oral histories, a fact that surprised me when it happened on a project I was working on. While living in the Arctic and working with the Gwich'in people, I accepted a position in London, England, as the Project Coordinator of the King's Cross Voices Oral History Project, which was to be conducted from 2004 to 2007. I relocated from living north of the Arctic Circle to living in central London. King's Cross is located in central London and it is the last physical and cultural landscape in which you might expect to hear about climate change, because of its seemingly total disconnection with a natural landscape. It is an urban, gritty physical landscape composed of railways, underground stations, Victorian industrial buildings dotted around both King's Cross and St. Pancras International railway stations, around which is woven a series of busy roads in the center of the city. King's Cross is now one of the largest construction sites in Europe and is being completely redeveloped. The goal of the project was to record the memories and experiences of those who had lived and worked in the area before the physical, social, and cultural landscape that was King's Cross was changed and lost forever to the new King's Cross.

As we started to record interviewees who had lived and worked in the area in what finally amounted to 312 interviews for the project, I was struck by a resonance between issues arising in the Gwich'in Elders project and those in the King's Cross project. Many similar issues were at the core of people's stories in both projects, although the physical location and environments could hardly have been more different. The similarities were striking and undeniable, a testimony to how, no matter where in the world we are, as humans we engage with our local environments.

Many people in King's Cross are from other countries and cultures. For many, English is a second, third, or fourth language. Many interviewees in King's Cross felt that their children, who were born in the United Kingdom, had little in common with, and could hardly even communicate with, their grandparents, or sometimes with their parents, who were still living in countries like Bangladesh and Somalia. The Gwich'in Elders had also repeatedly spoken of how their children and grandchildren could not speak the Gwich'in language, as a result of the children being sent to Residential Schools in the past or being taught in English today. Some interviewees in King's Cross, like the Gwich'in Elders, were also saddened that their children could not speak their native tongue. The London parents were troubled, as the Gwich'in Elders were in many cases, that they as parents could not understand the education system or what their children were learning in school, and they felt unable to assist their children with their homework.

For those King's Cross interviewees who were of British origin, what they shared with the Gwich'in Elders was the fact that many of their children had to leave the area (or in the Gwich'in case, leave the communities) to seek work elsewhere. Thus, the grandparents were denied regular visits and felt that they really didn't know their grandchildren. This contrasted sharply with the experiences of the older generations from both locations, who had been raised with multiple generations in the same household (or in the Gwich'in case, in the same seasonal camps). In both projects, many interviewees missed the places they had come from—not just the country, but the physical landscapes. And in some of the interviews at King's Cross, as in those with the Gwich'in Elders, the topic of climate change came up, although unsolicited.

Amid the busy pavement jungle in the heart of London, right behind St. Pancras International Station and King's Cross Station, is Camley Street Natural Park, a beautiful two-acre, internationally acclaimed, wild green space.[42] Susan Jellis, at the time a volunteer interviewer with the project, interviewed Irene Lucas, the first teacher at Camley Street Natural Park, in 2005, and Irene recalled how and why it was created in the early 1980s:

> Back in the 1950s—1960s, [Camley Street] was coal yards and some of the older visitors to the park remember the coal yards and the horses and carts going down the road. The land had been left empty for about twenty years when the GLC, Greater London Council, bought it to make a coach park [parking lot for buses]. There was quite a lot of local opposition to that and with the GLC Ecology unit, with Ken Livingstone at the head, and the fairly new London Wildlife Trust, it was decided to keep this piece of land and develop it into a nature reserve. It was to be the only permanent nature reserve in London. Work started back in 1983, end of 1983, and I started work as a teacher in the beginning of 1984. It was still being created;we had no building, so I was based in a local school in Somers Town and I would meet classes here everyday with a car full of spades, shovels, wheelbarrows, and the local schools were very involved in the creation of this site. For example, when they dug the hole to make the very large pond, we found lots of Victorian pottery, so we had a weekend dig and lots of local people, including the schools, came along and collected the pottery. Every school had their own collection and the then London Wildlife

> Trust, who managed the site, [and] the GLC Landscape architects planned [it] in consultation with the London Wildlife Trust. The first manager of the park was very keen on keeping the local community up-to-date and involved with the creation of the site. So every big thing that happened was open to the public and they were invited to come along and participate. They watched the liner go in the pond, the water go in, planted the trees, seeded the meadows, mulched the site. Although the creation took longer [with public participation], people were in touch with the process. The building arrived on Bonfire night [Guy Fawkes Night, in early November] 1984 and we moved in the following April. May 1985 was the official opening. (archive KXV-2005-049-02)

Fast forward 24 years to Tom Clarke, who is now the manager of the Camley Street Natural Park, and who observes a changing climate in his 2007 interview by Alan Dein:

> *Alan:* The people who created Camley Sreet back in the eighties, it sounds like their experiment has worked?
>
> *Tom:* Y-E-S and N-O! It depends what they were trying to achieve. It's been landscaped well. You could argue that the areas given to each habitat were too small, but it was a 2-acre site. The habitat that has done least well is the woodland. The climate has changed and it's much drier and hotter in the summers now. When you get a drought they are more severe so a lot of our trees are struggling to get beyond twenty or thirty years old, especially in the southern part of the site where there were some hydrological changes when they lowered Goods Way to go underneath St. Pancras. So we had a lot die off there as the water level dropped, because the road dropped as the water level went, we had a lot of trees died off with that. Also, long term we have to think whether woodland is a viable habitat here. Maybe we have to change that to adapt to the changing climate rather than watching all the trees go brown. You monitor it and wait and see and draw up contingencies. (archive KXV-2007-235-01)

This excerpt illustrates how, although the interviewer was talking about the creation of an urban park 24 years prior to the interview and about the management of it today, the effects of climate change and human-induced change creep into the conversation without being solicited. The King's Cross Voices Oral History Project's mandate was to work with the community members and local partners to record people's memories and life experiences in the area. The bulk of the project ran from 2004 until 2007, and it was finally completed in 2008.[43] This project was not aimed at documenting climate change or at a specifically changing natural landscape, yet these topics were very much part of the above interviews of people who had been involved with this two-acre section of King's Cross.

Through my review of the above projects, I hope to have demonstrated how oral history and recorded traditional knowledge in existing archives can be an untapped resource for indicators of change both in the natural environment and in the social fabrics of communities. Many people may have already unknowingly contributed to the oral history of landscape and climate change. I would argue that as a result of the ardent collection of community oral history since the Second World War, many audiocassettes and transcripts need to be digitized and placed into easily searchable databases, because they already contain information that can be used today in a variety of new and innovative projects.

Books that make use of such collections are beginning to be published. A case in point is the recent work of anthropologist Julie Cruikshank entitled *Do Glaciers Listen? Local Knowledge, Colonial Encounters and Social Imagination.*[44] Cruikshank shares with us an event that has echoed with her and has reverberated in her work since. While attending a conference in the Yukon in 1982, she experienced the following, as she reports in her book:

> Mrs. Annie Ned, then her late eighties, unexpectedly rose from her seat late in the afternoon to inject: "Where do you people come from?" she asked us all. "Outside? You people talk from paper. I want to talk from Grandpa." She then proceeded to speak about human and environmental history from her own experience of hunting, trapping and living there for almost a century. Her advice to "listen for different stories" has stayed with me.[45]

Thus in *Do Glaciers Listen?* Cruikshank listens to different stories as she reviews oral histories along with travelers' journals and colonial documents. She eloquently details how the aboriginal view of glaciers, which are animate and respond to human behavior in the aboriginal oral histories, conflicts with the notions of the Europeans, who believed they were an inanimate subject for empirical investigation and measurement. She argues that: "These stories may originate in the past but they continue to resonate with contemporary debates about history, science and colonial practices as well as with current struggles surrounding environmentalism, land rights, nationhood and national parks."[46]

In reviewing these assorted histories, how the glaciers have changed over the past 300 years is also revealed, an important marker for monitoring the way the glaciers are changing today as a result of climate change. Buried in oral history archives are oral histories that, although perhaps recorded for other purposes, give us background and clues to environmental changes occurring in the world today.

Acknowledgments

Leslie would like to thank Ingrid Kritsch, the Gwich'in Social and Cultural Institute, Tero Mustonen, and the Snowchange Cooperative for providing documents and assistance in the writing of this article. Many thanks also to Patricia Veltman for permission to use her photos of Igloolik.

Notes

1. Paul Nadasdy, *Hunters and Bureaucrats. Power, Knowledge and Aboriginal–State Relations in the Southwest Yukon* (Vancouver: UBC Press, 2003), 9, 10.
2. Gwich'in Social and Cultural Institute. *Gwich'in Traditional Knowledge: Study of the Mackenzie Gas Project Area* (Inuvik: Gwich'in Social and Cultural Institute, 2005), 15. Henceforth referred to as Gwich'in Social and Cultural Institute, *Gwich'in Traditional Knowledge.*
3. The Gwich'in Social and Cultural Institute has developed a more elaborate definition of Gwich'in Traditional knowledge, which it defines as: "that body of knowledge, values, beliefs and practices passed from one generation to another by oral means or through learned experience, observation and spiritual teachings, and pertains to the identity, culture and heritage of the Gwich'in. This body of knowledge reflects many millennia of living on the land. It is a system of classification, a set of empirical observations about the local environment and a system of self-management that governs the use of researchers and defines the relationship of living beings with one another with their environment" (Gwich'in Social and Cultural Institute, *Gwich'in Traditional Knowledge,* 15)
4. Paul Thompson *The Voice of the Past: Oral History*, 3rd edition (Oxford and New York: Oxford Univ. Press, 2000), 1.
5. "ELOKA," last modified August 30, 2010, http://www.eloka-arctic.org/about /index. (accessed August 30, 2010)
6. "National Snow and Ice Data Centre, Arctic Sea Ice News and Analysis," last modified August 30, 2010, http://nsidc.org/arcticseaicenews/ (accessed August 30, 2010).
7. The Mackenzie Gas Project proposes to develop natural gas fields in the Mackenzie Delta. The proposed pipeline system will stretch 1,196 kilometres (741 miles) from the Mackenzie Delta along the Mackenzie Valley in Canada's Northwest Territories. It will cross the traditional lands of the Inuvialuit, Gwich'in, and North and South Slavey peoples. Should the pipeline system be built, it will connect to existing pipeline systems in Alberta, thus connecting northern onshore gas fields with the North American markets. More information about the project can be found at http:// www.mackenziegasproject.com (accessed July 13, 2011). On March 10, 2011 the National Energy Board (NEB) issued a Certificate of Public Convenience and Necessity for the Mackenzie Valley Pipeline along with approvals for the other parts of the project. Although 270 conditions were attached to the decision, the Board believes that when combined with the project design, concerns regarding the environment impacts will be addressed. For more information see http://www .mackenziegasproject.com/moreInformation/upload/Issue%2015%20April%20 2011%20MGP_SF.pdf (accessed July, 13, 2011).
8. Gwich'in Social and Cultural Institute, *Gwich'in Traditional Knowledge,* 9, 10.
9. Northwest Territories Education, Culture and Employment, *Revitalizing, Enhancing and Promoting Aboriginal Languages. Strategies for Supporting Aboriginal Languages* (Yellowknife: Government of the Northwest Territories, 2001), 11.
10. Gwich'in Social and Cultural Institute, *Into the Next Millennium: The Five-Year Plan of the Gwich'in Social and Cultural Institute 1996-2001,* 16.

11. Gwich'in Social and Cultural Institute, *Gwich'in Traditional Knowledge,* 6. The proponents of the Mackenzie Gas Projected included Imperial Oil, the Aboriginal Pipeline Group (APG), ConocoPhillips, Shell Canada, and ExxonMobil. The study was funded by Imperial Oil and funded through the Mackenzie Project Environmental Group (MPEG). MPEG is composed of AMEC Earth and Environmental, Kavik-AXYS Environmental Ltd., Tera Environmental, and Golder Associates Ltd.
12. Gwich'in Social and Cultural Institute, *Gwich'in Traditional Knowledge,* 6. The Mackenzie Valley Resource Management Act, the Canadian Environmental Assessment Act, the National Energy Board Act, Gwich'in Land Claim Settlement Act, Inuvialiut Final Agreement, Sahtu Dene and Métis Land Claim Settlement Act all required compliance with regulatory requirements for using Traditional Knowledge in an environment and socio-economic impact process assessment.
13. Gwich'in Social and Cultural Institute, *Gwich'in Traditional Knowledge,* 7.
14. Ibid., 7, 20.
15. Ibid., 7.
16. Ibid., 7.
17. Ibid., 7, 21.
18. Ibid., 10.
19. Ibid., 10.
20. Ibid., 24.
21. Ibid., 28.
22. Ibid., 37.
23. Ibid., 62.
24. Ibid., 62.
25. Ibid., 63.
26. Ibid., 63.
27. Ibid., 85.
28. Ibid., 130.
29. Ibid., 131.
30. Ibid., 85. Ibid., 90.
31. Ibid., 90.
32. Ibid., 180.
33. Tero Mustonen, "Reflections on the Proposed Indigenous Peoples Climate Change Assessment," paper presented at Selkie Village, North Karelia, Finland, July 21, 2008. Henceforth referred to as Mustonen, "Reflections."
34. The scientific priority of Snowchange is currently in the following areas of the North: The Saami territories of Finland, Russia, Sweden and Norway; Murmansk Region in the Republics of Karelia and Sakha-Yakutia, Russian Federation; Savo, North Karelia and Kainuu, Finland; Iceland and Faroe Islands; British Columbia; Northwest Territories and Nunavut, Canada; Alaska, US (Mustonen "Reflections," 2008, 1). Tero Mustonen, "Eternal Kantele at the End of Time—Reflections on Retraditionalization of Traditional Knowledge in the Face of Rapid Ecological Changes in the Arctic" (paper presented at the 4th NRF (Northern Research Forum) Meeting, Oulu, Finland and Lulea, Sweden, October 5–8, 2006). For a map of the Arctic region see http://www.athropolis.com/map2.htm, accessed November 4, 2010.

35. Tero Mustonen, "Eternal Kantele" (see previous note).
36. Tero Mustsonen and Elina Helande, eds. *Snowscapes, Dreamscapes—A Snowchange Community Book on Community Voices in Change. The Snowchange Project* (Finland: Tampere Polytechnic, 2004). Henceforth referred to as Mustonen, *Snowscapes.*
37. Ibid.
38. The chapter is "Silaga Nauk?—Where Is My Weather?" by John Macdonald, in Mustonen, *Snowscapes,* 197–216.
39. The Inullariit Society won the 1998 Northern Science Award for its oral history work; see website for more comprehensive discussion of the project: http://dsp-psd.pwgsc.gc.ca/Collection/R102-4-2001-2E.pdf (accessed November 4, 2010).
40. John Macdonald, "Silaga Nauk?—Where Is My Weather?" in Mustonen, *Snowscapes* (Finland: Tampere Polytechnic, 2004), 197–216.
41. Mark Riley and David Harvey, "Oral Histories, Farm Practice and Uncovering Meaning in the Countryside," *Social & Cultural Geography* 8:3 (2007), 391–415.
42. "Camley Street Natural Park," last modified August 20, 2010, http://www.wildlondon.org.uk/Naturereserves/CamleyStreetNaturalPark/tabid/124/Default.aspx (accessed November 4, 2010).
43. The King's Cross Voices Oral History Project was funded by The Heritage Lottery Fund and the London Boroughs of Camden and Islington.
44. Julie Cruikshank, *Do Glaciers Listen? Local Knowledge, Colonial Encounters, and Social Imagination* (Vancouver: UBC Press, 2005).
45. Ibid., 9.
46. Ibid.

Archival material provided by:

Gwich'in Social and Cultural Institute, Archival Holdings, Yellowknife, NWT, Canada.

King's Cross Voices Oral History Project, Camden Local Studies and Archives, London Borough of Camden, London, UK.

Websites

"Snowchange," http://www.snowchange.org/ last modified August 25, 2010 (accessed July 13, 2011).

"Map of the Arctic," http://www.athropolis.com/map2.htm last modified 1/13/2010 (accessed September 4, 2010).

"Igloolik Place of Iglus," http://www.qia.ca/i18n/english/communications/commprofiles/igloolik.html last modified 2006 (accessed January 13, 2010).

"The Igloolik Oral History Project," http://dsp-psd.pwgsc.gc.ca/Collection/R102-4-2001-2E.pdf last modified January 13, 2010 (accessed September, 4, 2010)

http://nome.unak.is/nome2/issues/vol3_1/mustonen.pdf (accessed September 4, 2010).

"Mackenzie Gas Project," http://www.mackenziegasproject.com (accessed August 25, 2010).

PART 3

Introduction: Audience and New Technologies

Part 3 develops an interrogation of the oral history interview itself, building on observations developed earlier in the volume. Part 1 traced how the traditional association between orality and locality was disrupted and reconfigured as local voices were written down and transmitted to wider audiences, and part 2 considered new kinds of relationships between oral history and locality. Oral history enables local knowledge to be recorded and transmitted to wider audiences in oral form, rather than necessarily being transformed through writing. Part 3 continues to demonstrate how oral history can generate knowledge about particular localities, while it also considers how the oral history interview is itself a located activity, which depends on a listener or audience, and which need not necessarily take place as a one-to-one conversation, but can be staged in public. Interviews can themselves be considered located performances, while artistic practices and new technologies offer new ways of making projects public, and of moving them into a wider sphere.

Heike Roms and Rebecca Edwards in chapter 8 explore the history of performance art at specific locations in Wales. This chapter discusses how the authors' research project, "An Oral History of Performance Art in Wales," aims to utilize oral history's potential to uncover "lost histories," in this case histories of marginalized performances, via conversations with artists who have shaped the development of Welsh performance art since the mid-1960s. The conversations were staged publicly to call attention to the performative nature of the interview situation, and a number of these conversations were devoted to the question of locality and site. Site-specific performance work has a long history in Wales. In their attempts to document "live" performances, Roms and Edwards show how oral history can overcome some of the limits of written archives, giving us access to less-well-documented, nonmetropolitan, local scenes of art-making. Roms and Edwards also consider how written and oral sources can be used alongside each other to explore the complex way in which memory interacts with archival remains. Such remains of performances include the sites where they first took place, some of which were revisited in interviews and acted as triggers for memory and narrative. From the revisitations, there emerges a picture of the network of venues (and people) that supported performance work in the Welsh city of Cardiff. This picture is filled out further by encouraging audiences and others involved in performances to locate their memories on a large, walkable map of Cardiff.

Toby Butler's chapter continues to consider the experiences of audiences, but here the focus is on audiences/walkers who took part in two oral history trails or *memoryscapes,* in this case funded by the Museum of London with the goal of giving an insight into the recent history of the Thames riverscape. Chapter 9 explores the walker's point of view, using questionnaire responses and postwalk interviews. As Butler points out, location-based media have become increasingly popular and now reach a mass market through equipment such as the iPhone, and interest in sound walks or audio trails also continues to grow, but there has been relatively little qualitative evaluation of sound-walk practice from the point of view of the listener, so this chapter helps to fill the gap. It examines the way oral history, memory, sound, and the creative practice of the audio walk intersect with the listeners' experience and push at the boundaries of their sense of place. By making available the sound of the voices of local residents, for example, Butler proposes that oral history can encourage empathy, partly by challenging stereotypical views of people, because listeners cannot rely on the visual clues that they tend to use to rapidly make assumptions when first meeting someone, such as dress, home decoration, and body language. In doing so, Butler hopes that the memoryscapes avoid a problematic voyeuristic gaze, a gaze that can be characteristic of tourism. By encouraging empathy and understanding as well as providing information about the river's history, the voices give walkers a sense of connection with the locality. More than just a scenic landscape, the *Drifting* trail, in particular, challenges preconceptions about the river Thames and its people, by emphasizing its working-class, industrial history, which can provide a basis for further inquiry into the problems of industrial closure.

Like chapter 4 by Trower and chapter 5 by Thompson in part 2 of this collection, Butler's chapter (chapter 9), and especially Steven High's chapter (chapter 10), consider postindustrial localities. All four chapters incorporate the experiences and thoughts of industrial workers to varying degrees. Butler's and High's projects in particular provide alternatives to touristic and nostalgic views through the public dissemination of the oral history interviews in the form of sound trails and websites. High observes the growing number of research projects that have sought to bring mobility into the research process, encouraging scholars to engage with the materiality of built and natural environments, and involving such location-aware technologies as GIS (geographic information systems) mapping and GPS (global positioning systems). In this geographical context, High discusses his own project, an online memoryscape of a closed and demolished paper mill in Sturgeon Falls, Ontario. In the wake of the mill's closure, his team conducted 70 interviews with former workers, interviews that revealed a deep connection to the mill, as generations of family members had worked within its walls. Life-history interviewing provided an opportunity to explore the cultural meaning of displacement from the viewpoint of those most directly involved: the workers themselves.

With the help of the mill's blueprint and many photographs and documents gleaned from former workers, the author created a millscape, and peoples' stories were reconnected to the factory floor. Visitors can tour the mill virtually, traveling from one area to the next, hearing audio clips telling of work process, camaraderie, labor–management relations, workplace accidents, closures, and acts of resistance. High raises an interesting question, however, concerning whether an exclusively online memoryscape can immerse its listeners in place in the same way as a located memoryscape such as Butler's can do. He indicates that Internet and other "global" media may not always be the best way of reaching listeners, or of engaging with audiences, and that there is value—or there are different kinds of values—in operating on different levels, ranging from the local to the relatively global. Without endorsing the use of global media for the sake of it, then, High's project in a sense brings together the local and global: it is purposefully located in a specific place within a town in Ontario (a paper mill that is now destroyed and that has been recreated virtually), and at the same time it is disseminated on the World Wide Web to audiences located in an infinite number of places.

CHAPTER 8

Oral History as Site-Specific Practice: Locating the History of Performance Art in Wales

Heike Roms and Rebecca Edwards

Oral history's multifaceted connection with place, this chapter proposes, comes into sharper view when we look at it through the optic of performance. Oral history, place, and performance maintain a dynamic connection with each other that is mutually illuminating. This essay considers some implications of this connection by drawing on the example of our current research project, funded by the United Kingdom's Arts and Humanities Research Council, which has made extensive use of oral history in an attempt to engage with the history of performance practice in a particular local context. Under the title "'It Was Forty Years Ago Today...': Locating the Early History of Performance Art in Wales 1965–1979"[1] the project—for which, as the title implies, questions of place are of major significance—has employed different approaches to the placing of its oral history conversations: these include conversations staged in public, *in-situ* interviews, and installations that aim to locate audiences' memories. Underlying all three approaches is the proposition that oral history interviews can be regarded as instances of located performance, or even site-specific performance. We will argue that to foreground the performative dimension of an oral history conversation in this manner directs our attention more closely to the influence that its location exerts on the construction of its narrative. The ways in which artists have made use of performance's material bond with its setting can hereby serve as models for developing new ways of locating oral history conversations. And these new ways may help to create an oral history that, by being responsive to the sites where it takes place, offers in turn new insights into the contextual nature of performance.

Performing Oral Histories, and Oral Histories of Performance

Scholars of performance are increasingly drawn to oral history as an allied discipline with a mutual interest in the live encounter. In her introduction to *Remembering: Oral History Performance*, an edited collection that charts the many connections between oral history and performance, Della Pollock speaks of the unique synergy that the two fields enjoy: "Oral historians and performance scholars/practitioners are increasingly discovering shared and complementary investments in orality, dialogue, life stories, and community-building or what might more generally be called *living* history."[2] Indeed, oral history can itself be regarded as an instance of performance. Linda Shopes and Bruce M. Stave propose in the same volume, "As many oral historians know intuitively, the telling of stories is inherently performative: an interviewee puts on a show, creates an identity, within the context of talking to the interviewer."[3] Whilst such theatrical role-play for an interviewer-as-audience may have traditionally been thought of as getting in the way of a "truthful" account, it now emerges as that which constitutes the very nature of an oral form of historical evidence.

Jeff Friedman argues that oral history "is a performance that includes both the local embodied social situation and a more public and official historical posterity for whom the narrators stage their experiences. This additional layer requires a complex public performance from both the interviewer and narrator within the oral history event."[4] Taking a cue from performance studies, Friedman here moves beyond mere analogies with theatrical role-play toward a broader concept of performance as a form of structured behavior that involves both interviewee and interviewer as co-performers in an embodied, spatio-temporal encounter. From such encounters, oral history narratives emerge as contingent "truths" that are always dependent on the manner of their staging. Yet, as Friedman proposes, oral history's "staging" is not limited to the live exchange between interviewer and interviewee. Similarly, Ronald J. Grele suggests that in any oral history interview, the narrative is shaped by the awareness of the interviewee that "he [sic] not only speaks to himself and to the interviewer, but he also speaks through the interviewer to a larger community and its history as he views it."[5] Therefore, to approach an oral history interview as performance, we want to argue, implies first that one needs to be mindful of the particular *mise-en-scène* of the encounter between interviewer and interviewee. But second, it also urges us to be attentive to the manner in which this initial encounter prepares for the future encounters that various audiences may have with it (Friedman's "historical posterity")–in short, to be attentive to how oral history stages itself for its different audiences in the present and the future.[6]

Given the unique synergy and structural similarities between performance and oral history, it is perhaps little wonder that a considerable number of oral history projects have of late turned their attention to the particular histories of performance, especially those of the theatre and related artistic practices. Susan Croft, in a recent survey of such projects in the United Kingdom, concludes that

> the use of oral history to record aspects of British theatre history is a growing and widespread one... [Oral histories of theatre and performance] cover a whole range of material from theatre buildings to amateur theatre companies of long standing to the big companies, with their own archives, like Royal Opera House and the National Theatre, to contemporary queer performance festivals.[7]

Among these—both in Britain and elsewhere—are an increasing number that focus on so-called experimental, non-mainstream, or avant-garde performance work. Croft herself currently conducts an oral history of the British alternative theatre movement from 1968–1988, entitled "Unfinished Histories."[8] A similar focus, albeit filtered through the perspective of having been themselves key contributors to this history, is shared by Roger Ely and Cindy Oswin, who have both undertaken interviews with fellow theater and performance artists of the period. And "Towards an Oral History of Performance and Live Art in the British Isles"[9] has addressed the same field of artistic practice, but with a primary interest in exploring methodological approaches.[10] If Croft is right in stating that "more traditional, text-based forms of British theatre were perceived to be adequately documented through conventional means," leading to a situation in which "oral histories of theatre have been slower to emerge,"[11] it is not surprising that non-traditional forms of theater and performance have conversely been drawn to oral history as a method for engaging with their pasts.

The embodied and dialogic dimension of the oral history interview is considered especially productive with regard to artistic practices that have eschewed traditional dramatic narrative in favor of other forms of telling, most notably through physical expression, and that have frequently replaced the single author with collaborative creations (or, in the case of solo artists, have shown a greater awareness of the dependency of their performance work on the audience's collaborative act of witnessing). Such practices, the argument goes, have in the past been overlooked, marginalized, or insufficiently documented by scholarship focused on the written word and the singularity of the author–creator. The scholarly currency of these practices, however, has risen considerably over recent years, and interest in the experimental performance work of the 1960s and 1970s is especially strong, as evidenced by the aforementioned projects. This interest is further boosted by the fact that the artist generation that originated this work more than forty years ago is beginning to disappear, which has added greater urgency to the recording of its memories.

An aspect that is shared by all the listed projects is that they have been initiated by individuals who have come to oral history from performance rather than the other way round.[12] Their commitment to performance has led many of them to make particular use of the performative dimension of oral history, contributing to a growing self-reflexivity in the field concerning the performative methodologies of oral history work. Perhaps a little surprisingly for performance practitioners, this generally does not affect the staging of the interview event itself, which in most cases takes place in the familiar oral history format of an intimate face-to-face encounter. Rather, it affects the staging of its afterlives, as several projects use the interview as material for the generation of new performance work. Cindy Oswin's "On the Fringe" (2005–present),[13] for example, is a "performance lecture" on the history of the British alternative theater movement in the 1970s and 1980s that makes extensive use of excerpts from Oswin's interviews with fellow artists from the period.[14] Such performative approaches to the history of performance present a subgenre of the wider field of so-called oral history based theater and performance, which turn interview transcripts into dialogue and action for new stage works. Della Pollock has called oral history based theater a form of "re-performance" because it reperforms the "magnitude of the primary interview encounter by expanding it to include other listeners."[15] It attends to what Friedman has identified as oral history's "more public and official historical posterity" by allowing for an audience's repeated encounters with its narration through a variety of formats.

An Oral History of Performance Art in Wales

Our own oral history work has also been concerned in a self-reflexive manner with its performance. In our case, though, it is the staging of the interview event itself that has been at the center of this investigation. Our backgrounds are, respectively, in performance studies and in history, and our interest in oral history methodology emerged in relation to our current joint research project, "'It Was Forty Years Ago Today...': Locating the Early History of Performance Art in Wales 1965–1979." The project is part of a wider investigation into Wales's history of performance art, which Heike launched in 2006 under the umbrella title "What's Welsh for Performance? Beth yw 'performance' yn Gymraeg?" Roughly speaking, *performance art*—as distinguished from theater and the performing arts—evolved principally out of the traditions of fine art in the 1960s, when artists trained in painting and sculpture sought to extend and transgress the limits of their art forms by shifting their attention from the production of objects to the production of events.[16] Artistic practice of this kind has a long tradition in Wales. In 1965, art instructors organized the first "happenings" to occur in this country at Cardiff's National Museum of Wales; a festival of Fluxus art took place in Aberystwyth in 1968; that same year, Welsh painter Ivor Davies responded to the violence of the era with a performance featuring timed explosions and staged amidst similar "Destruction in Art" events at the Swansea University Arts Festival. Throughout the 1970s, from their base in South Wales, sculptor Shirley Cameron and drama graduate Roland Miller explored performance art's twin roots in fine art and experimental theater through their collaboration. New approaches to art teaching using performance as a mode of pedagogy evolved at the Cardiff School of Art and Design and the annual Barry Summer School during the same period. And the National Eisteddfod, the major Welsh-speaking cultural festival, included in Wrexham in 1977 a controversial performance art program involving famous European artists such as Joseph Beuys and Mario Merz, whose contributions were overshadowed by local artist Paul Davies's performative protest against the suppression of the Welsh language. One often searches in vain for traces of these events in accounts of Welsh art history and in publications on international performance art. Performance art in Wales has been twice overlooked: for a long time it represented a marginal art practice in a marginal place.

The attention that our research pays to this hitherto hidden history of performance art in Wales, however, is not meant to identify a distinctive strand of the art form that could be characterized as "Welsh performance art." Nor do we wish to reclaim its manifestations as lost masterworks. On the contrary, we seek to expand on the typical art historical focus on the close analysis of a single (and singular) work of art by attending to the wider context or scene from which such work emerged, and to the local infrastructures and international networks that produced and sustained it. By thus demarcating a limited terrain and considering it in greater detail, we also wish to highlight the manner in which even historical accounts of a genre-transgressing art form such as performance art have tended to restrict themselves to a certain canon of well-documented works (and that often means those created in the metropolises of art production), thereby neglecting local scenes of art-making. Through a case study focus on a multitude of performance activities in a geographically specific, socially and culturally defined place, we aim to examine the ways in which performance art as an artistic movement of international reach and influence was realized in different localized settings during its formative years. In Wales, this setting has been characterized by traditions of political radicalism, a lack of large art institutions, a small and multidisciplinary artistic scene, and a growing activism around issues of language and identity. It became therefore a fertile context for an art form that was ephemeral, interdisciplinary, politically engaged, and direct in its address to audiences. But although particular, Wales was not unique in this: the development of performance art in Wales both mirrored and refracted developments elsewhere.

In order to chart this history, our project combines a number of methodological approaches, most notably extensive archival research, accompanied by the compilation of an online searchable database of performance work that was presented in Wales between 1965 and 1979 by Wales-based and visiting artists (published at www.performance-wales.org), and a series of oral history conversations. We regard these conversations not merely as a way of filling the gaps that the archival record has left open; nor do we regard them as more truthful accounts of the performance work in question. Rather, we aim to subject archival documentation and oral testimonies to a comparative reading in order to examine the respective usefulness of both methods for an understanding of past performance practice. Such a reading can also help to reveal the complex manner in which memory interacts with archival remains in constituting our knowledge of the past. In this task, the performative dimension of the oral history interview becomes an important tool.

Heike has written elsewhere about the manner in which the oral history interview itself performs as a scene of historical evidence, and about what role past audiovisual documentation plays in this *mise-en-scène*.[17] In the following, we want to shift our attention to two related questions: Can we stage oral history conversations in different ways in order to generate different kinds of historical insight? And, what role does the location of the staging play in this *mise-en-scène*? Among the methodologies we have applied for this purpose are: conversations staged in public; in-situ interviews; witness seminar style group reunions at particular sites; reenactments of performances in their original locations; and installations that aim to situate audiences' memories. We have also undertaken more standard "life story" style interviews. What distinguishes these methodologies is, broadly speaking, their varying relationship with the location where the interview event takes place. A number of oral history conversations we have undertaken have been staged at selected sites in Wales that once served as locations for performance works. Such a located approach—what performance studies has termed a *site-specific approach*—has allowed us to go beyond analyzing the history of performance art as a series of individual pieces of work toward exploring its contextual dimensions.

Placing Performance, Locating Oral Histories

The different approaches to locating oral history conversations that we have worked through in our project have been inspired by the ways in which artists have explored and exploited performance's relationship with the places of its staging. One of performance's defining features is, after all, that it can and must "take place"—its embodied, material, interactive practice can only be realized if it is located somewhere. But the manner of this location is complex. In her study *Space in Performance*, Gay McAulay proposes that in traditional theater settings,"the spectator is continually tossed from awareness of... the here of the theatre space, and the (multiple) here of the fictional place(s)."[18] It is from the interplay between these two spatial dimensions and the "continual tossing of the spectator's awareness" between them that theater derives its particular representational strategies and pleasures. Nontraditional performance work, on the other hand, particularly so-called site-specific performance practice, is widely associated with a move away from the spatial conventions of traditional theater or gallery buildings—with their clearly defined separation between the realm of the art and the artists on the one hand and the space of the audience on the other—and into different kinds of sites (including streets, fields, and factories) and thereby into different cultural and communicative relationships.[19] Such a move, however, does not necessarily lead to the abolishment of performance's complex engagement with real and represented locations. Rather, site-specific practice allows for a reconfiguration of their relationship. It situates performance in "real" places[20] and frequently focuses its representations (through stories and actions), as McAuley has pointed out, on "the history and politics of that place."[21] It thus brings the present location into correspondence with (or sometimes in conflict with) its own past, engaging spectators in a playful method of historical inquiry by "tossing their awareness" between these two dimensions.

What then of the specific sites where oral history takes place? Whilst the recent attention to oral history's performative nature has generated extensive engagements with its corporeal elements[22], its located aspect has been less widely discussed. It is often implied, however. If we return, for example, to Friedman's citation at the opening of this chapter, we can infer that oral history also negotiates two spatial dimensions, what Friedman distinguishes as the "local embodied social situation" (the actual place of the interview) and "a more public and official historical posterity" (something like the abstract summation of all the potential locations in which the listening acts of future audiences will have taken place), and that both lay claim to the participants' awareness.[23] Oral history's address to future audiences, which we have identified above as one of its defining features, implies therefore a process of relocation: from the place of a private encounter to the realm of public engagement. To this we may add a third layer—akin to McAuley's represented places—namely, the past location(s) of this history that are evoked in the narration. We would like to propose that, following the example of site-specific performance, a mode of site-specific oral history too can explore and exploit the relationships between these different layers—the place of narration, the narrated place, and the place of an audience's encounter with the narration—in order to perform an historical inquiry that offers different (or additional) insights. We shall discuss how this has worked in practice in the context of our research project in more detail now.

Staging Interviews in Public: "An Oral History of Performance Art in Wales"

From 2006 to 2008, under the title "An Oral History of Performance Art in Wales,"[24] Heike undertook a series of conversations between herself as interviewer and a number of key artists who have shaped the development of performance art in Wales since the mid-1960s. Seven 2-hour conversations focused on a single event (the performance art festival at the National Eisteddfod in Wrexham in 1977); artistic oeuvres (Ivor Davies's "Destruction in Art" work in the late 1960s); Shirley Cameron and Roland Miller's collaborative performance work in the 1970s); institutions (Cardiff School of Art and Design in the 1980s and 1990s; the activities of the Centre for Performance Research); and on scenes (Cardiff's performance scene in the 1970s; contemporary artists' networks in Wales). The theme of place in all its variations emerged repeatedly throughout these talks: Why did artists settle or remain in Wales? What was the local scene like at a particular time? How did artists connect with artistic networks and scenes outside of Wales? How did they choose the places at which they showed their work? How did their work respond to the places at which it was shown? What were the cultural, social, and economic aspects that influenced their performance practice? What was its relationship to local audiences? Did Wales as a geographical or cultural entity have any relevance for their work?

The location in which the conversations were held was the same throughout the series:[25] the so-called Space Workshop at Cardiff School of Art and Design. The Space Workshop was itself an important site for the development of performance art in Wales: in the mid-1970s, Cardiff College of Art (as it was then called) became the first art college in Britain where students could specialize in time-based art (at the time referred to as the "Third Area," which encompassed performance, film, and sound art). It is also here—under the guidance of teachers such as John Gingell, Anthony Howell, and André Stitt—that students have since created a myriad of different performances, and here where in the 1990s the Cardiff Art in Time Festival, under the directorship of Howell, became an important forum for international performance work. This particular location, however, was only explicitly referred to once during the series of conversations that made up "An Oral History of Performance Art in Wales." In his interview about the history of performance at the school, Howell discussed several performances that he had witnessed in the space. He seemed to use the architecture of the room to call up from his memory the details of these works, evidently locating them imaginatively within the outlines of the present space.

> When I started...I asked for students to do a morning workshop...I think it paid off because people became really keen on quite difficult disciplinary acts inside their own performances, and they had the stamina and the sense that you could demand something of yourself...there was one girl...very, very good performer who used to love tying herself up in knots from which she herself could not untie herself...The point was that nobody else could tie her up, she had to self-inflict her inability to move. Her final piece was to erect a wall of lockers here [*points to the right hand corner of the Space Workshop*], get from the lockers to chains from which she dangled with her arms through the rings and then kick away the lockers. If she'd been left there she would have just starved to death. But she had put herself there. And then there was absolutely no instructions as to how to get her down. It was only through the good offices of other students saying "we'd better get Clare down." It was terrific, so much thought and guts had gone into it. I think that came out of that discipline, every morning working at action ideas, really taking action as seriously as a painter takes painting every day.[26]

Although "An Oral History of Performance Art in Wales" was not site-specific in the narrow sense, as it did not generally (with the exception of Howell's interview above) match the locations referred to in the conversations with the locations at which the conversations took place, the project was nonetheless attentive to the specifics of oral history's relationship to place. The series attempted to bring together the place of narration and the audience's encounter with it in the same space at the same time. This was done by staging the conversations as public events in front of a live audience; they attracted an average of about one hundred people per event (see Figure 1).

There were several implications that arose from thus breaking with the oral history convention of conducting interviews as one-to-one conversations in the intimacy of a private, mostly domestic setting. First, a domestic setting might seem the most straightforward and pragmatic choice, but it also privileges particular readings. It might lead one to believe, for example, that here we may be able to get a "truer" picture of the artist as a private person, beyond his or her public persona, whereas, as many have argued before, private and public memories are both the products of complex cultural mediations.

Second, the audience at the conversations also included collaborators on or witnesses of the past performances under discussion, and these people were encouraged to add their own memories, either orally or through written contributions. The artist's narration was consequently treated as one version (and an

Figure 1 "An Oral History of Performance Art in Wales," public conversation about the international performance program that took place at the National Eisteddfod in Wrexham 1977; John Chris Jones, Timothy Emlyn Jones, and Andrew Knight, interviewed by Heike Roms in Cardiff, February 22, 2007. Photo: Phil Babot.

important one) but not the only possible version of events, even where the artist's "own" work was concerned.

As Pollock and others have argued, oral history narratives do not "belong" to the teller, as such histories are always part of a wider cultural "forcefield of relationality."[27] This is especially true of narratives relating to performance art, as such art work is deeply contingent on its relationship with an audience. But just as in performance, where generally the very fact of an audience's presence, rather than the presence of specific individuals, impacts on the work, so in the conversations too, we propose, it was less the attendance of specific former eye-witnesses than the very fact of the conversations being staged in front of a public that influenced their performance. By inviting an audience to the conversations, the project attempted to make the usual "historical posterity," the wider audience community to which an oral history addresses itself, an actual co-presence in the same space as the interview itself. This helped to foreground the performative qualities of oral history, its contingency on the situation of its staging, its dialogic nature, its repetitive structure, and its public address. We recognize that such an approach is not suitable for all oral history work, as it may put some interviewees who are not familiar with speaking in public under undue pressure to perform. But in the case of artists, who are often used to accounting for their life and work in lectures, writings, or in interviews, and who have available to them the interpretations of their work through critics, such an approach can help to unsettle a little the usual perspective that these artists take on their work and can allow for new insights to emerge.

More than having an impact on the narration, however, we wanted the opportunity to utilize the public nature of the conversations to involve an audience with the narration in a manner that was essentially collective. It helped to engage audiences very directly in its historical constructions by performing such constructions live in front of them. And it turned private memories instantly into shared histories, and located performance art in Wales into a public space of debate and increased recognition.

It may be important to add here that "An Oral History of Performance Art in Wales" did not completely do away with the relocated "historical posterity" of the interview, with all that such posterity is able to offer in terms of a more considered critical reflection made from the distanced perspective of historical hindsight. The transcripts from the interviews have been published in book form,[28] and the video and audio recordings of all conversations will be made available in a selection of archives and oral history collections.[29]

In-situ Interviews: Revisiting Sites of Performance in Wales

"An Oral History of Performance Art in Wales" served as a pilot project for our current, more comprehensive research enquiry, "'It Was Forty Years Ago Today...': Locating the Early History of Performance Art in Wales 1965–1979." This enquiry has again made use of oral history and related conversational methods in a manner that has tried to harness their performative dimension. "'It Was Forty Years Ago Today...'" more specifically focuses on the origins and formative years of performance art in the 1960s and 1970s, a time of substantial artistic creativity and political radicalism. Methodologically, "'It Was Forty Years Ago Today'" has advanced a number of approaches that emerged from the earlier oral history work. These include the format of group interviews in the style of a "witness seminar," which has proven especially productive when referring to a single event or to a clearly defined scene, as it allows for multiperspective views of a particular set of circumstances. We have become increasingly interested in situating oral history conversations in locations that have an actual connection with their narrative. In the case of some of the group interviews we have undertaken, for example, participants have been reunited not only around a common event or scene, but also at a place that played a significant role in the history that they have been asked to recall.[30] This approach has been developed more fully into what we term *in-situ interviews.*

In-situ interviews take artists, administrators, and audience members back to the locations where they once made or witnessed performance work. The interviewee is brought back to the places that his or her memories revisit imaginatively, bringing into correspondence the place of the narration with the narrated place, or, in other words, bringing together the past and the present of a location. We have investigated two main manifestations of this approach. One focuses on a single location; for example, we have undertaken a series of in-situ interviews with different interviewees at Chapter Arts Centre in Cardiff, a key location for the history of performance art in Wales. Another manifestation concentrates on taking an interviewee to a series of connected places. Our intention with regard to the latter has been to explore how such an approach might assist our understanding of the infrastructural and contextual aspects of performance work, which by definition exceed the focus on one place alone.

To give an example: in November 2009, Mike Pearson, an artist and performance studies scholar, revisited the venues in Cardiff where he could remember watching and making performance work in the late 1960s and early 1970s.[31] Pearson came to Cardiff from Lincolnshire in 1968 to study archaeology, but soon became involved in performance, devising work, helping to stage other artists' work, and attending a range of performances that were shown in a variety of venues. Challenged to identify the main locations where performance art and related art practices occurred in the Welsh capital during this period, Pearson came up with seven sites (see Figure 2). These included a lecture theater in the former Arts Block of Cardiff University (now the Law Building), where in the late 1960s students put on a show by the Pip Simmons Group (in less-than-appropriate architectural conditions); the School of Engineering, where the late Geoffrey Axworthy programed a season of experimental theater in the early 1970s, before he became director of the university's newly built Sherman Theatre; the Sherman Theatre, which opened in 1973; the former Casson Theatre, now the Rubicon Dance School; Llanover Hall in Canton, home to numerous performance workshops and summer schools; and Chapter Arts Centre, still Cardiff's premier venue for contemporary art.

As happened in the aforementioned conversation with Anthony Howell, the various locations of these in-situ interviews often functioned as a trigger that helped Pearson to summon the memories of events that occurred in them. But the locatedness of these interviews also served a wider purpose. As Michel de Certeau has proposed, stories have the unique ability to "traverse and organize places; they select and link them together; they make sentences and itineraries out of them. They are spatial trajectories."[32] From the revisits and the stories they engendered, a picture of the complex and diverse ecology of venues (and people) that supported performance work in Wales in the late 1960s and 1970s emerged, as well as their organization and connection.

The frequent assumption is that performance art, as an innovative and radical art form, developed primarily outside of institutions. But the in-situ conversations with Pearson revealed that this is not the complete picture. The performance

Figure 2 In-situ interview by Heike Roms with Mike Pearson, Cardiff, November 27, 2009. Pearson revisited the main locations where performance art and related art practices occurred in the Welsh capital during the 1960s and 1970s. Photos: Heike Roms.

scene in Wales (like performance scenes elsewhere during that period) quickly began to develop its own institutions or, better put perhaps, its own infrastructure, which was made up of people, buildings, and a range of financial and social support systems.

As we have suggested above, the very material, spatio-temporal nature of performance demands that it "takes place." Performance artists have often been at the forefront of taking possession of new buildings in the name of art, or of placing their work in contexts that had no previous history of art-making. Of course, an oral history interview could have imaginatively revisited these locations and could have narrated their stories without actually going there. But by being in situ, the interviews also made manifest the changes that the locations had since undergone. Venues had changed their name, their purpose, their architecture, or had disappeared altogether. By thus connecting current places in Cardiff with the memories of their former manifestations of forty years ago, the in-situ interview helped to bring the specific local conditions and spatial extensions of both the historical and the contemporary scene into sharper focus.[33]

The in-situ interviews, unlike the public conversations, address themselves primarily to a potential historical posterity in the form of transcripts and recordings, rather than involving a copresent audience. However, we intend to rethink the ways in which performative forms of engagement can help to reshape an audience's encounter with the documents of oral history. In the case of the in-situ interviews, some of the recordings will be transformed into audio guides, which audiences can take to the locations in question.[34] Not only is this intended to enhance an audience's engagement with and enjoyment of the recorded oral histories, we also hope that it will encourage listeners to perform for themselves the form of located historical inquiry that these interviews represented, comparing and contrasting the narrated past with the physical present.[35]

Locating Audiences' Memories: "Mapping Performance Art in Cardiff"

One feature that characterized the public conversation series was its primary focus on the testimony of artists (and that of a few administrators). Although audiences were encouraged to add their own memories, it was the makers of the work that were the actual interviewees. As Robert Proctor has proposed, with regard to oral history interviews with architects, interviews with makers inherently privilege an authorial concept of an artist's role and often hope to gain a direct access to an artist's intention.[36] It is a perspective that is difficult to get away from, though. We are used to referring to the artist as the main authority on his or her work, even in relation to an art form such as performance art, where artistic intention is often very different from its realization and the notion of authorship is challenged by the collaborative presence of an audience. Yet, there admittedly was nothing inherently structural about the public conversation approach that would have prevented the interviewing of someone whose involvement with performance work in Wales had been primarily as an audience member. There were other reasons why this did not occur, which have to do with the particularities of staging performance art. Often audiences encounter works of performance art by accident, or, if they encounter them voluntarily, few records of their attendance are kept; at least such records weren't usually available for the time period that concerned us in our research. Performance art may be adept at creating its own infrastructures, but such infrastructures are often fluid and discontinuous. Whilst it is often not difficult to find a regular past attendee at a civic theater or gallery with the help of historical box-office records or mailing lists, locating audiences who have a history of seeing performance art work with some degree of continuity proves to be more challenging. We have begun to identify persons who witnessed certain performance events in Wales, with the help of local newspapers and social networking websites, but the process is time-consuming.

Furthermore, the comprehensive nature of an oral history interview is only really suitable for audience members whose experiences of performance art have been comparatively substantial. But what of the majority of audience members who have only vague memories of events caught out of the corner of their eye? We tried to engage with such memories through an interactive installation setup, which encouraged audiences to contribute their reminiscences, however small or imprecise, to a collaborative effort at remembering. Although not oral history in the strict sense, the approach nonetheless had at its core a conversational relationship that centered upon the oral narration of a history or histories. "Mapping Performance Art in Cardiff"[37] was shown on October 19, 2008, at Chapter Arts Centre in Cardiff, as part of its annual Experimentica performance art festival. Audiences were invited to share their memories of performance work in Cardiff over the last fifty years by locating them on a large, walkable map of the city. The idea for this approach again emerged out of the public conversation series. That series tested several ways of encouraging audiences at the conversations to part with their memories of performance work. Archive record cards were distributed with a request to fill them in, after-talk questions and feedback were actively solicited. But by far the greatest response was generated when audiences were asked to locate their memories on a small Ordnance Survey map of Wales.[38] It appeared to be much easier for people to remember where an event occurred than when it occurred, and the focus on the map seemed to lessen the pressure to have to recall with accuracy the details of their memories.

For "Mapping Performance Art in Cardiff," artist Kasia Coleman created an elegant, minimalist map of the center of Cardiff: the main roads and major buildings were outlined in pencil, waterways were marked out in tracing paper, and parklands appeared in grey cardboard (see Figure 3). The map, approximately 4.5 by 3 meters (14.6 by 9.75 feet) in size, was placed on the floor in one of Chapter Art Centre's performance spaces. It was surrounded with printouts from our archive, including a selection of 40 events from forty years of performance-making in Cardiff, and had a small viewing station, where visitors could watch the video documentation of the public conversation series. The project's online database, which records details of more than 2000 events of performance art in Wales, was also made available. The installation was open to the public for 8 hours from 2 p.m. to 10 p.m. It was advertised with the help of Chapter's Art Centre's monthly events brochure and Experimentica festival marketing, via specialist electronic mailing lists, on a number of relevant websites, and with leaflets that were distributed in and around Chapter on the day.

A number of visitors came especially for this event, including some that brought documentation of past performances with them to share. Others came across the installation as they were browsing other festival events or simply walking through the building. Around 100 visitors attended the event during the course of the day; some stayed only briefly, without making an active contribution, and some

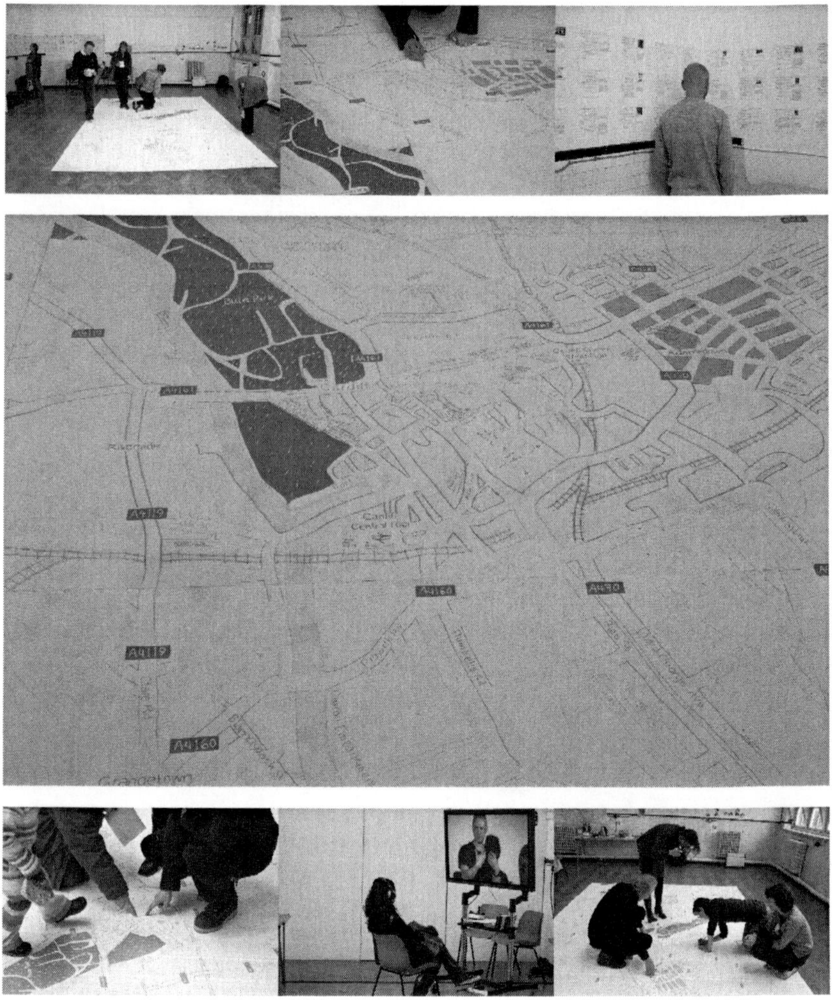

Figure 3 Visitors mapping remembered sites of performance art in Cardiff, October 19, 2008. Photos: Daniel Ladnar.

merely browsed or observed. But the majority contributed at least one memory to the map, with some visitors staying for several hours, drawing and discussing. Heike was present throughout the day, welcoming people as they entered the space, introducing the idea of the project, and engaging visitors in conversations about their memories. She was carrying an audio recording device, which recorded all conversations, and two video cameras filmed the activities on the map and in the space. The map was photographed at the end of the day, and photographs, video, and audio recordings were subsequently edited together for a short film documentation of the project, which has been shown at a number of art events since.[39]

Initially, the intention was for people to use the map merely as a reference and to write down their memories of performances they had encountered in Cardiff on a stack of archive cards that had been made available. But as soon as the first visitors entered the space, they stepped onto the map right away and started writing directly onto it. They jotted down memories, made little drawings, and gradually filled in the smaller streets and buildings that had been left out of the original version of the map. Most importantly, these activities became a conduit for dialogue–transforming the map into a tour, as De Certeau (citing a study by Charlotte Linde and William Labov on oral narrations of place) might have described it.[40] The conversations often involved Heike, but more frequently they occurred between audience members. Visitors discussed events they remembered, tried to help each other in identifying locations, and negotiated their memories together. Unlike the in-situ interview with Mike Pearson, which created a memory tour of Cardiff's performance scene at a given time, this map of performance art in Cardiff was more or less atemporal, although some visitors included dates in their accounts. The map nonetheless presented a form of historical inquiry, as it made manifest a number of aspects that related very directly to the history of performance art in Wales. It revealed in particular how certain locations in the town have repeatedly drawn performances to them. Areas of dense performance activity emerged, particularly around the central shopping precinct, where many street performances have taken place across the years; around the art school and venues such as Chapter; and also in certain private houses or defunct industrial sites. Infrastructures of connections between sites and networks of continued support came into view. And the map made material how, in a city as relatively small as Cardiff (with its 330,000 inhabitants), and with a nearly fifty-year history of artists creating performances in it, there is barely a place in the town that has not been touched by performance art at some point in its past.

Performing Audiences

This chapter has proposed that oral history interviews can be regarded as instances of located or even site-specific performance. Exploring and exploiting the performative dimension of an oral history conversation, we have argued, foregrounds the influence that its location exerts on the construction of its narrative. The ways in which artists have made use of performance's material bond with its setting can serve as models for developing new ways of locating oral history conversations. And these new ways may help to create a form of site-specific oral history that, by being responsive to the sites where it takes place, offers new insights into the contextual nature of performance.

To approach an oral history interview as performance implies that one needs to be mindful of its particular *mise-en-scène* and of the encounter between interviewer and interviewee. But more important, in our opinion, is the manner in which this performance forms the present and future encounters that different audiences may have with it. It is this aspect that has emerged most strongly from our inquiry. In its unique dependency on an audience's engagement, performance directs our attention to the fact that oral history's performance also does not merely involve interviewers and interviewees, but implicates a wider community of listeners. Finding new ways of locating and relocating not just the interview situation itself, but also an audience's encounter with it, can help to recognize the important role audiences play in shaping this complex performance we call oral history.

Notes

1. "'It Was Forty Years Ago Today…': Locating the Early History of Performance Art in Wales 1965–1979," funded by an *AHRC Arts and Humanities Research Council Research Grant* (Standard). Start date, 4 April, 2009; End date, 31 March 2011. Principal investigator: Heike Roms; Postdoctoral research assistant: Rebecca Edwards. http://www.ahrc.ac.uk/FundedResearch/Pages/ResearchDetail.aspx?id=142967
2. Della Pollock, "Introduction: Remembering," in *Remembering: Oral History Performance*, edited by Della Pollock (New York, Houndsmill: Palgrave Macmillan, 2005), 1.
3. Linda Shopes and Bruce M. Stave, Preface, in *Remembering: Oral History Performance*, edited by Della Pollock (New York, Houndsmill: Palgrave Macmillan, 2005), xi.
4. Jeff Friedman, "Fractious Action: Oral History-Based Performance," in *Handbook of Oral History*, edited by Lois E. Myers and Rebecca Sharpless (Lanham, New York, Toronto, Oxford: Alta Mira Press, 2006), 473. Henceforth referred to as Friedman, "Fractious Action."
5. Ronald, J. Grele, "Movement without Aim: Methodological and Theoretical Problems in Oral History," in *The Oral History Reader*, 1st edition, edited by Robert Perks and Alistair Thomson (London: Routledge, 1998), 44.
6. For a more comprehensive discussion of the relationship between performance and oral history see in particular the works of Della Pollock (*Remembering;* and "Moving Histories: Performance and Oral History," in *The Cambridge Companion to Performance Studies*, edited by Tracy C. Davis [Cambridge: Cambridge Univ. Press, 2008]. Also see Jeff Friedman ("Fractious Action;" see note 4; and "Muscle Memory: Performing Embodied Knowledge," in *Art and the Performance of Memory: Sounds and Gestures of Recollection*, edited by Richard Cándida-Smith [New York/London: Routledge, 2002]). Such work builds on the earlier performance-oriented scholarship of Richard Bauman; see, for example, Richard Bauman, *Verbal Art as Performance* (Prospect Heights, IL: Waveland Press, 1977) and Ruth Finnegan; see, for example, Ruth Finnegan, *Oral Traditions and the Verbal Arts: A Guide to Research Practices* (London: Routledge, 1992).

7. Susan Croft, "Oral Histories of Theatre: A Survey," March 2009, Society of Theatre Research website, http://www.str.org.uk/research/resources/oralhistory/index.html. Henceforth referred to as Croft, "Oral Histories of Theatre."
8. Susan Croft and Jessica Higgs (In Tandem TC), *Unfinished Histories—Recording the History of Alternative Theatre* website, http://www.unfinishedhistories.com (accessed July 1 2010).
9. Claire MacDonald, Sara Jane Bailes, Stephen Cleary et al., *Sounding Performance: Towards an Oral History of Performance and Live Art in the British Isles* website, http://www.soundingperformance.co.uk/ (accessed 1 July 1, 2010).
10. Comparable oral history projects outside the United Kingdom include the Switzerland-based *Performance Saga,* which has dedicated itself to interviewing women "pioneers" of performance art (see Andrea Saemann and Katrin Gröge, *Performance Saga* website, http://www.performancesaga.ch (last updated February 2010, accessed July 1, 2010), and *Crash Landing Revisited (and more)*, run by the Belgian writer and curator Myriam van Imschoot, which centers on conversations with participants of the long-running improvisational dance project (led by Meg Stuart), *Crash Landing;* see Myriam Van Imschoot, *Crash Landing Revisited (and more)* online wiki, http://crashlandingrevisited-andmore.wikispaces.com (accessed July 1, 2010).
11. Croft, "Oral Histories of Theatre."
12. Another common aspect that may be worth mentioning is that all these projects have been developed without major institutional backing.
13. Cindy Oswin, *On the Fringe* is "a personal history of British experimental theatre from the sixties to the eighties." For more information see Artsadmin, *Cindy Oswin* webpage, http://www.artsadmin.co.uk/artists/cindy-oswin (accessed August 1, 2011).
14. Myriam van Imschoot has similarly drawn on the conversations she undertook as part of *Crash Landing Revisited* to develop a series of performances, films, lectures, and installations, each of which reconfigures this material in new ways.
15. Pollock, "Remembering," 3.
16. For a brief history of performance art, see Roselee Goldberg, "Performance Art," in *From Expressionism to Post-Modernism (The Grove Dictionary of Art)*, edited by Jane Turner (London: GroveArt, 2000), 294–302.
17. Heike Roms, "Eventful Evidence: Historicizing Performance Art," *Maska* 117–118 (Issue: *History–Experience–Archive*) (Autumn 2008), 69–77.
18. Gay McAuley, *Space in Performance: Making Meaning in the Theatre* (Ann Arbor: University of Michigan Press, 2000), 86.
19. For a discussion of site-specific performance practice, see Nick Kaye, *Site-Specific Art* (London: Routlege, 2000).
20. Although the theatre too is a real place, of course.
21. Gay McAuley, "Local Acts: Site Specific Performance Practice," *About Performance* 7 (2007), 9.
22. See above all, the collection edited by Cándida-Smith, *Art and the Performance of Memory: Sounds and Gestures of Recollection* (New York/London: Routledge, 2002).
23. Friedman, "Fractious Action," 473.

24. Funded by a grant from the Arts Council of Wales/National Lottery Fund and supported by SHIFTwork, Cardiff School of Art and Design. For more info. see Heike Roms, *What's Welsh for Performance? Beth yw "performance" yn Gymraeg?* website, http://www.performance-wales.org
25. One conversation took place in Aberystwyth.
26. Anthony Howell, interviewed by Heike Roms, Cardiff, March 15, 2007; in: Heike Roms, *What's Welsh for Performance? An Oral History of Performance Art in Wales*, vol. 1 (Cardiff: Samizdat Press, 2008), 162–63.
27. Della Pollock, "Moving Histories," 124.
28. Roms, *What's Welsh for Performance?*
29. Copies of the interviews are to be deposited with the British Library Sound Archive, the National Screen and Sound Archive of Wales, the Live Art Archive at Bristol University, and the Centre for Performance Research at Aberystwyth University.
30. For example, four organizers and one audience member of the Aberystwyth Arts Festival 1968 were reunited at Aberystwyth University in January 2010 for a group conversation. Three members of the Zoo performance collective met at the former home of their late teacher and collaborator, John Gingell, in Cardiff in March 2010. Four ex-students of the Cardiff School of Art were interviewed at the School in July 2010. See http://www.performance-wales.org/it-was-40-years-ago-today/oralhistory-interviewees.htm.
31. Mike Pearson, interviewed by Heike Roms, Cardiff, November 27, 2009. (IWFYAT-Sited 1: "Performance in Cardiff 1968–1975: A Guided Tour." See http://www.performance-wales.org/it-was-40-years-ago-today/interviews/36_PearsonTourCardiff.htm
32. Michel de Certeau, *The Practice of Everyday Life*, trans. Steven Rendall (Berkeley: University of California Press, 1988), 115.
33. Being in-situ also prompted Pearson to remember sites of performance he had previously forgotten, such as a shop in Queen Street (Cardiff's main shopping precinct), now buried under the Capitol Shopping Centre, where artists Christine Kinsey and Bryan Jones put on art events in 1969 prior to their founding of Chapter Arts Centre.
34. The audio guides will be available from October 2011 through Chapter Arts Centre in Cardiff.
35. Heike has also undertaken reenactments of past performance events at the location of their initial performance in the presence of former eyewitnesses as well as of new audiences; these are forms of *in-situ* explorations that make use of the co-presence of audiences for their investigations. For more details see the project website, Roms, *What's Welsh for Performance? Beth yw "performance" yn Gymraeg?* http://www.performance-wales.org
36. Robert Proctor, "The Architect's Intention: Interpreting Post-War Modernism through the Architect Interview," *The Journal of Design History* 19:4 (2006), 295–307.
37. "Mapping Performance Art in Cardiff" was a Chapter Arts Centre/ Experimentica commission.
38. The idea was inspired by a workshop exercise devised by Dee Heddon at the Placing Performance Histories workshop, University of Glasgow, June 18, 2007,

as part of the *Towards an Oral History of Performance and Live Art in the British Isles* AHRC-funded network; see Claire MacDonald et al., *Sounding Performance* website, www.soundingperformance.co.uk/

39. Heike Roms, *Mapping Performance Art in Cardiff: A Documentary*, color video, 3 min.
40. De Certeau, *The Practice of Everyday Life*, 119.

CHAPTER 9

The Historical Hearing Aid: Located Oral History from the Listener's Perspective

Toby Butler

This chapter is concerned with how listeners respond to hearing oral history at specific places. It draws upon intensive evaluation of two experimental outdoor oral history trails (or *memoryscapes*) that were funded by the Museum of London in England. These trails explored two contrasting areas of the banks of the river Thames. Each memoryscape included almost an hour of oral history testimony relevant to the past and present of the cultural riverscape of the Thames in London. The oral history recordings were either made specifically for the project or came from the Museum of London archives. The audio trails were designed to be played on mobile media devices; the public could pick up a map and listening equipment at local libraries and tourist information centers, or download the audio recordings and maps for use on their own mobile phones or MP3 players.[1] Following a simple map, the listener would find specific points along the Thames Path National Trail and play the relevant track to hear a variety of local people talk about the past, present, and future of the riverscape they were experiencing.

I have published accounts elsewhere of how these memoryscapes were developed conceptually, and I have long argued that cultural historians, geographers, anthropologists, archaeologists, and others concerned with interpreting place would do well to engage with the possibilities of location-based media.[2] At the time of writing, location-based media are perceived by many in the computer and software industry to be the "next big thing" as the equipment that can deliver locational media (such as the iPhone and Android platform) has begun to capture the public imagination and reach a mass market. New devices and applications will develop, but as far as oral history is concerned, the experience will remain fundamentally similar whatever platform is used: you go somewhere and hear oral testimony at that location. To my knowledge, there has been little qualitative evaluation of this location-oriented use of oral testimony from the point of view of the listener, so I also hope that the responses made to this relatively early example of this genre will help to fill that gap and usefully inform future work in this exciting and rapidly expanding field.

The overarching concern of this chapter is to better understand what happens to listeners when they hear location-specific oral history. Where possible, I will reflect upon what the responses might mean in more general terms for place-based oral history practice. I start by examining how located memories can make places more significant and interesting by adding to our own mental map of our surroundings. Looking at this process more deeply, I go on to consider how the distinct qualities of listening to voice can evoke empathy and feelings of belonging to places, and can challenge preconceptions about the people who live there. More uncomfortable feelings such as voyeurism were reported by a few listeners, and I argue that practitioners would do well to be sensitive to this when working with this very intimate medium. Others described imaginative and playful responses to recordings. I consider these, along with the temporal aspects of the listener's experience. The past can be very powerfully mixed up with the present of the landscape the listener is experiencing, and this can make places more memorable as a result. Finally, I argue that it is now possible to incorporate oral history into all kinds of outdoor activity to provide some of the political, social, and historical realities of a landscape that people might otherwise miss.

As the listener's experience is my primary concern here, we need not consider the details of the trails themselves, which the reader can find online if they so choose (www.memoryscape.org.uk).[3] Suffice it to say that the *Drifting* audio trail explored a generally picturesque riverscape, which typifies the stretch of river from Hampton Court Palace to Kingston upon Thames, upriver in west London. A grassy riverside path follows the edge of a royal deer park and offers views of the opposite bank, which is mostly made up of riverside habitation, ranging from houseboats to bungalows and apartment blocks, the inhabitants of which were interviewed specifically for the audio trail. In contrast, the *Dockers* audio trail was almost entirely constructed from archive interviews with dock workers in the 1980s. It covers a much more industrial stretch of river on the Greenwich peninsula, on the east side of the city. This walk quickly leaves the stately architecture of Christopher Wren's riverside Greenwich Hospital to meander through places with a more industrial character: disused wharfs, rusting boats, and ruined cranes—the last traces of what was once the busiest dock in the world. The London docks closed over the 1970s and 1980s, and most trade moved upriver to deeper, containerized docks in the Thames estuary at Tilbury). These case studies will therefore have relevance to those considering using location-based oral history in green and pleasant lands, as well as in more gritty urban and suburban locations.

This chapter draws upon 147 questionnaire responses and postwalk interviews that the author arranged with participants throughout 2005. The walkers were self-selecting volunteers, willing to devote an afternoon to a walk, or were members of groups or classes who had expressed an interest in participating after an appeal for participants was made in the local press, radio, and online. The walkers were in no way representative of the general population so, to give some context, I will briefly outline the profile of the group. Overall, the age range of participants was fairly evenly distributed between 20 and 90; two-thirds were women and 16% of those who gave their ethnic origin came from non-white British backgrounds. Groups included students, healthy walkers (people who walk for exercise), museum curators, a partially sighted group, retirees, and local community members responding to walk advertisements. Twenty-four questionnaires were also received from individuals who experienced the walk on their own, either buying the trail CDs in the Museum of London shop or downloading the trail from the memoryscape website. Most

Figure 1 Walkers fill in questionnaires after completing the *Drifting* trail, Kingston upon Thames.

were from the more affluent social categories (ABC1 – clerical to professional). The majority lived in and around London, and most did not live in the local community where the walks were located. In terms of satisfaction, the experience was rated highly across the board, with 96% rating it 7 out of 10 or above. The average rating did not alter significantly between groups by background, sex, walk location, or whether the walk was undertaken alone or in an organized group. However pleasing these results, we must be wary of generalizing from such a small sample; but the qualitative responses of participants can tell us much more about their experience and can provide a base for further thought and investigation. After all, these are still the early, pioneering days of using oral history with location-based media.

The Cultural Riverscape of the Thames

The river Thames provided the walk setting, the research methodology, the interview topics, and whole *raison d'être* of the project.[4] The main aim was to increase public understanding, appreciation, and enjoyment of the Thames riverscape and its people. But with just an hour of recording to be used on each trail, the memoryscapes were necessarily partial. Some memories reflected the history of the river as the scene of events of regional, national, and international importance, such as Zeppelin raids, the Dunkirk evacuation, the economic role of the Port of London, and the international cable-laying industry. But, like memory, the liquid history of the Thames is not just in the past, but flows before our senses in the present. Urban sound walks/works by artists such as Janet Cardiff and Graeme Miller tend to "frame the negatory" by recovering landscapes and subcultures lost to urban development.[5] In my experiment, I was determined to incorporate the visible present of the river into the experience too. This was reflected time and again in the oral history recordings—in discussions of the merits of riverside housing development, the decline of industry, houseboat communities, and the pending residential development of the old wharfs. The river has a powerful and unpredictable nature of its own, which was explored with discussion of flooding and the dangers of the river. Finally, the river was the force, or actant, that physically and metaphorically bound the bewildering array of interviewees together. One reviewer described how the project builds "a larger role for the Thames as more than a threatened geographical location, but also as a cultural, spiritual and historical space that links people together rather than its usual role perceived by Londoners as a barrier to social engagement."[6]

So much for the theory. How did it work for the walkers in practice? Questionnaire responses suggested that the culture of the river was successfully put on the map for many of the walkers, particularly those that previously did not know the landscape well. The oral history trails changed their perceptions and challenged preconceptions, encouraging walkers to perceive the river differently:

> Normally when I walk I'm looking at the scenery. I'm an artist and I look at shapes and colour. Now I'll also think about the people.
>
> —Retired midwife, aged 63.

> Introduced me to a totally different side of the river—of which I'd only ever seen the "touristy" or "pretty" end—not as a working river.
>
> —Oral historian, female, aged 43

> It is livelier and more vibrant than I had thought.
>
> —Male student, aged 23

> The river becomes anatomised, it was fascinating to hear the attitudes of residents compared to water engineers and duck poachers.
>
> —Mask maker, male, aged 39[7]

This process of "anatomization" was a cumulative one of listening to dozens of river people; it might be characterized as being broadly educative as preconceptions were revised—the riverscape was alive rather than dull and disused, working as well as pleasing, and peopled as well as scenic. More than two-thirds of the respondents said that the walk had increased their understanding of the riverscape "a great deal," which was encouraging.

Of course, for those more familiar with this culture, or those that were themselves a part of it, there were fewer surprises. One example was Dennis, a rower in his seventies who had listened to the *Drifting* walk on the *Kingston Talking Newspaper*, a website for blind and partially sighted people. Dennis had been blind from birth, but knew the river well from rowing, walking, and running the *Drifting* stretch of river for more than 40 years. As he listened at home, his experience was not physical, but imaginative—the stories were slotted into an existing mental map of the river that had evolved over many years. This map seemed to be marked by the places and people that he knew best—the pubs and boat clubs that he knew well and people connected to them. He had many stories about the river. The locations and stories on the recordings seemed to provide points of reminiscence for his storytelling. Sometimes this would be direct—for example, he knew one of the people referred to in one track, which featured the reading aloud of a series of memorial plaques attached to benches along the river (*Drifting*, track 21), and commented:

> Manning lived by the river near Sunbury Lock. He had all sorts of skiffs and outrigger canoes, he was a great boating man. He belonged to the rowing club, the skiff club and the Thames Traditional Boat Society.
>
> —Dennis, retired, in his seventies

But the stories he told referred much more to the gaps, or places in between the sound points. Our two hours of discussion were filled with his own river-related memories, but it was difficult to get him to talk about the recordings. It seems they had not made a very deep impression, or they had no place on his mental map.

> *Interviewer:* Did you recognise the reference points, where they were?
> *Dennis:* Well I know the pubs very well. I was surprised you didn't push your float into the Swan [pub] actually [*laughs*]. Then you have got Thames Ditton Skiff and Punting Club which had two lions on their front lawn... One of the chaps that used to run the bar here, the Christie brothers, he used to run pub up at Thames Ditton.

The parts of the recording that he did mention were locations that had not featured in his experience—he mentioned the glass-fronted, prefabricated Huf Haus and the scene of an unofficial houseboat wedding, Cigarette Island, as two places that he hadn't realized were there until he heard the memoryscape:

> *Interviewer:* Did you get anything out of listening to the recollections?
> *Dennis:* I suppose it would be different to me as [I] knew the river so well, compared to someone who doesn't. The wedding I suppose went on a bit if you weren't involved in it but I didn't know about Cigarette Island or whatever you call it, I supposed I must have rowed past it a hundred times without knowing it was there really.

The experience did not seem as resonant for him in comparison to other blind and partially sighted people who walked the trail. Dennis's experience was also more passive in physical terms, as he listened to the recordings at home rather than while walking the trail. Yet his responses were extremely geographical, and new locations were introduced to his mental map. For such a mobile blind man, having a good mental map of the geographical location of things must have an importance that is hard for a sighted person to imagine. The gaps in the narrative that were an inevitable part of such a trail seem to have brought forward his own memories, which were deeply rooted in specific places—the pubs and rowing clubs along the route that he knew very well. His memory filled in the gaps (in the recording, and, in the context of our conversation, my knowledge). The process of listening to the memories seemed to be a kind of mental map-amending exercise for him (and for me in our conversation afterwards). The process of mental map-making without the "noise" of the visual brings into sharper relief the process of place-making that we all share; the little sensations, stories, and overlapping clues to previous lives and landscapes that breathe significance into our surroundings.[8]

The Power of Voice: Empathy and Accents

It was only after listening to the reactions to the walks that I realized that some people have some strong preconceptions as to the kind of people that might live in boats or riverside property. Some comments made about the *Drifting* walk showed that stereotypes did exist, but also that listening to their voices could have a powerful, empathetic effect that challenged the assumptions. It has been argued that oral history can be a powerful tool for social inclusion by challenging stereotypes, celebrating difference, and representing lost or marginalized voices.[9] I'd now like to explore how this process of sensitization or empathy works in the context of listening outdoors to place-specific oral history. Properties with a view of the river can fetch high prices and their residents are often within clear sight of the towpath. Here is an interview with Mike, a student in his twenties, after his walk:

> *Mike:* I always think of them (the bungalows) as like holiday homes almost. It is a bit surreal—I live in a terraced house, as far away from the water as I could be. I see them as luxuries, these people just live in them, these houses—they are all very—some of them have massive gardens—it is quite a different world, as it were.
>
> *Author:* Listening to those voices—has it changed in any way your perception of people who live by rivers?
>
> *Mike:* Absolutely. They sounded like . . . they might have been retired or whatever but they were ordinary people who just liked living there; it was just a dream of theirs to build a nice house by the Thames and live there. I guess I had never really thought about it, or heard anyone talk about it—it just answered a few questions as to—people do live in them, they are just normal houses.

Mike begins by explaining how difficult it is to relate to people who live in riverside houses. Mike's terraced house looks nothing like the detached riverside residences and, although I would not mind betting he lives near a river of some kind, in Mike's mind the river world is something that is entirely removed from his experience ("as far away from the water as I could be"). Mike mentions two things that help to change his point of view—first, the recordings humanized the people inside the houses, whom he previously had no connection with. They might be different from him ("retired or whatever"), but listening to their voices and the reasons why they liked the river seems to have transformed the bungalow owners from distant, perhaps indolent, rich individuals ("these people just live in them") into normal people that Mike could identify with ("they were ordinary people who just liked living there"). For Mike, a key element of this process was understanding and perhaps even sympathizing with their motives ("it was just a dream of theirs to build a nice house by the Thames"). It seems that the content of the recordings also provided some information that he lacked. From the various accounts of people living on the river, he surmised that the riverside properties here were not just holiday homes for the super-rich ("people do live in them, they are just normal houses").

I think this exchange reveals how the content of oral history recordings can inform and even transform the opinions of people that come from a starting point of having little or no knowledge of the kind of people that they are listening to. Outsiders can come away from the experience with a better-informed understanding of the culture that they have encountered. This might be seen as a relatively quick, one-way form of what an anthropologist would term *acculturation* or *culture contact.* A change has emerged when two different kinds of people interact with each other (albeit, in this case, in the listener's mind). Here is another response to the same location:

> They sounded like normal people that we know, they sounded really familiar, I don't know, before I didn't know what people, I didn't know what to expect from people that live by the river or live on boats, but they're pretty much normal people that I probably walk past everyday, so I was a bit shocked by that as well.
>
> —Joanne, aged 20, postwalk recording

In this case it is clear that the interviewee's style of speaking helped this process of normalization. All of the recorded postwalk interviews were in-depth, relatively unstructured and open—generally people were allowed to follow a train of thought for as long as they wished. This style of oral history interviewing is designed to make people feel at ease, and the resulting tone of the recordings is relaxed and conversational—what one respondent in his early twenties called "a laid-back atmosphere." I think this also has a part to play in the warmth of the interviews, as the technique encourages interviewees to convey something of themselves beyond rhetoric or factual information. As another walker observed:

> It was almost as if they were genuinely standing there and chatting to you, it didn't feel as if they were documenting anything, it was just a nice cosy chat.
>
> —Jane, aged 61, postwalk recording

This process of normalization was not restricted to people who were strangers to the area. Claire, age 33, had lived in a very well-known riverside house herself for many years—she used to be a live-in care assistant for an elderly lady in an apartment at Hampton Court Palace. Here are her comments from a postwalk interview:

> *Author:* This is a stretch [of river] that you know very, very well, having lived here; has it given you any new perspectives that you didn't have before?

Claire: Yes; I guess like everybody I form my own opinions about people and places as I go past them, so I have looked at all those posh houses on the other side of the river before, and sort of thought well very wealthy upper middle class/upper class people live in those houses, and I have whatever opinions vaguely formed in my mind about them, so it was kind of nice to get a perspective from them actually, and I felt much more empathy towards some of the people that were speaking on there than I maybe would have had by just seeing them which is kind of interesting. I suppose it challenged my own perceptions.

For Claire, the factual content of the recordings is less of an issue, because she is already familiar with the area and the river, but she gets a new perspective from hearing other people who live in her locality. In a similar way to Mike, her "vaguely formed" assumptions (this time class-based categorization) have been challenged by individuals speaking in a personal and specific way, rather than as a representative of any class or group. The fact that listeners cannot actually see the person concerned means that they cannot rely on all the visual clues and symbols of appearance, dress, home decoration, and body language that humans tend to use to rapidly make assumptions when they meet someone or see them interviewed on television. Claire has the feeling that the listening process encourages a more empathetic response in her than if she had seen the people concerned. In listening to a recording, there is little to take an instant dislike to, or make assumptions about, besides the content of the speech and the inflection, intonation, and accent of the voice.

In the questionnaire responses, many people remarked upon how the use of original voices gave the recording great authenticity. The recordings were perceived as primary sources of information and many people seemed to enjoy the opportunity to listen without much overt interpretation of what people were saying from an "expert." Instead, the interviewees themselves were the expert witnesses of their own lives, and the combination of hearing different views from people that had lived through what they were describing seemed to have provided a more authentic experience when compared to a more conventional guided tour. Here are some observations from people who walked the trails:

* A conventional tour is a more academic way of finding out new things. Here you have the real thing. You listen to different people's experiences and you reach your own conclusions.

—Curator, female, aged 35

* Gives personal views rather than one view, which can often be distorted or totally inaccurate.

—Retired female, aged 65

*Keeps one's attention. Get different points of view. Involves the local people and workers who know the place best, and love it generally.

—Anesthetist, female, aged 55

*It was [a] direct source of information—not reinterpreted by a guide.

—National Health Service finance officer, male, aged 49

* Interest; diversity; colour; personal perspectives. I learned! In listening, the giant at the core of our city acquired a human face for me.

—Retired female, aged 73

Again we can see pleasure derived from the liberation from a mediating voice. For some people, the figure of a guide is seen as monovocal, academic, processing, reinterpreting, shaping. In contrast, the voices of local people are diverse, colorful, knowing, loving, direct, and real.

Although accent can be a barrier to communication—one walker said that the accents of the different people sometimes made it difficult to understand everything—most people seemed to enjoy hearing a variety of different kinds of speech, particularly on the *Dockers* walk, which had a greater range of voices than *Drifting.* For some, accent helped place the memories in space and time. The following was an exchange with the group of blind and partially sighted people from Brighton after they had completed the *Dockers* trail:

Group Member: Hearing the old London thick rough London gritty accent fills in the picture of what life must have been like, like the man with boots.... Imagine little kids running to school barefoot and spending all day with no shoes.

Author: There was something very interesting you said about [how] hearing their voices somehow gave you a much better impression than, say, if it had been me [talking]—I could have read out a transcript in my voice and there would have been a difference?

Group Members: Yes because it was somebody that had experienced it.

*A real London accent.

* You could tell they were from London.

* It took you back in time.

Author: So it places it in time and space; so it sounds more like London and it sounds more of that time than if I had said it?

Group Members: Yes.

For Londoners, the cockney accent is not the territorial hallmark that it once was—the cockney diaspora includes large areas of Kent and Essex, but perhaps because the blind and partially sighted group were from outside London, the unfamiliar accent had a particularly resonant locational significance.

In the listeners' desire to make sense of what they are hearing, it struck me how the positionality of class stereotypes played such a big role—from the "posh houses" of Thames Ditton to the "rough London gritty accent" of the East End poor. Some people who live in the areas that are subjected to this kind of observation—and generalization—take great exception to it. For example, author and East London resident Jane Graves argues that the East End has been continuously and consistently subjected to a voyeuristic intrusive gaze that has changed little since the nineteenth century. East Enders have been encouraged to wear other people's masks—Cockney, Hood, Pearly King and Queen, Trickster—which has the effect of making the reality of an area that has "largely been the exclusive habitat of the 'poor'" invisible; or, if it is recognized, the outsider's view is often so laced with assumptions of superiority/inferiority that locals become little more than objects of pity, Graves observes.[10]

What place does the oral history heard on the walks have in this scenario? Are the walkers basically voyeurs, gazing for little more purpose than their pleasure? Gazing is certainly an important part of experiencing a memoryscape, but this seems to have worked in different ways on the different walks. Poverty is an important element of the *Dockers* walk—it certainly is not ignored, with several stories about children having no shoes and having to collect driftwood for heating. As the stories are clearly in the past and are told by the people who actually experienced the poverty, I do not think they evoke feelings of pity—but rather, feelings of wonder at how things have changed. This does not seem like an East End stereotype, or mask, either—the stories are too detailed, too real, too heartfelt for that.

On the *Drifting* route, some walkers experienced voyeuristic discomfort of a different kind. This seemed to come from a feeling of infringement of privacy. For one walker the wedding scene (*Drifting*, track 9) seemed a little too personal: Kate, a 21-year-old student, observed: "I kind of felt in a way like I was eavesdropping and I kind of didn't want to be."

Sue and Bethan, 20-year-old students, felt uneasy when they heard about the inside of the Huf Haus (mentioned above; *Drifting*, track 13), as they reported in their postwalk interview:

Sue: I found with the glass house, the guy that said he was in there and he saw how big the kitchen was and so on, and I saw a lady in the actual house at the time, and it was almost quite like you could be there, you could see the house and it was quite a private thing to be there, and that made me think "should we have this information of how big their house is," you know what I mean, like the kitchen and so on, but [it's] interesting to have that information.

Author: It made you feel a bit uneasy?

Sue: Yeah it made me a little, it was like he'd been in there and he'd said how big the kitchen was and like.

Bethan: It was almost like you were inside as well as outside.

> *Sue:* It's quite [the] sort of private information that I don't know if you should have, I don't know really.

Listening to the recordings in their native habitat also set up a further set of spatial problems concerned with privacy. This was particularly evident on the *Drifting* walk, which obviously used contemporary interviews; Sue and Bethan seem to have felt a dichotomy between public and private, as they observed. They heard detailed information about the interior of a house, which would have been unremarkable except for the fact that they were standing outside the house, looking through the windows at someone inside from the other side of the river. They were listening to a detailed description of the house, using earphones, almost surreptitiously, without the knowledge of the house owner. Being inside as well as outside felt like a trespass.

It would be hard to deny that staring through someone's windows is a voyeuristic act; the observer is gratified from the observation without the knowledge of the observed. I hope it is evident, however, that the memoryscape runs quite opposite to the kind of voyeurism described by Jane Graves; it involves listening, understanding, empathy, and respect for things that exist and have existed. Graves's battle, living in the shadow of Canary Wharf, is with the powerful outsiders who make no effort to understand what is there already before pronouncing its transformation; it is their "contemptuous gaze" which makes her working-class community feel powerless.[11]

Elsewhere on the *Drifting* trail, I was deliberately ambiguous about exactly where the speaker lived to avoid this kind of problem. An unintended consequence of this was the stimulation of imagination in some listeners. For example, the bungalow owners in the *Drifting* walk had requested that they did not want their specific house to be identified on the walk. For some listeners, it became a kind of game to imagine what they looked like and where they lived as can be seen in this postwalk recording:

> We got sidetracked a bit along the way as well because we were trying to work out where some of the people who were speaking lived, who were talking about the German house—just trying to listen to their accents and thinking, "Do you think they have a big house or a little house—is it that one?'
>
> —Teacher, female, in fifties

Here we can see that the listeners were trying to reconcile what little aural status clues they had—the accents of the house owners—and place them socially and spatially in the landscape before them. The lack of information slowed down their judgment to such an extent that they had turned their desire to categorize into a playful game. Imagining the appearance of people was another game that some people enjoyed—to the extent that one woman felt very strongly that she did not want to see pictures or video of the interviewees, as her imaginative journey would be spoiled. In her postwalk recording she observed:

> We wouldn't have wanted to see the interviewees because I think it is a bit like a book, when you read a book you have your own imagination of the characters, immediately they put it into film you think, oh he didn't look like that at all, I already know what he looked like!
>
> —Health development officer, female, aged 56

The last two accounts also show how some listeners created their own playful activities alongside the walking and listening experience. These might be understood as imaginative detours—the walker is imaginatively manipulating the characters in the spatial organization of the bungalows in a creative way. This process is a part of what De Certeau describes as the "long poem of walking," with its many spatial and experiential references, some of which are personal to the taste and imagination of the walker.[12]

The first instinct of a historian might be to locate oral history as precisely as possible to place, in order to unlock its full potential to tell us something real about a location. Yet here we discover that vagueness or ambiguity can be powerful too. The trail narration did not put great emphasis on precisely identifying the interviewees and the medium of the recorded voice masked, rather than revealed,

Figure 2 A memoryscape walker, listening to the *Drifting* trail at Molesey Lock.

many aspects of context and appearance. This, combined with the fact that people had a great deal of control over the process of listening (e.g.. by meandering, pausing, repeating or turning off the audioplayer) allowed room for listeners to get "sidetracked a bit along the way" with their own games or activities if they wanted to. When the skateboarder pulls tricks on familiar ground, new spatial and interpretive meanings are made; familiar surfaces are given new utility as handrails become toys; for a time, the conventional power relations of architecture can be played with, challenged, and subverted for the skateboarder's own ends.[13] It may not be as visually impressive to an onlooker as a skateboarder, but the walkers can actively create their own space for their own ends too, using the materials around them. Depending on the taste of the walker, the memoryscape can serve both as a catalyst and as extra material (story, character, memory) for imaginative (and memorable) encounters with place In this way the recording can be perceived to be like the skateboard—it might be used more conventionally as a way to enliven a journey, or it might be used an actant to pull some spatial or imaginative tricks.

The Historical Hearing Aid: Memories in Context

The Walkman and now the MP3 player and the mobile phone are commonly used apparatus to remove the consciousness of individuals from their environment. Conventionally, they have been used to provide a musical and mobile soundscape, which listeners often describe as either as a backdrop to the present or, with closed eyes and loud volume, as a curtain to block out the noise and stress of a city journey.[14] For some younger people, the sensation of listening to voices that were referring to the world around them, rather than to music, which is usually unspecific to their immediate surroundings, was very surprising:

> I think it's a bit difficult because normally you'd have music on, you're kind of blocking it out and you're focusing on what you are doing. When you're walking and listening and watching you have to be more careful, so I think it's weird, like a new sensation, cause you're listening to what the people are saying and concentrating, whereas when you're walking with music you're just having that background noise to block out the rest of the world, but with the headphones on you're concentrating on the words and where you are at that moment in time.
>
> —Female student 1, aged 20, postwalk recording

> It makes you like aware of your surroundings and like points out certain things so you're like looking around and taking in things more, rather than just walking along.
>
> —Female student 2, aged 20, postwalk recording

One woman commented:

> You visualise what it must have been like. You are literally walking along the paths/roads in the footsteps of the people who are speaking.
>
> —Administrator, female, aged 44

This reminded me of a strange sense of hyperreality I felt when experiencing *Linked,* a sound walk by artist Graeme Miller that featured recorded memories—I felt a powerful combination of carefully observing the present while receiving vivid experiences from the past.[15] In *Linked,* I thought that the musicality of Miller's composition, which consisted of repetitions, musicality, and sound design alongside the oral testimony, was a major element of creating intensely meditative sensation, but the physicality of walking and listening to oral history alone can have the power to create a similar effect. Another listener, Rob, a mask and puppet maker aged 39, nicely described this unfamiliar sensation in his post-walk interview:

> Another thing that strikes me about it is the ability of—the actual sensation of the words being inside your head. It is not like listening to the radio . . . you have actually got a sound chamber inside your head, and it is a very internal one. The whole experience of walking is that you have got the wind on your face, and you have got the sensation of just walking, and the crunching of the gravel underneath your feet, which is a very external one, and it brings the two into a very stark contrast, that internal world and the external world in a way which is very different to just doing a walk.
>
> Because you are hearing it through ear phones—I don't think many people listen to radio, to spoken voice through earphones that much—if you listen to radio, it is usually when you are doing something else and it is normally in a room as an activity, but when it is actually piped into you head, it is quite a different listening experience, because you are very aware of the outside world being excluded and so you have got a very personal thing going on. It is very close to having your own thought processes and being lost in your own thoughts.

For Rob, the synthesis was not between the past and the present, as it had been for me, but a spatially differentiated contrast between the inside and outside worlds. It is also apparent that the physicality and sensation of walking in the locality is a powerful part of the sensation of being connected to the place that is being discussed. Some walkers reported that seeing and listening to the environment that people lived in helped them to feel closer to the people they listen to, as they were subject to the same surroundings. It helped people to imagine episodes in the past and made them feel that they were physically participating in the experience. One man, aged 31, commented: "It makes one feel as though one is a part of what is going on."

Acts of Remembering and a Sense of Place

Several people remarked on how the experience seemed to concentrate the mind and help the act of remembering. A female charity researcher in her forties remarked that using all the senses made her much more likely to "anchor the memories in a multi-sensory experience" and to remember stories, in contrast to "looking at some objects behind glass in a climate controlled building." The process of remembering on the walk seemed connected to a place, even for those that had not visited the area before, as a female lecturer in her fifties observed:

> I thought that memoryscape is about the "stories" behind places [and about] architecture, the physicality of the cityscape; listening to the recordings brought those "stories" to life and transformed the Thames from a river to a rich cultural environment. [The] Thames became a "place" for me: an environment where people lived and worked, rather than just another river; also a historical site.

Respondents reported that using a variety of senses and using imagination, physically participating, and recognizing references in the landscape all helped to make the experience more meaningful and therefore memorable. Creating these connections, or links, to place seem to have had led to a feeling of closeness, or rootedness for some people. One retired female newcomer to London, aged 73, wrote, "Now I know a sense of a beginning attachment."

Rob described the process beautifully as "deepening my attachment to the river. Like roots shooting off into the soil." Several people talked about the experience adding a new reality, or a new dimension of reality to the existing landscape. Furthermore, anyone who visits the landscape again can use those links to remember something of the stories that they heard. As a 22-year-old male builder observed:

> *Memoryscape* has made me consider the part the river has played in so many people's lives. I think about this whenever I visit the river since listening to the recording *Drifting*.

Perhaps it is this aspect of the experience that could be of interest to those wishing to encourage feelings of belonging in a particular community or location, if memorable links can be made between individuals and the cultural topography of a place, past and present. In various ways, the walks introduce the listener to dozens of local people, both in the recordings and in the chance encounters that might occur on the walk itself. The significance of these encounters might only be reconsidered when the walker comes back to the place again in the future. I realized that it was too much to expect people to make complete sense of a long and involved experience immediately after a walk that is new, subtle, out of the ordinary, yet everyday. Perhaps more time to reflect and revisit is necessary to truly appreciate what has happened. Yi-Fu Tuan says that the beauty of a street lamp at sundown, or the bare earth packed firm by feet, can be touching and important to us, even though they do not impress themselves on our consciousness in the same way that, say, an artwork might:

> Intimate experiences, not being dressed up, easily escape our attention. At the time we do not say, "this is it" as we do when we admire objects of conspicuous or certified beauty. It is only in reflection that we recognise their worth. At the time we are not aware of any drama; we do not know that the seeds of lasting sentiment are being planted.[16]

Of course, there can be dangers in sowing seeds of lasting sentiment. A concern raised at the pilot evaluation was that the memories may be too nostalgic. A *Dockers* walker remarked:

> "I'd listened previously at home and it had sounded a tad sentimental *but* it didn't seem like this on the walk itself."
>
> —Lecturer, female, in her fifties

The senses are constantly interacting with the environment in a way that cannot work if you listen to the recordings at home, because what you are listening to and what you are experiencing in the same moment are inextricably linked. Without the juxtaposition of the present of place, the memories would have seemed flatter, one-dimensional, and sometimes sentimental. But on the *Dockers* walk, when combined with the sometimes harsh, elemental reality of the wharfs, any sentimentality is met by the reality of the working river—the huge lighter barges, the actual hold of a ship or the half-demolished pillar of a crane. The walk deliberately included large stretches without comment, in order to allow the walkers to absorb their surroundings. It is hard to feel nostalgic about the present. The landscape showed the walkers something of the dockers' workplace, which, like the work, was harsh, tough, and often boring as well as, at times, exciting and noteworthy. In this respect I hoped that the memories, often very significant pearls plucked from years of work and experience, found something of their true context again. The words were not writ large on video screens or exhibition spaces. The process was not of making more of, or magnifying, what was said, but almost making less of it, setting the oral testimony in the context of other people's memories and in the context of the landscape that contained them all.

The descriptions of the busy work that took place on the river were also juxtaposed with the wharfs and jetties that are, for the most part, no longer functioning (for example, see Figure 3). Perhaps the quietness and some of the desolation of a landscape in transition gave the walk more of a feel of a memorial than a celebration of the docks, sentimental or otherwise. One walker observed:

> I enjoyed the long stretches of quietness even though it's such a great city I felt the loneliness of the empty docks and wondered where all those people had gone.
>
> —Valerie, in her fifties

Cultural geographer Tim Edensor argues that industrial ruins have particular qualities that motivate us to celebrate surprising associations of the past in the present—unidentifiable objects, unsanitized images, strange nooks and corners that provide unexpected confrontations with sounds, atmospheres, and smells.[17] Although industry was still visibly present along much of the walk, the *Dockers* route shared many of the unsanitized, unmediated qualities of a ruin, which seemed to evoke a response in almost everyone. All but two of the walkers surveyed said that they found the industrial landscape interesting. Some, like Valerie above, said they enjoyed the dereliction and decay for the sense of loss that it gave. For one walker (a retired female) the landscape was a symbol of national decline, something far beyond the compass of the London docks. The wharfs were "all that is left of a time of British greatness and for all its faults a feeling of a better future," she observed. A few people enjoyed visiting desolation so much that it had obviously developed into some kind of hobby: A female lecturer in her fifties observed, "I like this postapocalyptic landscape! I look out for such

Figure 3 Lovell's Wharf on the *Dockers* trail, Greenwich peninsula. An apartment block has been built on the site since this picture was taken in 2005.

landscapes on days out, e.g. nuclear power stations etc." The questionnaire results showed that 49 out of 54 walkers on the *Dockers* route felt that the experience had made them more interested in exploring similar landscapes.

This kind of tourism is not without its critics. Steven High has traced the history of the urban exploration movement, which developed in North America, exploring deindustrialized structures such as disused factories and mills. In the urban exploration movement, explorers post experiences, photos, and information online about how to gain access and evade security measures. Having examined some of the relevant websites and chat rooms, Steven High argues that there is a danger that the adventure of treating such sites as "post-industrial playgrounds" and he notes that the uninformed fascination with the ruined industrial aesthetic can completely miss the political, social, and historical realities of industrial closure. "It is remarkable that urban explorers almost never ask why mills close. Nor do they reflect on the social impacts. These lie beyond their field of vision," High comments.[18]

My hope is that such an exploration, however shallow, does have the potential to pique interest and to be the starting point to further enquiry, if only the historical and social context were as easy to stumble across and explore as the industrial sites themselves. Location-specific oral history seems tailor-made to provide that kind of possibility, and wonderful online partnerships can be made. For example, after hearing about the *Dockers* trail on the radio, Charles Watson, the deputy manager of Alcatel Submarine Networks, which features in the *Dockers* walk, got in touch with me in an e-mail (August 3, 2005), where he noted:

> I am into a sport called Geocaching that you may, or may not, have heard of. It is a modern day treasure hunt that utilises a GPS to locate caches. Along your walk, there are seven caches and, in my latest hide details, I have put in a link to your web page.

Geocaching is a hobby that involves following clues and GPS reference points to find hidden containers, which have prizes or a log book inside.[19] It was immediately obvious that this unusual hobby had a strange connection—now made concrete by a hyperlink—with the trails that were also a series of little hunts with less tactile prizes (the recordings). So it seemed entirely fitting that these two games should be joined; why shouldn't memoryscapists hunt for objects as they listen, and geocachists hear some humanity while they track their quarry? A link to the geocaching website was included on the memoryscape links page in a reciprocal gesture of fellowship, and it isn't too hard to think of other outdoor leisure activities that located oral history recordings might complement in some way.[20]

When asked what features of the walk the respondents liked least, a few people felt that there should be more factual information about landmarks. A walker on the *Drifting* walk said that "the professionals were interesting. The others less so" (retired male, aged 61). Another wrote that the recordings were too personal, or "so focused on memories, not history, that it felt the useful history had been left out, almost in spite" (solicitor, female). Including contemporary themes and voices from a great range of people seemed to unsettle these walkers or prick their preconception of what this form of public history can be.

For the purposes of the experiment, I had made a decision to give as much time as possible to oral history and to leave out more conventional historical information, some which visitors could glean from information boards along the routes. But for the walkers quoted above, this wilful neglect of what they perceived as history and the implied questioning of what constitutes a proper expert in terms of interpreting our surroundings seemed unfathomable. It was also apparent that oral testimony alone generally can't cover all the factual information required. In designing subsequent trails, I find I am increasingly scripting historical and factual information to give the recordings some context and to provide the information that the oral testimony does not cover.

A few people found the *Dockers* experience too bleak and unnerving, as Ian wrote in an e-mail to me of April 11, 2006:

> I have to say that I found the *Dockers* walk to be unrelentingly depressing... the sense of being very isolated in an industrial wasteland was not to our tastes.

These responses suggest that many of the elements that some walkers liked most—the adventure, the industrial/post-industrial landscape, the authentic voices, the realism, the chance to meditate on the surroundings—could also be the reasons why some might dislike the experience.

Conclusion

Perhaps the most distinctive thing about these memoryscape experiments is the relatively unmediated use of oral history testimony "on location." Listener's responses suggested that the use of oral history in the landscape has real potential to challenge preconceptions and to give people who have not visited an area before a relatively rapid connection with their surroundings. Oral history recordings had the power to evoke strong feelings of empathy. Several people were surprised at this, considering that they were of a different age, class, or culture than the speakers. This "normalization" effect seemed to come from a combination of factors, including the content of the recordings, the style of speaking, and perhaps because the listener could not see the speaker. It is quite possible to develop "hooks" in the landscape (however ostensibly bleak), on which to hang memories and stories for the listener to hear. For newcomers, these stories can establish places of interest in their mental map of an area, however strange. For example, walkers enjoyed the adventure of exploring an industrial landscape and, as a result, most were more likely to explore such an area in the future. For locals or those with an existing knowledge of the landscape, the memories might add to, amend, or challenge their existing understanding and mental map of a locality.

Place-making was an important element of this experience; some people seemed to get a feeling of connection and rootedness to the locality by locating the stories and memories in the landscape, which aided the process of making the past present. The landscape contextualized rather than elevated memories; on the *Dockers* route, it seemed to serve as an antidote to sentimentality. Yet the intimate style of the oral history interview, combined with hearing recordings directly outside someone's house or workplace, made some people feel uncomfortable. As the memoryscape process involved listening, understanding, consent, and empathy, it should run contrary to an act of voyeurism, which is based on the powerlessness of the subject. Nevertheless, this is a useful reminder that the selection of testimony for place-specific work where individuals and their homes can easily be identified will need to be even more sensitive to the legal and ethical issues of privacy and defamation than might be the case for publications and exhibition spaces. There could also be some serious difficulties with locative oral history production systems that do not involve any kind of ethical or editorial consideration before online publication. This is not a simple process of liberating oral testimony from the archive and repatriating it back to the streets and houses it came from, as noble as that aim might be.

It may also be useful to compare this medium with other forms of exhibiting oral history. Most walkers were able to sustain their interest for as much as three or four hours, including an hour of oral history recordings, on each trail. This compares favorably to many museum-based video and audio displays and even oral-history-based radio and television documentaries.[21] It should be remembered that the walkers surveyed were self-selecting, so they may have been be more open to the concept than average, but their responses might suggest why this medium has such capacity for engagement. The multisensory experience of walking, the strong element of personal control over the listening process, the freedom to imaginatively play and to converse with others between listening points, the way that unmediated voices seem to share some characteristics of internal thought, and the authentic mixture of voice and place all seemed to help make the memoryscape experience absorbing over a long period of time. Overall, the walkers' responses suggest that place-based media that can draw upon oral testimony can be challenging, engaging, complex, multivocal, and accessible.

My experience of integrating memoryscapes with the existing activities of other river users, such as people doing geocaching and healthy walking, suggests that the medium can complement, inform, and enrich other forms of leisure activity. As locative media devices become ubiquitous, it will be fascinating to see how oral history practice develops place-based methodology with other partners to make our understanding of the cultural environment more interesting and complex. But of far greater significance will be the question of how we all, as listeners, adjust to the massive availability of location-specific material about the past. It might just change the way we perceive our place in the world.

Notes

1. The trails can be sampled online and maps and sound files can be downloaded from memoryscape.org.uk, and more community-focused trails can be found at portsofcall.org.uk
2. Toby Butler, "A Walk of Art: The Potential of the Sound Walk as Practice in Cultural Geography," *Social and Cultural Geography* 7:6 (2006) 889–908. Toby Butler, "Memoryscape : Integrating Oral History, Memory and Landscape on the River Thames," in *People and Their Pasts: Public History Today*, edited by Paul Ashton and Hilda Kean (London: Palgrave Macmillan, 2009), 223–39. Henceforth referred to as Butler,"Memoryscape."
3. See note 1 above.
4. The *Drifting* trail design process even used the current of the river to find interviewees for the recordings and the locations of each listening point along the way. For more details, see Butler, "Memoryscape."
5. Jeff Friedman, "Media Review: Drifting, from Memoryscape Audio Walks. Produced by Toby Butler," *Oral History Review* 33: 1 (2006), 107.
6. Ibid.
7. Questionnaire respondents were not asked to provide their names. The names of interviewees and focus group participants have been changed. Sex, age, and occupation are only provided in the text if the respondent provided that information.
8. Sue Clifford, "How Many Common Streams? Places, Cultures and Local Distinctiveness," in *Rivers of Meaning: Getting in Touch with the Thames*, edited by Rose Jaijee and Kelly Thomas (London: London Rivers Association, 2003), 18.
9. Rob Perks, "In Good Voice," *Museum Practice*, 25 (2004), 47.
10. Jane Graves, "Voyeurism, Silvertown and the East End," *Rising East* 4:4 (2001), 156.
11. Jane Graves? Ibid., 168.
12. Michel de Certeau, *The Practice of Everyday Life*, trans. Steven Rendall (Berkeley: University of California Press, 1984), 101.
13. Michel Nevin Willard, "Seance, Tricknowlogy, Skateboarding, and the Space of Youth," in *Generations of Youth: Youth Cultures and History in Twentieth-Century America*, edited by Joe Austin and Michael Nevin (New York: New York University Press, 1998). See also Iain Borden, *Skateboarding, Space and the City* (London: Berg, 2003).
14. For an in-depth study of the listener's experience see Michael Bull, Sounding Out the City: Personal Stereos and the Management of Everyday Life (Oxford: Berg, 2000).
15. Toby Butler and Graeme Miller, "Linked: A Landmark in Sound, a Public Walk of Art," *Cultural Geographies* 12:1 (2005), 77–78.
16. Yi-fu Tuan, *Space and Place: The Perspective of Experience* (London: Edward Arnold, 1977).

17. Tim Edensor, "The Ghosts of Industrial Ruins: Ordering and Disordering Memory in Excessive Space," *Environment and Planning D. Society and Space* 23 (2005), 829–49.
18. Steven C. High and David W. Lewis, *Corporate Wasteland: The Landscape and Memory of Deindustrialization* (Toronto: Between the Lines, 2007), 61–63.
19. See geocaching.com for further details and GPS coordinates of almost a million geocaches worldwide.
20. To give another example, the *Drifting* trail happened to be regularly used by a "healthy walking" group organized by Elmbridge Borough Council as part of their public health program. A chance meeting with the author led to the group trying the memoryscape and to the organizer offering the audio as an option in future healthy walks along that stretch of river.
21. The average time that a museum visitor watches a video is just over two minutes, and one study found that it very unusual for a museum visitor to listen to oral testimony at computers or listening posts for more than 20 minutes, although well-designed listening experiences (like ones providing comfortable armchairs) can improve matters. Beverley Serrell, "Are They Watching: Visitors and Videos in Exhibitions," *Curator* 45:1 (2002), 50–64; Frazer Swift, "London's Voices Exhibition Summative Evaluation," (London: Museum of London, 2002).

CHAPTER 10

Mapping Memories of Displacement: Oral History, Memoryscapes, and Mobile Methodologies

Steven High

We are born and have our being in a place of memory. We chart our lives by everything we remember from the mundane moment to the majestic. We know ourselves through the art and act of remembering. Memories offer us a world where there is no death, where we are sustained by rituals of regard and recollection.

—bell hooks, 2009[1]

How can we as social science researchers, harness the power of place in our methodology?

—Jon Anderson, 2004[2]

Rejecting the sedentary nature of current research practices, a growing number of scholars in the humanities and social sciences have embraced mobile methodologies and immersive technologies like global positioning system (GPS) activated or downloadable audio tours. The new "mobilities paradigm" is encouraging scholars to engage with the materiality of the built and natural environments.[3] While mobility risks becoming a mantra and is too often invoked uncritically, it offers us an opportunity to rethink oral history practice.[4] The walking interview, for example, has emerged as a core practice of geographers and artists interested in place identity and urban change.[5] The environment thus acts as a visual and auditory prompt to the stories being told whilst bimbling (aimless walking as a strategy to reconnect with the surrounding environment)[6], soundwalking (the mobile exploration of ambient sound)[7], or during the go-along (an interview done while walking, cycling, or driving through a person's neighborhood or home place).[8] "Walking, like telling stories, is the movement between places," writes Jane Ricketts Hein.[9]

Storytellers, however, are not the only ones on the move. The future story listeners can now download edited audio files onto iPods, MP3 players or smart phones, and can literally walk in the storyteller's footsteps. In some cases, global positioning system technology is being deployed to create an immersive storytelling space or mediascape.[10] This immersion is never complete though, producing a tension between past and present. There is tremendous political possibility in the space between. In mobile interviewing and listening, "the conversation inevitably becomes situated, that is, contingent on the surrounding visual and aural distractions, rather than on research questions."[11] All of these strategies serve to elicit spatial or place stories, a useful complement to life-history interviewing.

For the most part, geographers and artists have been at the forefront of these developments—not oral historians. The "Rescue Geography" project in the United Kingdom, for example, uses the walking interview and GPS to "capture people's understandings of places that are about to be radically altered by urban regeneration."[12] Many other projects have similarly focused on oral history and urban change. The most inspiring one, for me, is sound artist Graeme Miller's 2003 sound trail *Linked* (also discussed in Trower's general introduction), which challenges the building of the M11 motorway through Hackney in East London, displacing 1000 residents. The sound trail consists of "recorded memories from people who had lost their homes in the process of the motorway construction, broadcast from lamp posts."[13] Miller, a former resident himself, explains this project as a final act of defiance: "at the simplest level and motivation I was going to put the houses back," he wrote.[14]

By contrast, many oral historians have been slow to embrace new media and to harness the power of place. We have been so fixated on the interview that it seems that we have spent remarkably little time thinking about what to do with the recordings.[15] Most of us are much more comfortable authoring in text than in sound. Michael Frisch has called this loss of orality at such an early stage, oral history's "deep dark secret."[16] There has likewise been surprisingly little cross-pollination between oral history and geography. According to geographers Mark Riley and David Harvey, place has been "largely treated by oral historians in a superficial, Euclidian, manner—a frame for research rather than an active part."[17] This predisposition is beginning to change, as evidenced by this volume.

Doreen Massey's path-breaking 1995 article, "Places and Their Pasts" serves as an essential point of entry into the cross-disciplinary scholarship on place. She writes that the "identity of places is very much bound up with the histories which are told of them; how these histories are told, and what history turns out to be dominant."[18] For Massey, place is no empty container where the "stuff" of history happens. Rather than a thing, it is a process that is both spatial and temporal.[19] In consequence, places are much more than points on a map but are envelopes of time as well. A sense of place would be impossible without memory, "the recollection of personal history grounded in a particular landscape or set of landscapes."[20] Memory maps, Joan Schwartz notes, "are not so much about space on the ground as place in the mind."[21]

What happens when these remembered and highly emotional attachments are severed? What becomes of a site of memory when it ceases to exist in the built or natural environment? "The landscape has been the central stage for the proof and spectacle of radical transformation," writes geographer Alistair Bonnett. "The eradication of old buildings, old place names and old monuments, and the construction of new places, new names and new monuments, provided the most visible symbols of revolutionary intent."[22] Discursively, "displacement" has become so commonplace that it has been shorn of its emotional content and cultural meaning. Displaced workers are effectively reduced to a static category or object. The same could be said of the DPs, or displaced people, who came to North America after World War II, or the fishing families "resettled" by the state in 1960s Newfoundland. The language is rather distant and strangely immobile.

As we will see here, memoryscapes and sound walks allow us to explore places in new ways—what Toby Butler has called the "multisensory experience of place."[23] Memoryscapes, Jeff Friedman writes, "attempt to suture space and time together through the aural experience of oral history interviews and ambient sound."[24] Although Butler defines memoryscapes narrowly as "outdoor trails that use recorded sound and spoken memory on a personal stereo or mobile media to experience places in new ways," I would go further and add immersive websites that explore place memory and spatial stories through mental mapping.[25]

There is a danger, however, in many of the memoryscapes and audio tours that I have familiarity with in that they suppose a stable and unitary local community. Accordingly, they tell unifying stories that are largely devoid of internal division. We must ask ourselves if there is a place for more controversial or less consensual stories in these immersive spaces. How do we represent the complexity of social relations and the fluidity and multiplicity of communities themselves? In answering these questions, we must keep in mind how these interpretative acts came into being: from whom, by whom, for whom. What is the process behind the finished product? What choices were made and why? This paper explores these issues in relation to an online millscape that I created with Michael Klassen of the now-demolished corrugated paper mill in Sturgeon Falls, Ontario (available at: http://storytelling.concordia.ca/high/sturgeon_falls/). The Millscape's potential as a site of memory for former workers and as a site of historical interpretation for others will be considered, as will the politics of memoryscapes and audio tours more generally.

Place, Memory, and Belonging in Sturgeon Falls, Ontario

Looking back, it is hard to argue with those who suggest that single-industry towns are a pervasive feature of Canadian society.[26] The Canadian Association of Single-Industry Towns calculated that there were over 1000 resource-dependent communities in the country in 1987.[27] As most are located in the provincial northlands, they are characterized by small populations and geographic isolation. The central fact of life in these towns, according to Alex Himelfarb, is dependence.[28] Forty years ago, Rex Lucas identified four stages in the development of single-industry towns: construction, recruitment, transition, and maturity.[29] Changing times, however, led Himelfarb to add a fifth stage: decline.[30]

Economic change on the resource frontier has historically been understood in terms of the boom-and-bust cycle. After 1945, it helped explain hard times in good times. This economic cycle of extremes has been replaced, of late, by a sense of inevitable decline. Northern Ontario, my home region, provides a good example of this paradigm shift. The region comprises fully 90% of Ontario's land area, but only 786,500 of its people. Outmigration and an aging population have meant that the region's population is in decline, fully 4.5% from 1996 to 2001.[31] The decline of the region's primary and secondary manufacturing industries has been dramatic, dropping from 28% of the region's workforce in 1981 to just 16% in 2001. Jobs in forestry and mining have dropped a startling 47% in that time.[32] As a result, only 5% of the region's jobs were in forest manufacturing in 2001. A giant wave of mill closures has since struck Northern Ontario with devastating force, displacing thousands more.

Like many single-industry towns across Canada, Sturgeon Falls has been ravaged by the deep crisis in forestry. The town is located four and a half hours' drive north of Toronto, in the Canadian Shield. The mill had been the town's major employer for more than a century when Weyerhaeuser abruptly closed it in 2002. Many local families had ties to the mill going back three generations and had multiple family members working there at one time or another. The deep connection to the mill was evident throughout the interviews that we conducted with former workers and local management. Virtually everyone used home and family metaphors to describe their attachment to work, to coworkers, and to the mill itself. Emotions were never far from the surface. It may have been "nothing personal" for the multinational corporation that was leaving town, but it was intensely personal for those left behind.

The bonding of people with their places of work insures that periods of major economic change are also periods of major spatial change.[33] The power of place was everywhere apparent in the interviews conducted. It infused people's language and structured their stories in numerous ways. A mill closure challenged their sense of place at the deepest level, depriving them of a social structure in which they felt valued and validated.[34] Mill worker Randy Restoule spoke for many when he explained the loss that he felt: "I felt a deep loss. The fact that everyone else was leaving... All your friends are gone. And like I said before, the reason that you keep going in a job is because of friends."[35] Displaced workers lose much more than a paycheck the day their mill or factory goes down—they lose a sense of their place in the world around them.

The diversified mill's decline came gradually over a quarter century. One by one, the mill's production lines fell silent. By 2002, corrugated paper was its only product. The mill's linkages to area farmers, who had long supplied the mill with its wood fiber, were cut in the early 1990s, when it converted to recycled paper. Over time, the mill's workforce had been whittled down from a high of 700 to just 140. Even so, the December 2002 closing was devastating for the town's remaining mill families and was universally viewed as the end of an era. Today, all the major employers in this town of 6,000 are in the public sector. The largest blue-collar employer is now a small lumber mill, ranked fourteenth largest overall, with 51 employees—slightly ahead of the local McDonald's restaurant.[36]

The Making of the Sturgeon Falls Millscape

It is no surprise then that the mill loomed large in the oral narratives. For more than a century, the mill dominated the social, cultural, and economic life of Sturgeon Falls. Its water tower and smokestack cast their shadow over the locality. The mill's subsequent demolition and the shredding of "boxes and boxes" of mill records, some dating back to the 1920s, were acts of cultural erasure. Several workers we interviewed pointedly asked why the company had not donated these records to the local museum. After all, the mill had been owned by Weyerhaeuser for only 3 of its 104 years of existence. Whose history was this? We don't often associate mill and factory closings and the resulting dislocation with violence, but the hurt and pain recorded in these interviews is all too real.

Although my motivation for building an online millscape was in response to the company's attack on memory, it was also inspired by the historical labor of two former mill workers. Hubert Gervais and Bruce Colquhoun spent years researching the history of the mill for its 1998 centenary, gathering newspaper clippings, photographs, and facts into the Mill History binder—the biggest binder that I have ever seen. This giant memory book testified to the strength of workers' attachment to the mill and to their sense of collective belonging. With the closure, however, the binder became something more: a surrogate for the mill itself. In the aftermath of the closure, the binder circulated amongst the former workers, enabling them to revisit their former lives in the mill or to show visiting relatives or a grandchild what it was like to work there. I have argued elsewhere that, much like a family photo album, it provided a continued connection to the past for this memory community.[37] To flip through its pages facilitated the social act of remembering and helped the mill workers to share their memories with others.

My research project was born the day that I met Bruce Colquhoun and his big black binder. Over the next three years, we interviewed 50 former employees of the mill, as well as a dozen city politicians and economic development officials. We gathered thousands of pages of mill documents recovered in people's basements—a box here or a file there—as well as newspaper articles and a scattering of archival material found in public archives. Working with documentary photographer David Lewis, we gained entry into the mill as it was being prepared for demolition and took dozens of photographs. We also took individual portraits of a half-dozen former mill workers. This rich oral and visual record resulted in two exhibitions. The first, *Corporate Wasteland*, was a traveling exhibition that toured galleries and museums throughout Ontario and Michigan. The second, *Le Moulin* (*The Mill*), was created as a permanent exhibition at the Sturgeon Falls House Museum. All of the interview recordings were donated to the museum as a permanent contribution to the town's history and will help counter the company's destruction of memory. I find Robert Bevan's work on the intentional targeting of buildings for destruction in times of war or genocide particularly useful in thinking about what happened in Sturgeon Falls.[38]

It was at about this time that my students at Concordia University began to experiment with downloadable audio tours and mobile methodologies. In 2006, Nancy Rebelo and Jasmine St.-Laurent produced the Bus 55 audio tour (http://stortelling.concordia.ca/memoryscapes/) for my Working Class Public History seminar. Saint Laurent Boulevard, or "the Main," has long been known as Montreal's immigrant corridor. To tell this story, the students interviewed members of the city's Chinese, Portuguese, Italian, and Jewish communities and developed a 35-minute audio track that is downloadable to an MP3 player or iPod. Participants then board city bus #55 in the Old Port and listen to these stories as the bus rolls northward. The idea is that you look out upon the city with new eyes. Their project caused something of a media sensation in Montreal and has inspired many other student projects.[39] Mobile methodologies have since become an integral part of our training of oral and public historians at Concordia. As I write this, students enrolled in my Oral History and Urban Change course are experimenting with immersive mediascape software, 3-D modeling, and various forms of "map-mashups."

Given these changes to my teaching practice, it was only natural that I would undertake my own memoryscape or audio tour. My opportunity came in 2008 when Michael Klassen, a recent graduate in landscape architecture, came to work with me at the Centre for Oral History and Digital Storytelling. Michael's MA thesis explored memoryscapes as a way to harness the power of place, and he was interested in forging a connection with oral historians. Over the next year, we created the Sturgeon Falls Millscape, using the mill's floor plans, aerial photos, and insurance maps, as well as the photographs of David Lewis. Audio clips were embedded in the photographs and can be played individually or concurrently, simply by moving your cursor onto one of the hard hat symbols.[40]

With the help of the mill's blueprint, we set out to connect people's stories to the factory floor. Visitors can tour the mill virtually from one area to the next, hearing audio clips telling of work process, camaraderie, labor–management relations, and workplace accidents. To demarcate change and conflict, we located stories about the mill's closing and the aftermath outside the factory gate and beyond the fence line of our virtual mill, where cars were often parked during the demolition of the mill. Old timers would sit there for hours, watching the mill go down.[41] Stories of resistance are there too, located at the factory gates where protesters demanded that the mill be reopened in the weeks and months following the mill's closure.

The main navigation map is the primary point of entry into the Sturgeon Falls Millscape. In hovering over the side portals, you highlight the relevant location on the mill's blueprint in red. Clicking on it brings up another browser window, taking you into that specific part of the mill. You can then navigate to other areas or return to the main navigation map. The resulting memoryscape is composed of twenty-two specific sections, or departments, within the mill, such as the main office, the paper machine room, the paint line, the boiler house, and the water tower. The millscape also includes moments in time, or key themes, such as layoffs, floods, the 1930s (when the mill was closed), and the last roll of paper to be produced at the mill. The black-and-white photographs by David Lewis provide the backdrop for much of the journey.

Most, though not all, of these specific sites include audio clips from the interviews we conducted. In the main office, for example, we hear from personnel manager W. E. (Ed) Fortin and superintendent Gerry Stevens, both of whom provide a bird's-eye view of the plant and its workforce. A more personal story is told by staff member Ruth Thompson, about how she was hired in at the mill. The interviewees associated with the office area speak on a variety of topics, but there is usually a discursive line drawn between "workers" on the shop floor and "company people" in the office.

Of course, the issues raised on the shop floor itself often differ. In the paper machine room, for example, we hear stories of workplace accidents, job insecurity, and the work process itself. Denis MacGregor and others told us about the tragic death of a coworker, who died on the job from a heart attack. Decades later, you can still hear the anger in their voices as they retell how local management refused to stop the paper machine. The men had to stay on the job, even as the dead man was being carried out. It did not seem to matter that the man had another family member working there. In sharing this particular story, former workers were telling us a great deal about labor–management relations. Yet most still took pride in their work and emphasized the skill required to do their jobs. Their achievements were even more admirable, considering the aging and obsolete equipment that the company gave them to work with.

Job insecurity was a constant theme running through the interviews. Many of the layoff stories culminated in the 2002 mill closure and its subsequent demolition. We located the layoff stories inside the map of the plant, but moved off-site when it came to the plant shutdown stories that followed. In the "Ottawa Street" section of the memoryscape, for example, we hear about Denis MacGregor's ring:

> I usually wear that [a thirty-year ring given for service], but the guys at the mill give me a hard time. But I say, "Hey, I earned that." So nobody is going to tell me if I can wear it or not. I could take the insignia off, maybe I would, because I really hate those guys. I don't hate the state. I hate Weyerhaeuser.

Although the Sturgeon Falls mill was not a bastion of left unionism, that does not render it insignificant from a labor history perspective.[42] In many ways, it was a typical North American mill during its century of production. Local mill workers unionized during the First World War, but only walked off the job on three occasions that I am aware of. In two of these instances, it was part of wider strikes against the Spanish River Company in the early 1920s and against Abitibi Pulp and Paper in the mid-1970s. Not a single worker that we interviewed recalled the first strike—all traces of this early period of trade unionism appear not to have survived the mill's closure between 1930 and 1946, which devastated the town. Workers remembered the later strike in the 1970s, but it was recalled as a failure by nearly everyone we spoke to.[43] The third strike, a wildcat, was mentioned only in response to our direct questions. Their reticence to speak of the matter is understandable, as the walkout in protest of the company's decision to promote an unpopular union member as foreman had resulted in a nasty legal fight, pitting union member against union member. There were therefore no working-class martyrs to remember in Sturgeon Falls—no obvious Luigi Trastullis or Dona Marias to point to.[44] As a result, the union was peripheral to almost all of our interview conversations and thus peripheral to the memoryscape that we created. It was only after the mill's closure that the story of labor militancy became audible.

One of the challenges that we faced in making the Sturgeon Falls Millscape was how to represent change over time. The mill's floor plan and the aerial photograph used to structure the memoryscape appear stable, even permanent, masking the often dramatic changes in production and work process. The mill that we see before us was built in stages, and many of its sections served different functions over the postwar decades. What was once the paint line later became a warehouse; what was once the hardboard mill became the recycled pulp plant, and so on. How then to locate stories of work processes that no longer existed on the 1990s-era floor plan? We must therefore treat the millscape as a palimpsest where "history appears spatialized and built space temporalized."[45] The demolition of the mill encouraged others to see the mill in these terms. Former mill worker Hubert Gervais visited the site each and every day during its demolition, taking a total of 1,200 photographs. In our interview, he noted that it was as though the demolition company were intentionally working back through time as they worked their way from the newer parts of the plant to the older parts. For him, it was as though time had suddenly gone into reverse.

From Ruins to Ruination

What then are the politics of the Sturgeon Falls Millscape? Is it a digital eulogy for a vanishing way of life, or something with more political edge? How do we represent displacement? In "Imperial Debris," Ann Laura Stoler reflects on the meaning of ruins and ruination in the context of imperial history. It is vitally important in this context, she argues, to work against the melancholic or nostalgic gaze that aestheticizes rubble into ruin.[46] In the European imagination, ruins are often "enchanted, desolate spaces" or treated as dreamy "icons of a wistful, romantic loss."[47] In emphasizing ruination, Stoler shifts the focus from "left over" relics to those "left with" what remains. To ruin "is to inflict or bring great and irretrievable disaster upon, to destroy agency, to reduce to a state of poverty, to demoralize completely." Accordingly, ruination is an "act perpetrated, a condition to which one is subject, and a cause of loss." It is a "political project that lays waste to certain peoples and places, relations and things."[48] Hence, ruins are "not just found, they are made" and not made by anyone, mind you—"large scale ruin-making takes resources and planning."[49]

Reading Stoler's words, I was struck by their applicability to the ruination of the Sturgeon Falls mill and to our efforts to represent this act perpetrated by Weyerhaeuser. In my opinion, our memoryscape is a study of both ruins and ruination. In embedding audio clips from our interviews with mill workers and managers in the photographs themselves of the ruined mill, we hoped to destabilize their meaning—to see them, perhaps, from the vantage points of those most directly affected. The emotion-laden stories of former mill workers, and their anger against the corporation that did this to them, provide a different reading of what we are seeing. As Stoler writes:

> Asking how people live with and in ruins redirects the engagement elsewhere, to the politics animated, to the common sense they disturb, to the critiques

> condensed or disallowed, and to the social relations avidly coalesced or shattered around them. What material form do ruins of empire take when we turn to shattered peoples and scarred places rather than to their evocations and enchantments?[50]

Oral history provides us with an invaluable opportunity to see ruination from the point of view of those most directly affected. It allows us to shift from *learning about* these places from a safe distance to *learning with* those who live there—to understanding what happened and why in conversation.

Conclusion: Towards Immersive Spaces

"Memory appeals to us," writes Kerwin Lee Klein, "partly because it projects an immediacy we feel has been lost from history."[51] It is the immediacy of the experience that gives memoryscapes and audio tours their emotive power. At their best, audio tours allow us to experience places in new ways and thereby "reawaken [a] poetic and emotional connection to place," as Foth et al. note.[52] That said, there are substantive questions about the ability of online memoryscapes to immerse visitors in place. If my students are any indication, and I think they are, visitors tend to surf these websites, sampling bits and pieces to get a sense of it all. They don't spend a great deal of time "doing" the virtual tour. One therefore has to ask if an exclusively online memoryscape is the right place for deep listening. Or, at the very least, how can we slow things down? Should we follow the lead of some multimedia artists[53] in New York City, who insist on the *in-situ* experience rather than circulating their performances on DVDs or on the Internet? Of course, not everyone can get to Sturgeon Falls to see the site for themselves. Sturgeon Falls is not New York City.

If the immersive potential of memoryscapes is severely limited when the stories are heard at a distance, I also think that the tension between past and present is lost almost entirely. Imagine an audio tour in Sturgeon Falls where visitors listened to these stories on an iPod as they walked around the perimeter of the site. The effect of hearing these stories *in situ* would be significant, as the chain-link fence now encloses an empty field.[54] The hypothetical walking listener would likely be moved by the experience and by the sight of this act of destruction. The stories would now be heard in relation to this absence. We therefore have to continue to think of how we can employ new media to create immersive spaces online. Virtually all of the existing scholarship on mobile methodologies requires us to be there. Recent work in immersive gaming, however, may provide part of the answer.[55] Players often spend a great deal of time in these games, in sharp contrast to the tendency to "surf" while online. At the very least, it is a much more structured experience.

In the meantime, I worked with the Centre d'Histoire de Montréal on a June 2011 exhibition entitled *Quartiers disparus,* or *Vanished Neighbourhoods.* It will interrogate the memories of loss attached to those working-class neighborhoods demolished in the 1960s to make way for Montreal's Ville Marie and Bonaventure autoroutes, as well as for new government complexes. Inspired by the work of Canadian historian Joy Parr, we are organizing group interviews with former residents, using old insurance maps and expropriation photos to prompt memories.[56] The exhibit was built up from there. We now intend to conduct audio walks of Pointe-Sainte-Charles and other formerly industrial districts adjoining the Lachine Canal. Should we secure funding, we would also like to develop a sound art project along the lines of Graeme Miller's *Linked* or Alexei Blinov and Armin Medosch's *Hidden Histories* projects, both in the United Kingdom. We hope that the resulting tensions between past and present will raise fundamental questions about economic change.

We are likewise taking a hard look at immersive mscape software, which uses GPS-activated audio and photographic files to interpret a site.[57] All of these mobile methodologies offer oral and public historians the possibility to track subjective, partial, and individual trajectories through time and space. One might even follow Christian Nold's lead and experiment with emotion mapping, gauging people's emotional responses to the environment using biomedical monitoring devices and GPS technology.[58] No matter how we approach the exhibition and the accompanying audio tours, we believe in the profound connection between life stories and place. According to Michel de Certeau, stories "traverse and organise places; they select and link them together, they make sentences and itineraries out of them."[59]

Notes

1. bell hooks, *Belonging: A Culture of Place* (New York: Routledge, 2009), 5.
2. Jon Anderson, "Talking Whilst Walking: A Geographical Archaeology of Knowledge," *Area* 36.3 (2004), 257. Henceforth referred to as Anderson, "Talking."
3. Jane Ricketts Hein, James Evans, and Phil Jones, "Mobile Methodologies: Theory, Technology and Practice," *Geography Compass* 2:5 (2008), 1266–85. Henceforth referred to as Hein, "Mobile."
4. I am sometimes dismayed by the ready equation of mobility with progress, as something to be celebrated. In emphasizing mobility rather than displacement, scholars sometimes assume it is a voluntary act. Tim Cresswell. *On the Move: Mobility in the Modern Western World* (London: Routledge, 2006).
5. Mimi Sheller and John Urry, "The New Mobilities Paradigm," *Environment and Planning* A 38 (2006), 208. The "mobility turn" is evident in the journal *Mobilities,* founded in 2006. See also Alison Blunt, "Cultural Geographies of Migration: Mobility, Transnationality and Diaspora," *Progress in Human Geography* (2007), 1–11.

6. "Bimbling afforded the opportunity to reminiscence and be reminded of these events, or to prompt other life-course memories." Anderson, "Talking," 257.
7. Re. soundwalking, some scholars believe that everyday noise can prompt memories and stories during the walking interview. "We have been struck, listening to our recorded tours, not only by the extent to which everyday sound gives texture to settings, making places the places that they are, but also by the ways in which sound has acted to configure the routes respondents have shared with us." Tom Hall, Brett Lashua, and Amanda Coffey, "Sound and the Everyday in Qualitative Research," *Qualititative Inquiry* 14:6 (2008), 1019–40.
8. Re. the go-along, Richard M. Carpiano describes it in "Come Take a Walk with Me: The 'Go-Along' Interview as a Novel Method for Studying the Implications of Place for Health and Well-Being," *Health and Place* 15 (2009), 263–72. I have certainly done interviews while driving and walking in the past, and I organized a chapter of one of my books around the stops selected by Gabriel Solano, a former Detroit autoworker interviewed by me on two occasions. See Steven High and David Lewis, *Corporate Wasteland: The Landscape and Memory of Deindustrialization* (Toronto: Between the Lines, 2007).
9. Hein et al., "Mobile," 1277.
10. mscape software was developed by Mobile Bristol (UK), a partnership between the University of Bristol and Hewitt-Packard. It is a digital tool downloadable to a Personal Digital Assistant that sonically "tags" the built or natural environment in order to create an immersive experience for the visitor. "Simply put," writes Stuart P. Stenton, "a mediascape plays multimedia content (image, audio, or video) on a mobile device in response to context triggers." See, for example, "The Riot of 1831" voice dramatization of Queen Square in Bristol, which allows you to "move around the square to listen to the everyday stories and accounts of the rioters who protested." See Stuart P. Stenton et al., "Mediascapes: Context-Aware Multimedia Experiences," *IEEE Computer Society* (July–September 2007).
11. Lyndsay Brown and Kevin Durrheim, "Different Kinds of Knowing: Generating Qualitative Data Through Mobile Interviewing," *Qualitative Inquiry* 15:5 (2009), 920.
12. Hein, "Mobile," 1278.
13. Toby Butler and Graeme Miller, "Linked: A Landmark in Sound, a Public Walk of Art," *Cultural Geographies* 12 (2005), 77–88.
14. Ibid.
15. Steven High, "Telling Stories: Oral History and New Media," *Oral History* 38 (Spring 2010), 101–12.
16. Michael Frisch, "Three Dimensions and More: Oral History Beyond the Paradoxes of Method," in *Handbook of Emergent Methods,* edited by Sharlene Nagy Hesse-Biber and Patricia Leavy (New York: Guildford Press, 2008), 222.
17. Mark Riley and David Harvey, "Talking Geography: on Oral History and the Practice of Geography," *Social and Cultural Geography* 8:3 (June 2007), 1–4.
18. Doreen Massey, "Places and their Pasts," *History Workshop Journal* 39: 1 (1995), 182–192.
19. A similar point was made about the concept of class in the introduction to E. P. Thompson, *The Making of the English Working Class* (New York: Vintage, 1963).
20. Marlene Creates, quoted in Joan M. Schwartz's preface to the book, "Constituting Place of Presence: Landscape, Identity and the Geographical Imagination,"

in Marlene Creates, *Places of Presence: Newfoundland Kin and Ancestral Land, Newfoundland, 1989–91* (St. John's: Killick Press, 1997), 1–18.

21. Joan M. Schwartz, "Constituting Place of Presence: Landscape, Identity, and the Geographical Imagination," preface to Marleen Creates, *Places of Presence: Newfoundland Kin and Ancestral Land, Newfoundland 1989–91* (St. John's: Killick Press, 1997), 1–18.
22. Alastair Bonnett, "The Dilemmas of Radical Nostalgia in British Psychogeography," *Theory, Culture & Society* 26:1 (2009), 49.
23. Toby Butler, "Memoryscape: How Audio Walks Can Deepen Our Sense of Place by Integrating Art, Oral History and Cultural Geography," *Geography Compass* 1:3 (2007), 360–64. See also Toby Butler, "A Walk of Art: The Potential of the Sound Walk as Practice in Cultural Geography," *Social and Cultural Geography* 7:6 (December 2006), 889.
24. Jeff Friedman, "Review of Drifting for Memoryscape Audiowalk," *Oral History Review* 33:1 (2006), 107.
25. Toby Butler, "Memoryscape: How Audio Walks Can Deepen Our Sense of Place by Integrating Art, Oral History and Cultural Geography," *Geography Compass* 1:3 (2007), 360–64.
26. Alex Himelfarb, "The Social Characteristics of One-Industry Towns in Canada," in *Little Communities and Big Industries: Studies in the Social Impact of Canadian Resource Extraction*, edited by Roy T. Bowles (Toronto: Butterworths, 1982), 16. Henceforth referred to as Himelfarb, "Social."
27. James E. Randall and R. Geoff Ironside, "Communities on the Edge: An Economic Geography of Resource-Dependent Communities in Canada," *Canadian Geographer* 40:1 (Spring 1996), 21.
28. Himelfarb, "Social," 16.
29. Rex Lucas, *Minetown, Milltown, Railtown: Life in Canadian Communities of Single Industry* (Toronto: Univ. of Toronto Press, 1971).
30. Himelfarb, "Social," 16.
31. Ray D. Bollman, Rolland Beshiri, and Verna Mitura, *Northern Ontario's Communities: Economic Diversification, Specialization and Growth* (Statistics Canada, Agricultural and Rural Working Paper Series No. 82, 2006).
32. Ibid.
33. Doreen Massey, *Spatial Divisions of Labour: Social Structures and the Geography of Production* (London: Macmillan, 1984), 11. Scholars increasingly view spatiality as actively produced and "as an active moment within the social process." See also David Harvey, *Spaces of Global Capitalism* (London: Verso, 2006), 77. Henri Lefebvre's tripartite division of space as material (space of experience and perception), as conceptual (space as conceived or represented), and as lived (sensation, imagination, emotion) has been particularly influential in this regard. See Henri Lefebvre, *The Production of Space* (Oxford: Wiley-Blackwell, 1991) and his *The Survival of Capitalism: Reproduction of the Relations of Production* (London, Alison and Busby, 1976).
34. Kathryn Marie Dudley, *The End of the Line: Lost Jobs, New Lives in Postindustrial America* (Chicago: University of Chicago Press, 1994), 47.
35. Randy Restoule, interviewed by Kristen O'Hare, 5 August 2004.
36. The employment list can be found at www.westnipissingouest.ca/demographics.html (accessed August 2009).

37. Steven High, "Placing the Displaced Worker: Narrating Place in Deindustrializing Sturgeon Falls, Ontario," in *Placing Memory and Remembering Place in Canada,* edited by James Opp and John Walsh (Vancouver: University of British Columbia Press, 2010), 159–186.
38. Robert Bevan, *The Destruction of Memory: Architecture of War* (London: Reaktion Books, 2006); see the introduction.
39. Several dozen student projects can be accessed on the website of the Centre for Oral History and Digital Storytelling, see http://storytelling.concordia.ca
40. The process of audio clip selection was made easier by the fact that I had already created a database of 16 hours of interview material using Interclipper database software. For more on what we learned building this database, see Steven High and David Sworn, "After the Interview: The Interpretative Challenges of Oral History Video Indexing," *Digital Studies* 1: 2 (2009).
41. This was, and is, a very common sight in deindustrializing areas. See Steven High and David Lewis, *Corporate Wasteland: The Landscape and Memory of Deindustrialization* (Toronto: Between the Lines, 2007), 23–40.
42. Australian historian Lucy Taksa suggests otherwise in "Labor History and Public History in Australia: Allies or Uneasy Bedfellows," *International Labor and Working Class History* 76 (2009), 82.
43. The mill's closure between 1930 and 1946, which caused an exodus of families and pushed the municipality into bankruptcy, caused a rupture in memory. Nobody interviewed recalled stories about the early days of trade unionism or work in the mill.
44. Alessandro Portelli, *The Death of Luigi Trastulli and Other Stories* (Ithaca: State University of New York, 1990); Daniel James, *Dona Maria's Story* (Durham: Duke University Press, 2000).
45. Andreas Huyssen, "Nostalgia for Ruins," *Grey Room* 23 (Spring 2006), 6–21.
46. Ann Laura Stoler, "Imperial Debris: Reflections on Ruins and Ruination," *Cultural Anthropology* (Spring 2008), 5.
47. ibid., 5
48. Ibid., 8.
49. Ibid., 17–18.
50. Ibid., 9–10.
51. Kerwin Lee Klein, "On the Emergence of Memory in Historical Discourse," *Representations* (Winter 2000), 129.
52. Marcus Foth, Helen Klaebe, and Greg Hearn, "The Role of New Media and Digital Narratives in Urban Planning and Community Development," *Body, Space & Technology* 7:2 (2008).
53. New York City's Washington Square saw the erection of an interactive storytelling installation with a mix of videotaped stories and archival photographs—people had to visit the site. Karl J. Mendonca, Marcus Pingel, Charles Yust, "Document: An Oral History of Washington Square Park," *MIT5: Creativity, Ownership, and Collaboration in the Digital Age* (27 April 2007). http://web.mit.edu/comm-forum/mit5/papers/Medonca.pdf (Accessed February 15, 2010).
54. Two of the best projects that I have encountered that combine mixed media and oral history are *Urban Tapestries* in London (http://urbantapestries.net)

and *Crossing the Boulevard* in Queens, a borough of New York City (www.crossingtheblvd.org). A more traditional linear narrative for an audio tour can be found in the new Alcatraz Cellhouse Tour, launched in 2007 for the Parks Service by Antenna Audio. It lasts 42 minutes and includes only the voices of those who "were there." Antenna Audio. www.antennaaudio.com/content/view/556/31/ (accessed December 2009).

55. See the website of Kevin Kee's Simulating History Lab at Brock University in Ontario, Canada: http://simulatinghistory.com/resources/
56. Joy Parr, Jessica Van Horssen, and Jon van der Veen, "The Practice of History Shared across Differences: Needs, Technologies, and Ways of Knowing in the Megaprojects New Media Project." *Journal of Canadian Studies* 43:1 (2009), 39. See also Joy Parr, *Sensing Changes: Technologies, Environments, and the Everyday, 1953–2003* (Vancouver: University of British Columbia Press, 2009).
57. mscape software was used in Montreal in 2005 by the Mobile Digital Commons Network, which interpreted the social history of Place Émilie-Gamelin using GPS-triggered sound and images. According to Michael Longford, the project "examined the ways in which memory can be inscribed in space, drawing on field recordings, oral history, and archival materials to form a layered mediascape." See Michael Longford, "Territory as Interface: Design for Mobile Experiences," *W: Journal of the Mobile Digital Commons Network* 2:1 (2006), 3–5.
58. Christian Nold, "Bio Mapping / Emotion Mapping" at http://www.biomapping.net/ (Accessed February 15, 2010). See also Hein et al., "Mobile," 1273–74.
59. Michel de Certeau, *The Practice of Everyday Life* (Berkeley: University of California Press, 1984), 115.

Index